INDUSTRIAL DESIGN
MATERIALS AND MANUFACTURING

Jim Lesko

JOHN WILEY & SONS, INC.
New York, Chichester, Weinheim, Brisbane, Singapore, Toronto

This publication is designed to provide accurate and authoritative information in regard to the subject matter covered. It is sold with the understanding that the publisher is not engaged in rendering professional services. If professional advice or other expert assistance is required, the services of a competent professional person should be sought.

Library of Congress Cataloging-in-Publications Data

Lesko, Jim.
    Industrial design materials and manufacturing / Jim Lesko.
       p.   cm.
    Includes index.
    ISBN 0-471-29769-0
  1. Design, Industrial. 2. Manufacturing processes. 3. Materials.
  I. Title.
TS171.4.L47   1998
745.2—dc21   97-33670

Printed in the United States of America.

10 9 8 7 6

CONTENTS

ACKNOWLEDGMENTS

The idea for *Industrial Design Materials and Manufacturing* began about 1975 when Professor Born asked me to teach the subject at the University of Cincinnati. I had the good fortune of having an exceptional group of students, including John Bucholtz, Mike Galleger, and Sam Lucente, whose enthusiastic response to my organizational structure of the subject convinced me that a simple visual text was necessary to get the interest of artistically trained students. Many of the existing texts and journals on the subject do a great job for those students whose interest is in the amount of detail presented, with an emphasis on quantifiable arguments and explanations. I learned from these texts and journals, and they remain a necessary part of the learning process for design students. But impatient industrial design students who want to understand concepts, need an overview—read a summary, see examples, and go on to the next topic in some logical manner. Design students seem to sense that they will not have the prime responsibility in selecting materials or in specifying the manufacturing process in the design of products, but intuitively they understand that they must be conversant on the subject and that materials and manufacturing methods will be a determinant in part design.

Today there is a growing excitement and exploration in materials and manufacturing in the design community because of the recent explosion of ideas engendered by the advances in technology. The recent show *Mutant Materials in Contemporary Design* organized by Paola Antonelli, Associate Curator at the Museum of Modern Art and the *Material Connection* conceived by George Beylerian are outstanding examples of this renewed energy focused in this essential aspect of design. Within the Industrial Designers Society of America, Dave Kusuma was instrumental in organizing the Materials and Processes Group and in bringing the Society of Plastics Engineers and IDSA together for meetings and conferences. In order to aid in materials education these two groups got together to provide a designer's tool box with samples of the various parts for students to study.

For years I hoped that someone else would produce such a text. After 15 years or more teaching the subject I realized that no designers were presumptuous enough to try to develop a text for industrial design students, so I began to assemble my notes. While at Pratt Institute, I received a Mellon grant to produce a structure for the information that should be included. During this first phase several students assisted me, including Deborah Zweiker and Eileen Lee. Without the advantage of the computer, we labored most of the summer laying out the organizational charts and making the many lists of information. While I was at Carnegie Mellon University, Professor Alex Bally, Head of Industrial Design; and Professors Greenberg and Paxton of Materials Science reviewed my preliminary concepts and provided many suggestions and much encouragement.

While I am responsible for the use I made of the information that I received it was impossible to complete this undertaking on my own. In fact, this book is the work of many people: many students who sat through the lectures and provided feedback, and the manufacturers and suppliers who graciously took much time and patience with me in trying to insure that I received the information I needed. There are many who stand out, who went way beyond that call of duty.

This book would not have been completed without Ed Eslami who on a number of occasions rescued me from panic and whose calm assurance, clever drawings, and graphic layout brought the book out of the morass that it was in at times. I am grateful

for his help and his exceptional talent. Many students helped with research and drawings including Kyang Haub Kang, Tong Jin Kim, and Minghsiu Yang.

Mr. Don Blair of Talbot Associates was with me almost from the beginning, and later Mr. Jeff Talbot joined him to provide hours of discussion, stacks of brochures, and many sources of information on casting. Ms. Christine Lagosz and her associates at Trumpf, Inc., Mr. Bill Guftner of US Amada Ltd., Steven Friedman of Peterson, Walter Ackerman of Risdon, John Matthews of ESAB Welding & Cutting Products, and Bob Cook of Bridgeport Machines were just some of the great individuals who provided all the information I requested on metal forming and cutting. Don Douty reviewed the introduction to the metals sections and provided valuable information and encouragement.

Dave Kusuma and Michael A. D'Onofrio, Jr. and their associates at the Bayer Corporation, Jack Avery, George Whitney, and their associates at GE plastics, Steve Ham, Dave Beck of Pappago, Victor Gerdes and his associates at the Stevens Institute, and Bill Fallon of Sikorsky provided impor-

tant parts in building the plastics section. I am thankful that the publisher of the *Injecting Molding Handbook* by Rosato & Rosato and the *Plastics Engineering Handbook* by the Society of the Plastics Industry for allowing me to reproduce many drawings.

I am grateful to my colleagues, Professors Schile and Krebs for their corrections and suggestions. There were obviously many others who plowed through my drafts and patiently corrected my errors. There are many others who contributed their expertise, and their thoughts are here somewhere inside. It was the enthusiasm and willingness to help on the part of nearly everyone that I contacted that kept me going. All played a part. I am grateful to all.

I am grateful for the support of my wife who sat alone while I struggled with revision after revision and unending letters, faxes, and calls. I am thankful that my publisher stayed with me as new responsibilities and the chaos of relocating caused numerous delays. Finally I would like to acknowledge the support of Miss Kitty who oversaw every word I typed. Her affection and loyalty kept me sane. It is difficult now without her.

Manufacturing Methods		Forming			Cutting				Joining				Finishing		
		Liquid State	Plastic State	Solid State	Sheet Cutting	Chip Forming	Non-Chip Forming	Flame/ Laser	Solder/ Braze	Weld	Adhesive	Mechan-ical	Formed	Cut	Coatings
Metals	Ferrous	All	All	All	All	All	All	All	All	All	All	All	All	All	All
	Non-ferrous	All	All	All	All	All	All	Most	All	All	All	All	All	All	All
Plastics	Thermoset	All	No	No	All	All	Some	Some	No	No	All	All	All	Most	All
	Thermoplastics	All	All	Most	All	All	Some	Some	No	All	All	All	All	All	All
Rubber & Elastomers	Thermoset	All	No	No	All	Some	Some	Some	No	No	All	All	All	Some	Some
	Thermoplastics	All	All	All	All	Some	Some	Some	No	All	All	All	All	Some	Some
Engineering Materials	Manufactured Carbon	All	No	No	No	All	Some	No	No	No	Most	Most	Some	Some	Some
	Glass	All	All	No	All	Some	Most	No	Some	All	Most	Most	All	Some	Some
	Engineered Ceramics	All	Most	No	No	Some	No	No	No	No	All	Most	All	Most	Most
	Refractory Hard Metals	All	All	No	No	Most	Most	Most	All	No	Some	Some	Some	All	Some
Natural Materials	Fibers	All	Most	All	All	All	No	Some	No	No	Most	All	Some	Some	Some
	Wood Products	Some	Some	No	All	All	Some	Some	No	No	All	All	Some	All	All

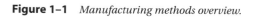

All Processes Most Processes Some Processes No Processes

Figure 1–1 *Manufacturing methods overview.*

INTRODUCTION

Need for a Materials and Manufacturing Primer

The industrial designer, whether on a design team or acting alone as a design consultant, is responsible for the appearance and form of a product. If the form of a product is to some degree the result of how it was manufactured, it follows that the designer must have a good understanding of all manufacturing processes available, in order to have confidence that the proposed manufacturing process is the most economical and appropriate. If designers are unaware of certain available processes, they will be limited in their creative potential, like a composer writing a symphony totally unaware of the color and full range and capability of two or three instruments.

Design Education

Industrial design students should have an understanding of materials and manufacturing methods early in the curriculum—ideally in the sophomore year. This is important because as projects are assigned, students need to visualize and develop forms that ultimately will be manufactured (even if theoretically). Without a comprehensive knowledge base of materials and manufacturing possibilities, students can only fantasize and flounder along, limited by ignorance of the subject and oblivious to the variety of possibilities available. With a good knowledge base the student can propose an array of possible design solutions and have some confidence that they can be manufactured. There are a number of excellent engineering

texts available, but these may be too detailed and complicated for the needs of the average student. However, this primer is not, and is not intended to be, an alternative to the standard engineering texts on the subject. It would be wise for the student to acquire such a text at some point. This primer is intended to give an overview in simple and visual terms, not to provide all of the information required for a full understanding. It will, however, serve as a guide and introduction to this rather complex field. (Figure 1–1).

As it should have been from the beginning, concurrent design and engineering has become a reality. It is now more important than ever that industrial design students understand industry standards and materials and manufacturing. Often in a product de-

Figure 1–2   *Young designer.*

sign review, changes especially concerned with design for manufacturability (DFM) can be proposed and normally must be approved quickly. If the designer is unprepared to defend the rationale for a proposed design, he or she may lose control of important design features and is reduced to being an observer as design changes are debated and approved. In fact the designer should be prepared to present and defend proposals that not only improve the appearance and performance of products but are more economical and elegant in their manufacture than what was proposed or exists. Unfortunately, concurrent design and engineering education is absent from many design and engineering curriculums. It is therefore incumbent on the industrial design student to learn some of the language and concerns of manufacturing engineering (Figure 1–2).

MANUFACTURING PROCESSES

Form is the Resolution of Function

Design is in essence a search for form. "Form follows function" has been on the banner of designers since the Bauhaus. However this famous statement suggests that function leads and form follows, relegating form to a subordinate position. Restated, it might read "form is the resolution of function," where function has two major components: (1) performance specification demands, including all user-friendly aspects, and (2) cost and manufacturability. The former refers to human factors—those concerned with the abilities and limitations of the product's user. The latter refers to the physical aspects of the product, including material selection and manufacturability. "Form is the resolution of function" suggests that form is dynamic and interactive, whereas "form follows function" implies that form is passive, following behind function as the primary de-termining factor in a design. Using the re-vised "form is the resolution of function," manufacturability is understood in its right-ful place as an equal determinant in the de-sign process.

Form is realized or made visible in a material or a combination of materials, which are shaped by tools. In creating a form, the designer is by default selecting a manufacturing process. Normally the de-signer creates models to demonstrate a con-cept in substitute materials—not the actual material—and by so doing is removed from a real understanding of the way the manufac-turing process will impact the material and form. If the designer creates forms on paper using pencil or marker, there is a danger that he or she is not only removed from an under-standing of what the actual manufacturing ramifications are but is another step re-moved from dimensional reality and mater-ial behavior altogether. It takes a real-world understanding of materials and manufactur-ing methods to create successful products. This cannot be accomplished in a studio: It requires teamwork with materials and man-ufacturing engineering development and support. The Aeron chair, by Donald Chad-wick and William Stumpf (Figure 2–1), is an excellent example of a successful product whose form is not only a celebration of ma-terials and manufacturing but is the essence of function for human need. No individual aspect of this design could have been pro-posed without satisfying all factors involved. The form evolved after years of trial and error, then a number of major successes— like the Ergon—the predecessor of the Aeron. The materials selected and in fact in-vented (because nothing existed that met the need), the production process selected, and the form were developed interdependently,

Figure 2–1   *Aeron chair (Courtesy of herman miller inc.).*

Materials and Manufacturing

Industrial Design Materials and Manufacturing is an overview of the key processes and salient related supporting information intended for (student) industrial designers. It is limited to engineering materials (excluding natural materials such as wood,* stone, and so on). The goal is to distill the key information on the subject, organize it, and present it as simply as possible (Figures 2–2 and 2–3).

Existing texts attempt to be inclusive, with extensive technical information geared to engineering. This primer, however, summarizes the processes important to industrial design and presents them as simply and graphically as possible. It is an overview and as such makes no attempt to present all available manufacturing processes; rather, it is limited to the key processes and the salient related supporting information. It is intended to be an industrial designer's guide to manufacturing and a methodology for organizing the information on the subject.

in an optimization process in which the best possible solution was determined after deliberation and exhaustive search and testing.

Perhaps the violin is the absolute epitome and essence of a product in terms of materials and manufacturing. No other human invention is so absolutely perfect in its resolution. If made by Stradivarius, nothing can match it in its ability to reach the sublime. Of course it takes a master to play it properly: There is no use playing a Stradivarius unless the music is written by a master such as Bach or Beethoven.

---

*Some wood products are included.

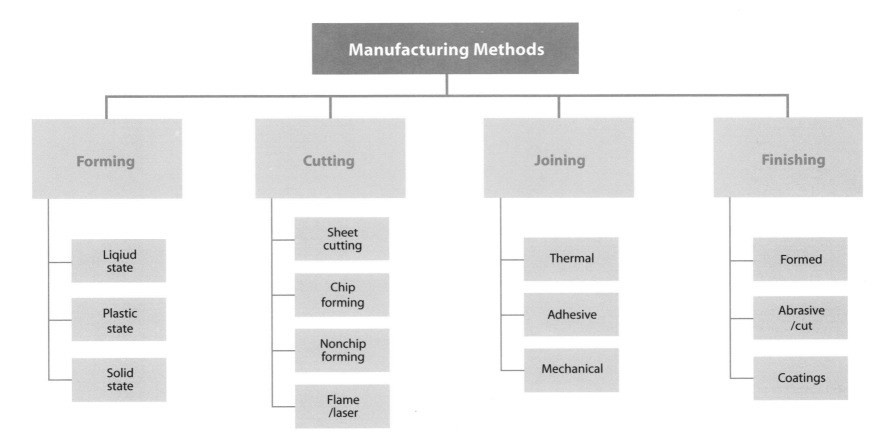

Figure 2–2 *Manufacturing methods.*

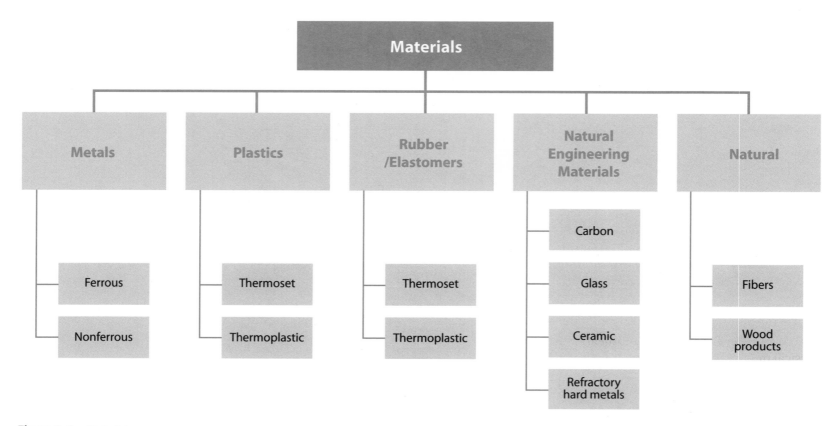

Figure 2–3 *Materials.*

METALS

Pure metals are composed of atoms of the same type. Metal alloys are composed of two or more chemical elements, of which at least one is a metal. The majority of metals used in engineering applications are alloys. Metals are generally divided into ferrous and non-ferrous. Each metal has specific mechanical and physical properties that make it ideal for a specific application. Metals are combined into a number of alloys, creating various mechanical properties tailor made for a variety of specific needs. Fairly recently, metals have become available in powdered form, making them simpler to alloy and in some cases providing alloys that were not previously possible (Figure 3–1).

3.1 PROPERTIES OF METALS

Mechanical Properties

There are two kinds of properties—mechanical and physical.

Mechanical Properties

Material behavior and concern for the mechanical properties of materials is traditionally the main responsibility of engineers. However, it is important for the industrial designer to know at least the basic terms for describing materials.

When traveling in a foreign country, it makes sense to at least try to learn a few words in the language of the people you are visiting. The same is true when working with engineers. In addition, properties are listed in technical sheets that describe materials and how they will perform under specified conditions.

Understanding a few basics about the properties of metals and how metals behave will give the designer some insight into why certain shapes work best for a given application and how to get the best performance out of a material.

Brief Definitions of Mechanical Properties

Hardness is the ability of a material to withstand penetration and scratching. Hardness and brittleness are related. Warm bubble gum is not hard: A hard sphere dropped on it will penetrate into the gum (Figure 3–4). But a ball will not penetrate the surface of glass. If the sphere hits the surface with great force, it will shatter the glass.

Brittleness is the opposite of ductility. If bubble gum is frozen, it becomes brittle and can break your teeth or shatter if you hit it with a hammer. Glass is a good example of a brittle material.

Hardness is important in liquid-state and plastic-state forming. For example, in making a sword (which is forged), it is im-

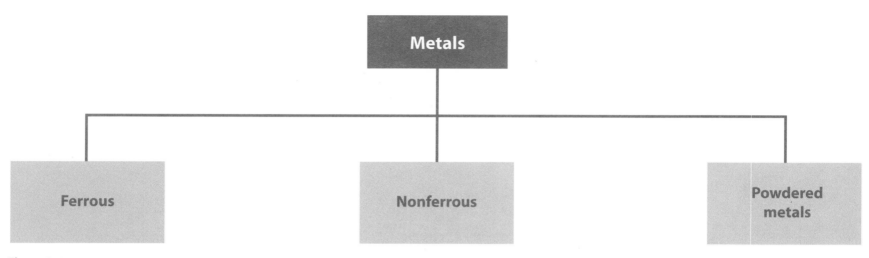

Figure 3–1 *Metals.*

portant to have hardness in the steel blade in order to get a sharp edge. But a sword must also bend. If the sword is hard and brittle (hardened state) it will shatter if it is bent—an undesirable characteristic. The sword must also be flexible. Through clever heat treatment and manipulation of the properties, it is possible to have hardness *and* flexibility—the precise but contradictory mechanical properties required for a great sword.

Ductility is the ability of a material to withstand plastic deformation without rupture. Again, bubble gum is a good example. As it is chewed it does not break up but is molded by the teeth into a new shape. Ductility is important in discussing bendability and drawability in solid-state forming.

Compression is a measure of the extent to which a material deforms under a com-

pressive load prior to rupture. Again, warm bubble gum is a good example. No matter how hard you squeeze it or step on it, it flattens but does not rupture (the reason why foundations for buildings are not made of bubble gum). A foundation requires a strong material with outstanding compressive strength—such as concrete. Concrete has good compressive strength, but under a very heavy load, it will crack. It is brittle.

Bending is characterized by the outside fibers of a beam being placed in tension and the inside fibers in compression.

Torsion is the application of torque to a member to cause it to twist about its longitudinal axis. A crankshaft must be made of metal with superior torsional strength or it will fail under the stress it is subjected to in an engine.

Shear strength is the maximum load a

material can withstand without rupture when subjected to a shearing action. Bubble gum has very little shear strength; it will shear very easily.

Strain is the change a material undergoes during elongation or contraction. It is given as a measure of deformation under load.

Metals exhibit elastic as well as plastic behavior, both of which are necessary for the forming process. These unique behaviors allow most metals to bend and draw during the shaping process (Figures 3–2 and 3–3).

Elasticity describes the recovery of a material back to its original shape and size after being deformed, when a stress is removed. This is called *elastic behavior* because the deformation the material experienced is not permanent. The stress/strain curve (Figure 3–5) graphically records how a

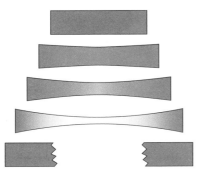

Figure 3–2 *Elastic behavior.*

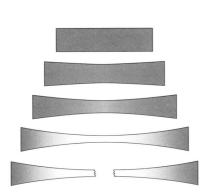

Figure 3–3 *Plastic behavior.*

Figure 3–4 *Indentation for hardness test.*

material stretches and then fractures. A good example of pure elastic behavior is demonstrated by a rubber band (Figure 3–2). When stretched, it deforms—it is elongated and the cross section is reduced. When the force is removed, the rubber band returns to its original shape. If the force exceeds its elastic limit, then the rubber band snaps or ruptures. But there is no change in the cross section of the rubber band—there is no plastic deformation (Figure 3–2).

Plastic behavior is quite different from elastic behavior. A good example of pure plastic deformation can be demonstrated by gum. When gum is stretched, it deforms and the cross section changes—it thins out. This is called *necking*. When the force is relaxed, the gum does not return to its original shape.

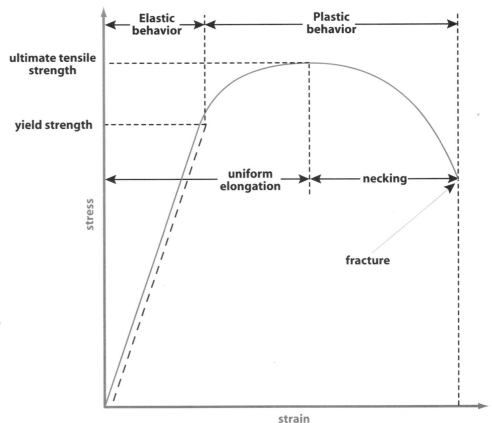

Figure 3–5 *Stress vs. strain curve.*

This is called *plastic deformation* (Figure 3–3).

Tensile strength is the maximum (pulling apart) load that a material can withstand prior to fracture.

Yield strength is the stress at which a material exhibits a specified permanent deformation.

Percent elongation is the increase in length over the original length.

Figure 3–6 *Optical inspection of glass products using the physical properties of color, transparency, and density.*

Physical Properties

Brief Definitions of Physical Properties

The following *physical properties* are inherent aspects of a material that are generally not easily altered. Physical properties generally remain intact, whereas mechanical properties are changed through heat treatment.

Opacity/transparency: Ability to transmit light (Figure 3–6).

Color: Inherent reflected wavelength.

Density: Weight per unit volume (specific gravity).

Electrical conductivity: Ease with which a material conducts a current.

Thermal conductivity: Ease with which heat flows within and through a material.

Thermal expansion: Expressed in units of 1/°F or 1/°C. Generally, the coefficient of thermal expansion is inversely proportional to the melting point of a material—higher-melt-temperature materials have less expansion. Steel is a significant exception.

Magnetic/nonmagnetic/ferromagnetism: Alignment of iron, nickel, and cobalt atoms into domains.

Melting point: Energy required to separate a material's atoms.

Corrosion resistance: Ability to resist surface deterioration caused primarily by oxygen, chemicals, or other agents. (Degradation in plastics can also be caused by ultraviolet light, moisture, and so on.)

3.2   FERROUS METALS

Crystals

Crystals are formed when ferrous metals solidify from a molten state and their atoms are arranged into orderly configurations that are face-centered cubic (fcc), body-centered cubic (bcc), or body-centered tetragonal (Figures 3–8, 3–9, and 3–10). This crystal arrangement, which is determined by the rate at which the metal cools from a liquid

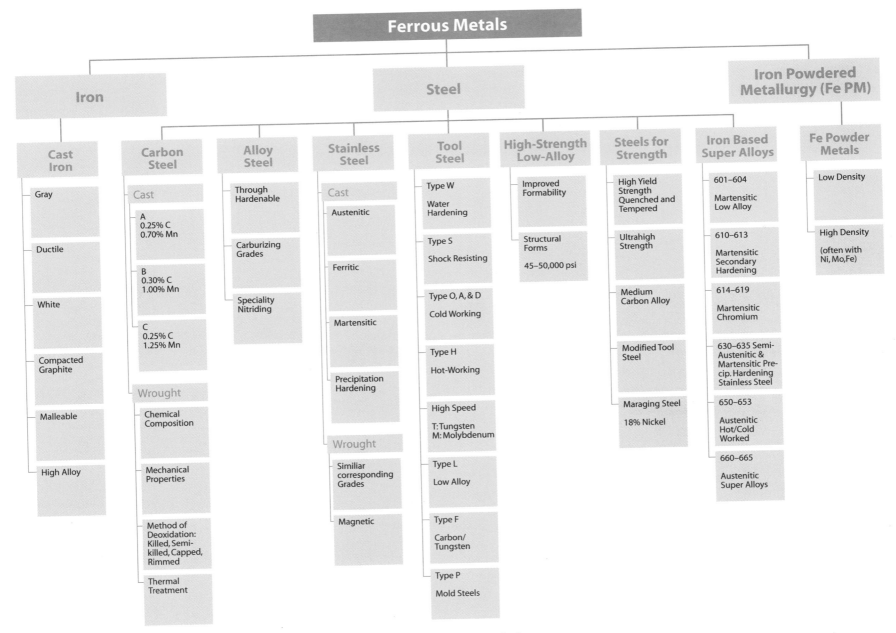

Figure 3–7 *Ferrous metals chart.*

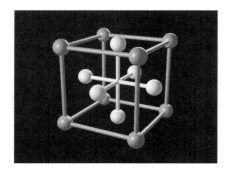

Figure 3–8 *Austenite or gamma phase at high temperature FCC—Face-centered cubic lattice in iron.*

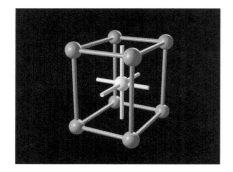

Figure 3–10 *Martensite—Body-centered tetragonal lattice is formed when iron is quenched, causing it to be stressed and distorted.*

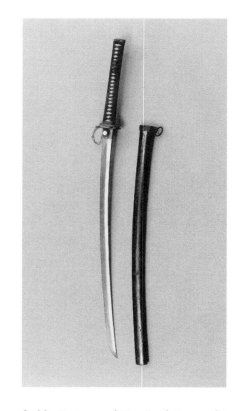

state to the solid state (called a phase transformation), establishes whether the metal will be brittle and stressed or soft and ductile. How metals behave during manufacturing and how they perform in service depends on their chemical composition,

atomic structure, and heat treatment history. Post-heat treatment of steel is one of the most commonly used methods of enhancing mechanical properties. The processes available are described as through, surface, or case hardening. To harden a metal after heating, it is necessary to quench, or cool, it quickly. Besides enhancing the hardness of a metal with a quick chill, generally considered a positive change, quenching affects other mechanical properties, such as increased brittleness—generally considered a negative change. When a metal freezes quickly it is said to be stressed (as you would be if you stepped off a plane from Florida in New York in the middle of winter). On the other hand, if the change occurs slowly at room temperature, the metal is said to be stress relieved (also called normalized, tempered, or annealed).

Figure 3–11 *In Ascent of Man, Jacob Bronowski argues that technology is at the foundation of human advancement. He presents the Master sword-maker Getsu, using ancient metallurgy and ritual to forge a steel billet, as an example of how technology was passed down through the ages. A sword must be flexible, and yet it must be hard in order to hold a sharp edge. To achieve these conflicting attributes, the billet is cut, then doubled over again and again so as to make a multitude of inner surfaces, with well over thirty thousand layers. At the last stage the sword is covered with clay of different thicknesses, so that when it is heated and plunged into water it will cool at different rates, which hardens the sword and fixes the different properties within.*

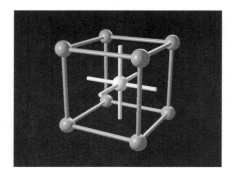

Figure 3–9 *Ferrite—BCC—Body-centered cubic lattice formed by slowly cooled iron at room temperature. Wide interatomic spacing makes this structure soft and ductile.*

Hardening

Hardness is an important mechanical property for certain applications, such as hardness to resist cutting of a steel chain. But steel becomes brittle as it is hardened. For example, hardened steel chain, if not properly heat-treated, may snap while lifting a load. So heat treatment must be done carefully, with a full understanding of the desired results. In case-hardening, only the surface is hardened, while the interior remains unaffected. This is important if the part has to resist wear but dampen vibration, or bend easily and maintain a sharp edge—as in a sword (Figure 3–12).

Heat Treatment for Carbon and Alloy Steel for Uniformity and Grain Refinement

Annealing produces a soft structure with good ductility and formability.

Normalizing produces a uniform structure with good ductility and grain refinement.

Sphereoldize annealing produces the softest structure, with maximum ductility and improved machinability.

Stress relieving reduces internal stresses and minimizes subsequent distortion, leaving the original structure unchanged.

For Through Hardening

Quench and tempering improves toughness and tensile and compressive strength. It also increases hardness and provides improved wear resistance.

Austempering is similar to quench-and-temper, with minimum distortion after heat treating. No temper cycle is usually required.

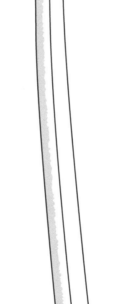

Figure 3–12   *Drawing of Samurai sword blade with hardened areas indicated .*

Martempering is similar to quench-and-temper, providing high strength with minimum distortion.

Precipitation hardening, a low-temperature process with no quench required, provides the least distortion of all hardening processes.

For Case Hardening

Gas carburizing improves fatigue strength, wear resistance, torsional strength, and bend strength.

Carbonitriding is the same as carburizing except that the case is shallower and harder on the surface, with less distortion.

Gas nitriding provides the best wear resistance and anti-galling surface of all hardening processes. It improves fatigue and torsional strength, with less distortion than all other case-hardening processes.

Soft nitriding is the same as nitriding but can be applied to a wider variety of steels, providing slightly softer surfaces.

Induction hardening provides the deepest case of all case-hardening processes, with the greatest load-carrying capacity. It also improves wear resistance, fatigue, and torsional strength.

Iron

Irons are available as cast or wrought. All cast irons contains at least 2 percent carbon and from 1–3 percent silicon. The six kinds of iron are:

Gray iron is used in automotive engine blocks, gears, flywheels, disc brakes and drums, and large machine bases. A supersaturated solution of carbon in an iron matrix,

Figure 3–13   *Early hand iron with interchangeable wood handle.*

gray iron has excellent fatigue resistance and an ability to dampen vibration—important for applications such as machine tools. Although gray iron has poor tensile strength and a lower impact strength than that of

Figure 3–14   *Early hand iron. The expression "too many irons in the fire" probably originated when these irons were heated by a cast iron coal stove.*

most other cast ferrous metals, it has a high compressive strength (Figures 3–13 and 3–14).

Ductile iron, or nodular iron, applications include crankshafts and heavy-duty gears because of its machinability, fatigue strength, and high modulus of elasticity. But it has less vibration-dampening capacity than gray iron. Ductile iron contains trace amounts of magnesium, which improves the stiffness, strength, and shock resistance over gray iron.

White iron is specified where wear and abrasion resistance are required for applications such as clay-mixing and brick-making equipment such as crushers, pulverizers, and nozzles; railroad brake shoes, and rolling-mill rolls. White iron gets its name from the whitish appearance of the metal, caused by chilling selected areas of gray or ductile iron in the mold.

Compacted graphic iron (CGI) is used in automotive engine blocks, brake drums, and exhaust manifolds and high-pressure gear pumps. It has a strength and dampening capacity near those of gray iron, with high thermal conductivity and machinability superior to those of ductile iron.

Malleable iron is used for heavy-duty bearing surfaces in automobiles, trucks, railroad rolling stock, and for farm and construction machinery. Malleable iron is white iron that has been transformed by a heat-treatment process, providing a malleable and easily machined iron.

High-alloy irons are ductile, gray, or white irons that contain up to 35 percent alloy content. High-chromium irons are oxidation and wear resistant. Nickel irons are nonmagnetic, have good corrosion resistance, and an extremely low coefficient of thermal expansion.

Steel

Carbon, alloy, stainless, tool, high-strength low-alloy, steels for strength and iron-based super alloys are the general kinds of steel. Nearly a million tons of steel are produced in the United States every week (Figure 3–15). Carbon steel (especially cold-rolled sheet and mill products), stainless (mostly sheet and standard shapes), and tools steels (for molds) are of interest to industrial designers. Other types of steels are used in construction, in heavy industrial equipment, and in other specialized applications. The following discussion on steel will be somewhat limited to steels used in products and applications that involve industrial designers.

Carbon steel (or common steel) is an iron-based metal containing carbon and small amounts of other elements. Steel is available as cast or wrought mill products such as sheet, angles, and bar and tube, from which finished parts are formed, cut, and/or joined. The method of deoxidation is important in steel making. Molten steel contains oxygen, and how oxygen is removed or killed—is allowed to escape as the steel solidifies—determines the properties of steel. In addition, the combined effects of several elements influence steel's properties—its hardness, machinability, corrosion resistance and tensile strength. There are four types of carbon steel (based on method of deoxidation): killed, semi-killed, rimmed, and capped.

Killed and semi-killed steels are created by adding deoxidizing elements such as alu-

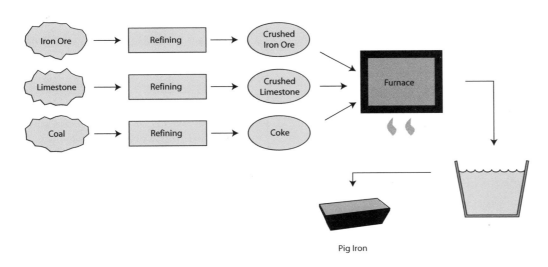

Figure 3–15 *In the production of steel, refined iron ore and limestone are heated by coke (coal baked in an oven, removing sulphur and other impurities) in a blast furnace. Slag is removed, and the molten iron is transported to steel-making furnaces.*

minum and silicon, which combine chemically with the oxygen in the steel. Killed steels are specified for forging, for hot or cold rolled sheet, and for casting.

Rimmed steel is characterized by a gaseous effervescence when solidifying, resulting in relatively pure iron in the outer rim. It is subject to property changes through aging. The skin of rimmed steel is free of carbon, which makes it ductile and is often specified for cold-forming applications.

Capped steel has characteristics similar to those of rimmed steels but is intermediate between semi-killed and rimmed steels in behavior and properties. Because of their soft, ductile surface skin, which is thinner than that of rimmed steel, capped steels are suited for cold-forming applications.

Alloy steels are specified when high strength is needed in moderate to large sections. Their properties are enhanced by specific amounts of alloying elements. Alloy steels are heat treated to increase properties such as tensile strength, which can be raised from 55,000 psi to 300,000 psi.

Stainless steels have a minimum of 10.5 percent chromium as the principal alloying element. The four major categories of wrought stainless steel based on their metallurgical structure are: austenitic, ferritic, martensitic, and precipitation hardening. Cast stainless-steel grades are generally designated as either heat resistant or corrosion resistant (Figure 3–16).

Austenitic stainless steels are commonly used for processing chemicals and food and dairy products, as well as for shafts, pumps, fasteners, and piping in sea water equipment where corrosion resistance and toughness are primary requirements.

Ferritic wrought alloys are used for automotive exhaust systems and heat-transfer equipment for the chemical and petrochemical industries. These alloys are magnetic, with moderate toughness and corrosion resistance.

Martensitic stainless steels are typically used for bearings, molds, cutlery, medical instruments, aircraft structural parts, and turbine components. They are magnetic and can be hardened by heat treatment. These alloys are normally used where strength and/or hardness is the primary concern, in a relatively mild corrosive environment.

Precipitation-hardening stainless steels are used for aircraft components, high-temper springs, fasteners, and high-pressure

Figure 3–16 *The Unisphere was designed by Gilmore D. Clarke for the 1964 World's Fair in New York City. It has 500 pieces of stainless steel and weighs 900,000 pounds. The Unisphere was a gift of the United States Steel Corporation. The base was designed by The Peter Müller-Munk Office.*

pump parts. The precipitation-hardening process produces very high strength in a low-temperature heat treatment that does not significantly distort precision parts. These alloys are used where high strength, moderate corrosion resistance, and good fabricability are required.

Tool steels are metallurgically "clean," high-alloy steels that are used for tools and dies and for parts that require resistance to wear, stability during heat treatment,

strength at high temperatures, or toughness. Tool steels are often specified for critical high-strength or wear-resistant applications. To develop their best properties, tool steels are always heat treated.

Shock-resisting tool steels (type S) are used for pneumatic tooling parts, chisels, punches, shear blades, bolts, and springs subjected to moderate heat in service. They are strong and tough, but not as wear resistant as other tool steels.

Hot-work steels (type H) are used for high performance aircraft parts such as primary airframe structures, cargo-support lugs, catapult hooks, and elevon hinges.

High-speed tool steels (type T/M) make good cutting tools because they resist softening and maintain a sharp cutting edge at high service temperatures.

Type P mold steels are created specifically for plastic and die-cast tooling.

High-strength low-alloy steels (HSLA)

FN–0205–35

- Minimum Yield Strength
- Percent Combined Carbon (by weight)
- Percent Major Alloy
- Basic Element

Figure 3–17b *Powdered metal coding designation developed by Metal Powder Industries Federation.*

Figure 3–17a *Powdered metal parts (Courtesy of Metal Powder Industries Federation).*

Prefix letter codes for the elements used in P/M

A	aluminum
C	copper
CT	bronze
CNZ	nickel silver
CZ	brass
D	molybdenum
F	iron
FC	copper iron or steel
FN	nickel iron or steel
FX	infiltrated iron or steel
FL	pre-alloyed ferrous material (except stainless steel)
FM	pre-alloyed ferrous material
G	free graphite
M	manganese
N	nickel
P	lead
S	silicon
SS	stainless steel (pre-alloyed)
T	tin
R	titanium
U	sulfur
Y	phosphorus
Z	zinc

are used for transportation equipment components where weight reduction is important. Because of their strength they can be used in thinner sections, providing increased strength-to-weight ratios over those of conventional low-carbon steels.

Steels for strength are heat-treated constructional alloy steels and ultrahigh-strength steels that are used in situations where weight-saving is an advantage. Some have added toughness and weldability.

Iron-based superalloys are iron, nickel, and cobalt-based alloys which are specified for high-temperature applications. They are available in all conventional mill forms as well as special shapes available for most alloys.

3.3 POWDERED METALLURGY

Powdered metallurgy (P/M) has provided new processes and new metal alloys that can significantly reduce weight while providing enhanced mechanical properties. P/M parts are used in sports products; electronic and office equipment components such as actuators, sprockets, levers, fasteners, bearings, impellers, cams, and gears; and for automotive engines, transmissions, and chassis, as well as off-road vehicles (Figure 3–17a). Parts are formed by a compaction process and then sintered. They can then be forged in a second step for greater strength. Additional forming processes include injection molding, hot isostatic pressing, and cold isostatic pressing. In addition to conventional iron and steel alloys, the list of available powders includes new classes of tool steels and cermets, and alloys of aluminum, copper, nickel, titanium and other nonferrous metals.

The P/M coding system, developed by the Metal Powder Industries Federation (MPIF), includes (1) a prefix indicating the major alloying constituents, (2) four digits that indicate chemical content, and (3) a two-digit code that indicates minimum yield strength for as-sintered material, sometimes followed by "HT," indicating minimum ultimate tensile strength for heat-treated material. Ferrous alloys begin with an F (for iron) followed by a letter designating the next major noncarbon alloying element (Figure 3–17b). Unalloyed carbon steels and irons have only an F in the prefix with the percentage of the major alloying element is designated by the first two digits. The last two digits designate the percentage of metallurgically combined carbon. Stainless-steel alloys are an exception; they begin with SS followed by the standard stainless-steel designations.

3.4 NONFERROUS METALS

Metals account for a large percentage of the elements, but only a few are normally used in manufacturing consumer and industrial products. Nonferrous metals offer a wide variety of mechanical and physical properties, have a wide range of melt temperatures, and differ greatly in cost and performance (Figure 3–18). Many of the same manufacturing methods used with ferrous metals are also used to form, cut, and join nonferrous metals and their alloys. However, the reaction of nonferrous metals to these processes is often more severe, and the mechanical properties of the cast and wrought forms of the same alloy may vary greatly.

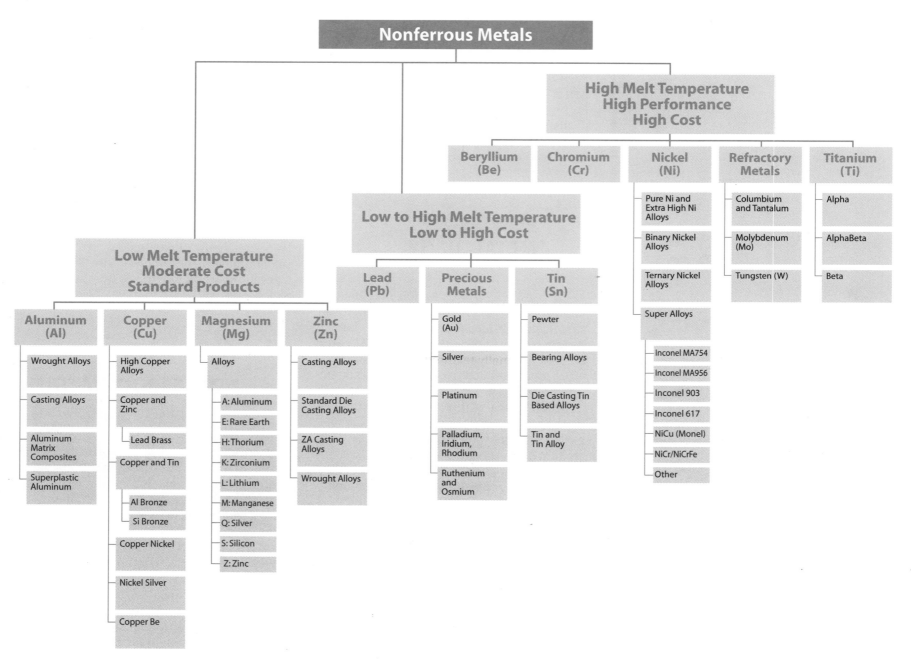

Figure 3–18 *Nonferrous Metals.*

Low Melt Temperature Metals

Low-Melt-Temperature Standard Product Metals

Aluminum is one of the most commonly used metals and is particularly important in industrial design. It has a high strength-to-weight ratio, good formability, and its own anticorrosion mechanism. When exposed to air, a hard microscopic oxide coating forms on the surface, sealing the metal. Aluminum and most aluminum alloys, available in commercial forms, can be easily formed, cut, joined, and finished. Aluminum is an efficient electrical conductor, reflects radiant energy throughout the entire spectrum, and is nonsparking and nonmagnetic. It is available in two forms: as wrought products or as castings or ingots. Each category has its own numerical designations.

The wrought designations have four numbers plus a suffix that indicate a temper, finish, and/or coating. The first number indicates the major alloying metal, the second digit indicates modifications of original alloy or impurity limits, and the last two digits identify the alloy or aluminum or alloy purity (Figure 3–19a).

Wrought Aluminum Alloy Designations

1xxx Aluminum (99% or greater), excellent corrosion resistance, high electrical and thermal conductivity, good workability, low strength, not heat treatable

2xxx Copper, high strength-to-weight ratio, low corrosion resistance, heat treatable

3xxx Manganese, good workability, moderate strength, generally not heat treatable

4xxx Silicon, low melting point, forms dark-gray oxide film, generally not heat treatable

5xxx Magnesium, good corrosion resistance and weldability, moderate to high strength, not heat treatable

6xxx Magnesium and silicon, medium strength; good formability, machinability, weldability, and corrosion resistance; heat treatable

7xxx Zinc, moderate to high strength, heat treatable

8xxx Other

Aluminum Association Designations for Finishes

M   Mechanical finishes
M1X As fabricated surface
M2X Buffed surface, usually bright and shiny
M3X Directionally textured in one direction
M4X Nondirectionally textured in a distinct but random pattern
C   Chemical finishes
C1X Non-etched cleaned, usually with preparatory chemical cleaners
C2X Etched surface, including chemical milling
C3X Brightened, often clear anodized afterwards
C4X Conversion coatings, including chromates, phosphates
A   Anodic coatings
A1X General, includes sulfuric, chromic, and hard anodize
A2X Protective and decorative—generally below 0.4 mil thick
A3X Architectural Class II—between 0.4 and 0.7 mil thick
A4X Architectural Class I—over 0.7 mil thick

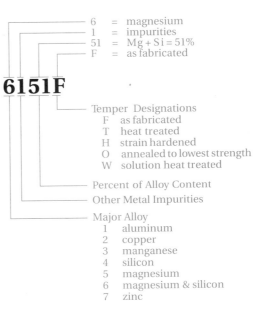

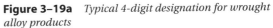

6 = magnesium
1 = impurities
51 = Mg + Si = 51%
F = as fabricated

6151F

Temper Designations
F as fabricated
T heat treated
H strain hardened
O annealed to lowest strength
W solution heat treated

Percent of Alloy Content
Other Metal Impurities
Major Alloy
1 aluminum
2 copper
3 manganese
4 silicon
5 magnesium
6 magnesium & silicon
7 zinc

Figure 3–19a *Typical 4-digit designation for wrought alloy products*

Figure 3–19b *Aluminum castings from mold awaiting trimming*

R   Resins and other organic coatings—paints, powder, plastics
V   Vitreous coatings—porcelainizing and ceramics
E   Electroplating and other metal coatings

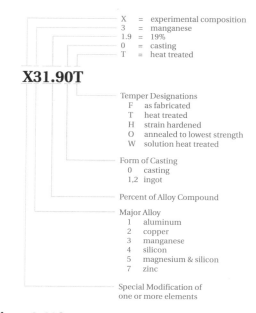

X = experimental composition
3 = manganese
1.9 = 19%
0 = casting
T = heat treated

X31.90T

Temper Designations
F   as fabricated
T   heat treated
H   strain hardened
O   annealed to lowest strength
W   solution heat treated

Form of Casting
0   casting
1,2   ingot

Percent of Alloy Compound

Major Alloy
1   aluminum
2   copper
3   manganese
4   silicon
5   magnesium & silicon
7   zinc

Special Modification of
one or more elements

Figure 3–20A *Typical four digit designation for cast aluminum.*

Figure 3–20B *The Pensi Collection, Toledo Stacking Chair, (Courtesy of Knoll).*

Temper Designations

F   As fabricated
O   Annealed
H   Strain hardened
W   Solution heat treated
T   Heat treated to T62—solution heat treated and then artificially aged (specified for stress relieving and to improve dimensional stability. The number following the T indicates the variation in cold-working and/or thermal treatments.

Aluminum casting alloys are identified by a four-digit system. The first digit indicates the major alloying element. The 100 series indicates a minimum of 99 percent pure aluminum. The second and third digits in the 100 series indicate the exact minimum aluminum content. The 200–900 series designate various alloys, with the second two digits assigned to new alloys as they are registered. The fourth digit indicates the product form. Castings are designated 0; ingots are designated 1 or 2. Letter prefixes before the numerical designation indicate special control of one or more elements or a modification of the original alloy. Commercial casting alloys include heat-treatable and non-heat-treatable compositions. Heat-treated alloys carry the temper designations 0, T4, T5, T6, and T7. Die castings are not usually solution heat treated because the temperature can cause blistering (Figure 3–20A).

Cast Aluminum Alloy Designations

1xx.x Aluminum (99% minimum)
2xx.x Aluminum—copper
3xx.x Aluminum—silicon, with copper and/or magnesium
4xx.x Aluminum—silicon

Copper is known for its ease of forming and joining, excellent electrical and thermal conductivity, attractive color, and excellent corrosion resistance. Copper (Cu) and its alloys have relatively low strength-to-weight ratios and low strengths at elevated temperatures, and unless stressed relieved, some alloys are susceptible to stress cracking. Brass (Cu + Zinc) and bronze (Cu + Tin) are available in many standard shapes and are used extensively in the plumbing industries and in fine art casting. Copper alloy compositions are designated by a five-digit identification number preceded by C as part of the Unified Numbering System (UNS) for metals and alloys. C10000–C79900 are assigned to wrought compositions, and C80000–C99900 to casting alloys.

Magnesium is an important metal for product design because it is the lightest structural metal available. Typical gravity-filled castings are aircraft engine components and wheels for racing and sports vehicles. Die-cast examples are chain-saw and power tool housings and attache-case frames. Because of its light weight, magnesium is used extensively in the transportation and recreation industries. It has an excellent combination of low density and good mechanical strength, which gives it a high strength-to-weight ratio. Magnesium alloys can absorb energy elastically and have moderate strength, which provides excellent dent resistance and a high dampening capacity. Magnesium has good fatigue resistance and performs well in applications involving a large number of cycles. The metal is sensitive to stress concentrations, so partial design should avoid notches, sharp corners, and abrupt section changes. These rule-of-thumb design features should be observed as a matter of course, but magnesium is particularly sensitive, so added care should be observed in designing parts that will be subjected to stress. Magnesium can be machined faster than any metal, is easy to hot work, and welds easily. It has good corrosion resistance and can be finished by painting or plating.

Magnesium is almost always alloyed when used in structural applications. Common magnesium elements are: A (aluminum), E (rare earths), H (thorium), K (zirconium), L (lithium), M (manganese), Q (silver), S (silicon), and Z (zinc). These alloys are designated by an American Society for Testing Materials (ASTM) system that uses two letters and two numbers that cover the chemical compositions and tempers. The letters of the designation identify the two alloying elements specified in the greatest amount, and the numbers indicate the respective percentages. The letters and numbers are arranged in order of decreasing percentages, or alphabetically if the amounts are equal, followed by a final serial letter indicating some variation in composition. In the alloy AZ31B, for example, the A indicates that the alloy contains aluminum and the Z indicates that it also contains zinc. The 3 means that there is 3 percent aluminum and the 1 means that there is 1 percent zinc. The B designates a variation of the basic alloy AZ31.

Zinc alloy die-cast components are used in numerous products that range from automotive components, building hardware products such as electrical boxes, and industrial tool components to toys. Zinc has moderate strength and ductility. Because it has excellent corrosion resistance, it is used as a coating for steel, called galvanized steel. It extends the life of materials such as rubber and plastics, is used as an aging inhibitor, and as activators and stabilizers for plastics. It is also used as an additive in wood paints. Zinc die-castings have good tensile properties. Zinc can be cast in thin sections with good dimensional accuracy. Rolled zinc can be worked by common fabricating methods and finished by painting or plating (Figure 3–21).

Low to High Melt Temperature Metals

Low to High Melt Temperature/Low- to High-Cost Metals

Lead is toxic but it is very useful because it resists attack by corrosive chemicals, many soil types, and marine and industrial environments. It is also impervious to X-rays and gamma radiation. Its uses include chemical applications and storage batteries. Lead is an efficient sound deadener for industrial and commercial applications because of its high internal dampening characteristic. Its low

Figure 3–21 *Galvanized (zinc-coated steel) highway structures.*

melting temperature, ease of forming, and ease of salvage from scrap make it a useful metal as long as care is taken in its use. Many solders are lead-tin alloys.

Precious metals are organized into three subgroups: silver and silver alloys; gold and gold alloys; and the platinum metals—platinum, palladium, rhodium, ruthenium, iridium, and osmium. Most of these are available as sheet, tape, foil, wire, tubing, gauze, and other forms. Gold and silver are used for coins and jewelry in industrial and high-tech applications where the ultimate in corrosion resistance or electrical conductivity is required. Precious metals are virtually corrosion resistant. Platinum is able to perform in temperatures up to 3200°F without corrosion. The range of melting temperatures for precious metals has a low of 1763°F for silver to a high of 5533°F for osmium.

Tin has a low melting point and is easily alloyed, usually with antimony, copper, lead, and zinc. It is used in many solders and as a "tinplate" coating for steel. Tin work softens and is too weak for mechanical applications.

High Melt Temperature Metals

High Melt Temperature, High-Performance, High-Cost Metals

Beryllium is used in military-aircraft and space-shuttle brake systems, reentry body structures, missile guidance systems, mirrors and optical systems, satellite structures, and X-ray windows. Beryllium has a low density (two-thirds that of aluminum), high specific heat, high strength, excellent dimensional stability, and is transparent to X-rays. It is expensive and has a low impact strength when compared to other metals. Beryllium particles or salts can present a health hazard and are toxic if inhaled.

Chromium is known to industrial designers as a decorative finish-plating metal that also provides corrosion resistance. Chromium is used to harden steel, improve its resistance to abrasion and wear, and provide corrosion resistance (see stainless steel).

Nickel and its alloys are used in applications that require corrosion resistance or strength at elevated temperatures. Casting alloys can be machined or ground, and many can be welded or brazed. Most wrought products can be formed, cut, and/or joined on standard shop equipment with a few modifications or special techniques. Nickel is a common plating metal.

Refractory metals are used in applications requiring high temperature strength and corrosion strength, with melting points above 4000°F. Tungsten, tantalum, molybdenum, and columbium, the four refractory metals, have alloys available in mill forms. Pure tungsten is used for lighting filaments and for electrical contacts in automative ignition systems. Tungsten-carbide is used for wire drawing dies, cutting tools, and rotary drilling and mining bits.

Titanium is used for surgical implants and for marine and chemical equipment hardware. Sheet and plate work harden during forming. Minimum bend-radius rules are about the same as for stainless steel, and are cold- or warm-formed at temperatures of 800°F to 1400°F. Titanium sheet can be sheared or punched on standard equipment. Castings can be produced by investment or graphite molds in a vacuum furnace.

Zirconium is commonly used for heat exchangers, drying columns, pipe and fittings, pump and valve housings, and reactor vessels. It is used for chemical processing because it resists strong acids and alkalis. Zirconium can be formed or punched on standard shop equipment with a few modifications or special techniques, and it has better weldability than some of the more common aluminum or steel alloys.

METAL FORMING

There are three ways to form metals:

1. In a *liquid state* (or casting), where the metals are melted by heat and poured into a mold. The process is an efficient way to get metal where it is required. There are, however, some problems associated with the process, such as a tendency for a porous structure and warpage. Nonetheless this process is often the most efficient one available, especially for complex parts.

2. In a *plastic state* (or forging), where bars and preshaped parts are heated below the melting point, making them easy to form. Forging processes are often labor intensive, but the advantage of these processes is the enhanced strength achieved in the part. Some high-volume production processes can be automated.

3. In a *solid state*, normally limited to sheet, rod, and tube, usually done at room temperature. Although these processes are normally labor intensive,

new developments with computer-controlled tooling and sheet handling has drastically cut time and costs (Figure 4–1).

4.1 LIQUID STATE FORMING (METAL)

Liquid State Forming

Liquid state forming or *casting* is one of the earliest manufacturing processes. It is often the most economical way to manufacture a complex object, putting metal where it is needed in a desired thickness with a minimum of required secondary operations. There are many casting processes available. Selecting the optimum method to produce the desired part depends on a number of delimiting factors such as the material to be cast, all related costs, size, quantity, tolerance, section thickness, physical/mechanical properties, design features or complexity, machinability, and weldability. Competing processes, production time, and consumer/customer preference also play a role in the final decision (Figure 4–2).

Liquid or molten metal is cast in assembled mold halves made of sand, plaster, ceramic, and ferrous and nonferrous metals. Obviously the metal cast has to be of a lower melt temperature than the mold material or a refractory material—one that can withstand the temperature of the molten metal. A pattern made of wax, wood, plastic, or metal is used to create the mold void in expendable molds (Figure 4–3). The mold cavity in nonexpendable tools is machined in solid materials.

Expendable molds are those destroyed during part removal, so drafts and undercuts are not required during the casting process. However draft and the elimination of undercuts are still required to remove the pattern from the mold. Surface finish and appearance considerations are also important factors in casting.

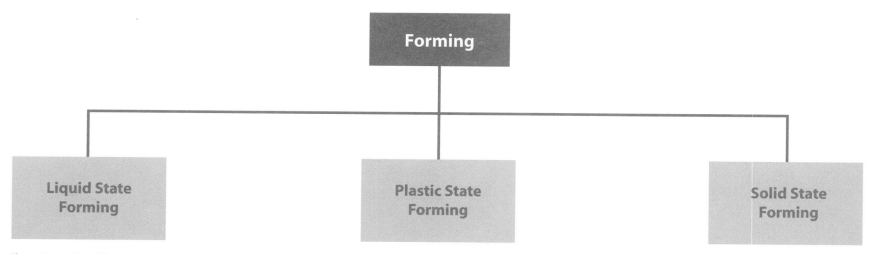

Figure 4–1   *Metal forming.*

Nonexpendable molds (also called tools or dies) are expensive and require large production quantities to make them economically feasible. They also usually require a greater lead time in order to prepare the molds, and last-minute changes to the molds are extremely expensive, if not impossible. Nonexpendable molds also have other disadvantages: A draft is required in order to eject the part from the mold, and undercuts are not possible unless there are movable cores or a side action that moves obstructions out of the ejection path. In some cases cores can be made of expendable materials. Die-casting machines are expensive. (*Note:* Some molds are made of flexible materials—such as rubber—and do permit undercuts with little or no draft. These molds are limited to very low melt temperature metals and plastics.)

Although centuries of casting experience have taken much of the mystery out of the process, it is still fundamentally an art and little should be taken for granted. During the initial design phase of the product/part, the designer should seek out foundries, pattern makers, material suppliers, and sales representatives with a proven track record. Special attention should be paid to their recommendations.

A major dent occurred in the volume of casting following World War II as a result of the many technical advances in welding and the explosive evolution of engineering plastics. The lower cost and sophisticated technology made welding an economically more competitive alternative to casting. As plastic technology improved, it provided many advantages over metal casting, particularly in consumer products. Because of concern for

Electro Magnetic Interference (EMI) and Radio Frequency Interference (RFI)—particularly in business equipment, and because of other important mechanical and physical property advantages of metals, and other new developments in metal casting—there is a resurgence in these processes, and it is an error to routinely overlook metal casting for part development.

Molds, Cores, & Patterns

Molds

Generally all molds have much in common (*see* Figure 4–4). Usually there are two parts, the drag [lower] (1) and cope [upper] (2), or male and female in hard molds that are joined at a parting line (3). There is a pouring basin and sprue (4) with a runner (5) leading

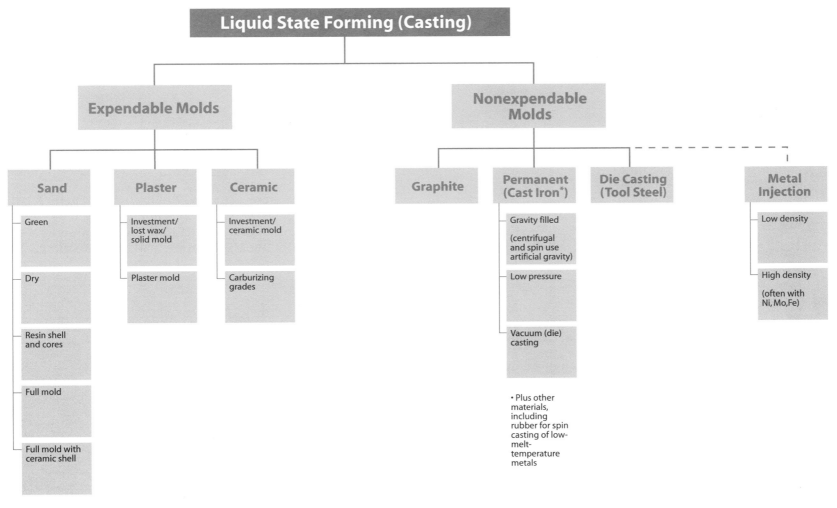

Figure 4-2 *Liquid-state forming.*

Figure 4–3   *Skilled pattern maker milling a pattern or tool. (Courtesy Talbot Associates).*

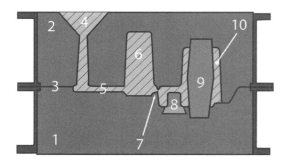

Figure 4–4   *Schematic of a sand mold with cores .*

to an ingate (7) at the part cavity (10)—also called the negative—created by a pattern. A hollow in the casting is created by a core, either a set core (9) or a ram-up core (8) (called a [moveable] side action core in hard molds). Cores are made of sand or of solid materials in hard molds.

Figure 4–4, a schematic section of a sand mold, includes a riser (6), which is slightly higher and heavier in cross section than the part cavity in the mold. Its purpose is to allow the turbulent molten metal to settle and enter the part cavity smoothly, to ensure that the part cavity fills completely, and to act as a reservoir of liquid metal to feed the casting as it shrinks, avoiding internal shrinkage porosity. Any gasses trapped in the

mold, being light, will flow to the highest point (in the riser), out of the cast part. All parts shown, including the riser, have a draft, because they were formed by a pattern. Sand molds are destroyed to remove the casting, so no draft is required. Draft is required to remove the pattern when the mold is made, so a draft must be designed into the pattern for that purpose.

Patterns

A pattern (also called a positive) is made of wax, wood, plastic, or metal and is used to create the mold void. (In hard molds the void is machined out of a solid block.) A pattern is a likeness of the final product or cast part, but must be larger, to account for shrinkage of the casting during cooling. A skilled pattern maker can give the designer valuable insights into the art of casting (Figure 4–3).

Cavities

The number and type of cavities in a mold or die (hard molds) classifies it as a single-cavity (one-part), multiple-cavity (a number of

parts), combination (of different parts), or a unit die. The unit die is interchangeable with other units for a variety of part combinations to be cast (Figure 4–5).

Casting Design Principles

Although casting processes offer a variety of possibilities of size, shape, and a spectrum of castable metals, there are a number of elementary principles and some rule-of-thumb guides that must be followed. The designer must be aware of how solidification is affected by part geometry and changes in cross-section area. Draft, which affects appearance, is required in most casting.

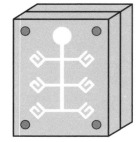
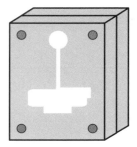
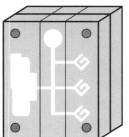
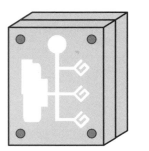

Figure 4–5   *Single-cavity, multiple-cavity, combination, and unit dies.*

The internal grain structure of the casting is affected by the cooling rate. Cooling begins at the outer wall and proceeds inward to the center. Changes in thickness will alter the cooling rate and can cause warping, hot tears, and shrinkage. Therefore, the designer should maintain a uniform wall thickness or change thickness gradually, offset or stagger connections, and avoid square corners or areas of material build-up.

Sharp corners and angles should be avoided, and gradual curves and fillets should be used to ensure uniform liquid metal flow. Flat areas should be avoided, because they have a tendency to warp and often result in poor surfaces. A draft is required, and the part line should be simple rather than complex and located at the corners or edges rather than on a surface, especially a flat surface.

Machining Allowance

The interior of a casting is apt to be more porous than the outer wall. If a hole in a part is required, it should be cast in using a core. It should not be drilled unless necessary. If a close tolerance is required, a machining allowance must be provided to mill out a cast hole or to provide for flat surfaces. Machining will also be required to provide a smooth bearing surface to reduce wear. The surface of raw castings is primarily determined by the mold material.

Automated Casting

If the production rate warrants it, most mold-making and casting processes can be automated with many mold stations capable of 100 or more castings per hour. Computer control is used to provide a variety of robotic metal-pouring operations to remove the castings and position them for gate-sprue removal at a shearing station. Figure 4–6 shows a typical automated mold-making process.

4.1.1 Expendable Molds/ Waste Molds

Expendable (waste) molds are destroyed when removing the casting.

Sand Casting

Green sand molds are made of moist sand packed into wooden or metal pattern halves. The mold is assembled with or without cores, molten metal is poured into the resulting cavity, and the mold is broken to remove the part (Figure 4–7).

Dry sand molds are used primarily for large, heavy castings. The sand is coated with refractory material and is dried, making it stronger than wet sand molds. The refractory material helps protect the sand from excessive heat.

Figure 4–6 *Automated mold making (Courtesy of Talbot Associates Inc.).*

Figure 4–7 *Gravity fill of sand molds (Courtesy BOOSE Aluminum Foundry, Co.).*

Figure 4–8 *V-Process sand mold (Courtesy of Missouri Steel Castings).*

Vacuum molding, or V-process, is an innovative new process developed for large castings (Figure 4–9). Heated plastic film is drawn across the molds with an applied vacuum (Figures 4–8 and 4–10).

Resin shell molds are made of fine sand mixed with thermosetting plastics. The mixture is blown onto a hot metal pattern, creating a thin shell. The mold parts are assembled with or without cores, molten metal is poured into the resulting cavity, and the molds are broken to remove the part.

Resin shell cores are made of fine sand mixed with thermosetting plastic. The molds are heated, melting the plastic which binds the outer surface of the sand. The inner sand is removed, leaving a shell.

EXPENDABLE MOLDS/WASTE MOLDS

Advantages

• Few limitations on size or shape
• Inserts can be part of the mold
• Molds are inexpensive

Disadvantages

• Limited dimensional accuracy
• Poor surface quality
• Thin sections are impractical
• Machining usually required

Figure 4–9   *Sand-mold steel castings (Courtesy of Missouri Steel castings).*

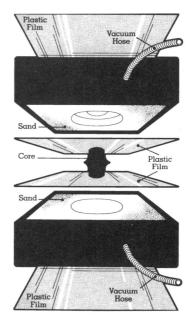

Figure 4–10   *V-Process mold (Courtesy of Missouri Steel castings).*

Full Mold Casting

Full mold casting, also called evaporative pattern casting, is somewhat like investment casting except that the positive is made of styrofoam instead of wax and is left in the sand or investment. Molten metal is poured into the mold, vaporizing the foam pattern and thus saving the burn-out step. No draft is required and undercuts are possible.

Replicast ceramic shell (CS) *molding,* a new variation, uses a thin ceramic coat over the styrofoam patterns that is backed up by dry sand, sometimes using a vacuum to lock the sand grains into a hard, strong mold (Figures 4–11–4–13). One version eliminates the pattern with a thermal treatment prior to pouring the metal, eliminating the resulting contaminating gasses.

Advantages of Replicast (CS) Molding

- Improved surface quality
- Improved casting integrity
- Improved casting yields
- No sand contact
- Superb dimensional accuracy
- Reduced cleaning requirements
- Reduced machining
- Long-term dimensional repeatability

Investment Casting

Investment casting (also called lost wax, precision casting, or solid mold*) is made of plaster that is 70–80 percent gypsum and 20–30 percent fibrous strengthening (Figures 4–14 and 4–15). This earliest of casting processes has changed little. The steps are:

1. The part to be cast is made of wax.
2. Runners and sprue are attached and held in a flask.

---

*The term *solid mold* is used in industry—*investment* and *lost wax* are used in art casting foundries and art schools.

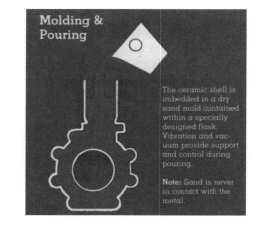

Molding & Pouring

The ceramic shell is imbedded in a dry sand mold contained within a specially designed flask. Vibration and vacuum provide support and control during pouring.

Note: Sand is never in contact with the metal.

Figure 4–13 *Drawing of the replicast casting process (Courtesy Missouri Steel Castings).*

Figure 4–11 *Replicast process castings (Courtesy Missouri Steel Castings).*

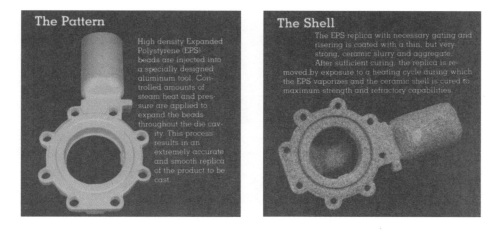

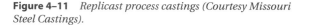

The Pattern

High density Expanded Polystyrene (EPS) beads are injected into a specially designed aluminum tool. Controlled amounts of steam heat and pressure are applied to expand the beads throughout the die cavity. This process results in an extremely accurate and smooth replica of the product to be cast.

The Shell

The EPS replica with necessary gating and risering is coated with a thin, but very strong, ceramic slurry and aggregate. After sufficient curing, the replica is removed by exposure to a heating cycle during which the EPS vaporizes and the ceramic shell is cured to maximum strength and refractory capabilities.

Figure 4–12 *Replicast CS photographs of a pattern and shell (Courtesy Missouri Steel Castings).*

INVESTMENT CASTING

Advantages

- Superior surface quality
- Thin wall or section, intricate parts
- Minimum or no draft angle required (except for pattern)

Disadvantages

- Limited to nonferrous metals
- Limited in size

Typical Parts

- Precision parts, scientific and medical instruments, tools
- Sculpture, jewelry, aerospace parts, airborne electronics

Figure 4–14   *Aluminum investment casting (Courtesy of Talbot Associates Inc.).*

Figure 4–16   *Pouring metal (Courtesy of Armstrong Mold Corporation).*

3. Investment is poured into the flask surrounding the assembly leaving access to the sprue and pouring basin.

4. When the investment is set, the flask is inverted and heated, melting the wax, which drains from the mold, leaving a cavity or void.

5. The flask is righted and liquid metal is poured into the void via the pouring basin.

6. When the metal solidifies, the plaster or ceramic is broken away and the runners and vents are removed from the cast part(s) (Figure 4–15).

Plaster Molds

Plaster slurry is poured onto the cope and drag pattern halves and allowed to set. The mold is then removed from the patterns,

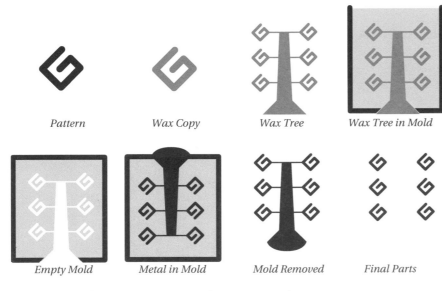

Pattern   Wax Copy   Wax Tree   Wax Tree in Mold

Empty Mold   Metal in Mold   Mold Removed   Final Parts

Figure 4–15   *Schematic representation of investment casting process.*

PLASTER MOLDS

Advantages

- Short lead time, superior surface quality, thin wall or section
- Intricate parts, minimum or no draft angle (except for pattern removal)

Disadvantages

- Plaster molds limited to nonferrous metals
- Limited in size, not good for heavy sections

Typical Parts

- Precision parts, often used to prototype for die-casting
- Sculpture, jewelry

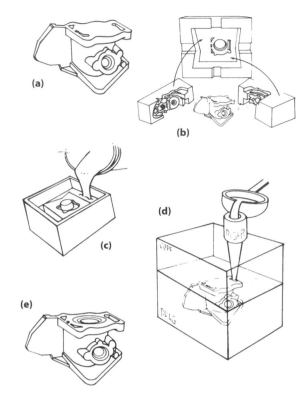

Figure 4–17 *Plaster mold casting process (Courtesy of Armstrong Mold Corporation).*

baked to remove moisture, and assembled. The metal is poured into the resultant cavity (Figure 4–16). The mold is broken to remove the casting (Figures 4–17 and 4–18).

Ceramic Shell Casting

Ceramic shell casting, a development of investment casting, is similar to the original process except that the wax pattern or tree to

CERAMIC SHELL CASTING

Advantages

- Superior surface quality
- Cheaper than solid molds
- Thin wall or section
- Intricate parts
- Minimum or no draft angle
- Can be used for most metals
- Can cast larger parts compared to solid molds

Disadvantage

- Labor intensive

Typical Parts

- Precision/scientific/medical instruments, parts, and tools
- Gun parts, jet engine parts, missile firing parts
- Sculpture

be cast is coated with a number of layers of a ceramic material, forming a shell around the wax. The process is shown in Figure 4–19, numbers 1–6. After the part is cast, it is trimmed, cleaned, and then inspected to ensure that it will meet specifications (Figure 4–20).

Ceramic Molds

Ceramic molds are made the same as plaster molds except that they are baked at 1800°F to produce hard, stable molds. High-melt-temperature metals can then be poured into the cavity of the assembled mold (Figure 4–21). The mold may be broken to remove castings,

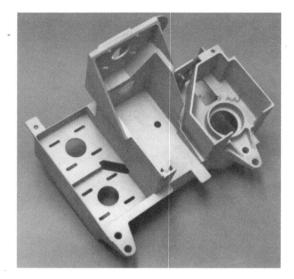

Figure 4–18 *Plaster mold casting (Courtesy of Talbot Associates Inc.).*

CERAMIC MOLDS

Advantages

- Short lead time, superior surface quality
- Thin wall or section, intricate parts
- Minimum or no draft angle (except for pattern)
- Can be used for ferrous and other high-melting-point metals

Disadvantages

- Limited in size, labor intensive, expensive (nonferrous metals cast less expensively in plaster molds)

Typical Parts

- Precision parts, scientific/medical instruments and tools, sculpture

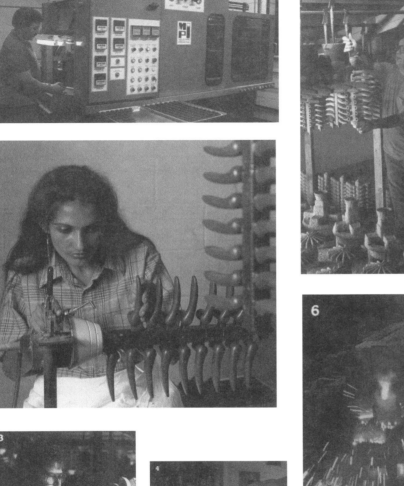

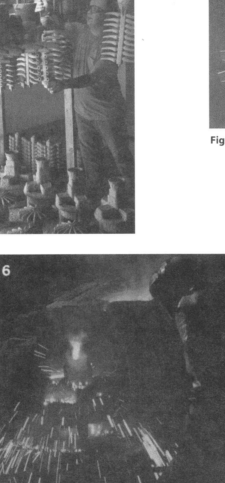

Figure 4–20   *Investment castings (Courtesy of Lamothermic Corp.).*

Figure 4–19   *Photographs of the Perision ceramic shell mold-making and investment-casting process [lost wax process] (Courtesy of Lamothermic Corp.).*

but in most cases, especially with low-melt-temperature metals, the molds are reused if there are no undercuts and if the molds are not degraded by the heat of the casting (Figure 4–22).

4.1.2   Nonexpendable Molds

Graphite Molds

Graphite molds (Figures 4–24–4–26) are solid molds machined in graphite, which is refractory and does not require a ceramic mold wash as with permanent molds. The metal used is usually ZA-12 zinc alloy, in castings from 1 ounce to 10 pounds (a limited amount of aluminum is cast in graphite molds, but it degrades the mold and the mold life is much shorter). The process requires a suggested minimum draft of 2°, with a wall thickness of 0.12 to 0.25 inch. The normal size limit is $12 \times 14 \times 5$ inches. Production ranges of 500 to 20,000 per year are most economical for most parts.

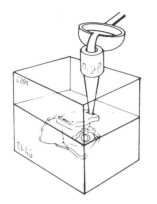

Figure 4–21 *Visualized mold (Courtesy Armstrong Mold Corporation).*

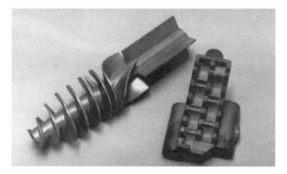

Figure 4–22 *Ceramic mold casting (Courtesy of Talbot Associates).*

Permanent Molds

Permanent molds are often cast in iron or are machined in various metals (Figure 4–27). Cores can be metal, sand, or sand shell. Castings are limited to aluminum, zinc, some brass, bronze, and lead. The molds are usu-

Figure 4–23 *Aluminum investment casting. Gear carrier for VTOL aircraft (Courtesy of Talbot Associates Inc.).*

ally coated with a ceramic wash prior to being gravity filled.

Low-Pressure and Vacuum (Die) Casting

In *low-pressure casting,* molten metal is forced by 5 to 15 pounds of air pressure from a heated crucible through a feed tube into the mold. Bottom fill eliminates much of the turbulence of typical gravity-fill casting. After the cast part solidifies, pressure is reduced and excess metal returns to the crucible. The advantages of low-pressure casting include increased density and uniform grain structure, which insures good casting repeatability and good tolerances (Figures 4–28 and 4–31).

Vacuum (die) casting, originated, developed, and patented by Aurora Metals, is used to produce castings that require precision and strength. In this process a steel die is enclosed in an airtight bell and submerged into the molten metal. A vacuum is drawn within the chamber, causing the metal to flow up the sprue and into the cavity (Figures 4–29 and 4–30).

PERMANENT MOLDS

Advantages

- Good grain structure, fewer impurities
- No porosity, moderate tool cost
- Cost is mid-way between that of sand and die casting

Disadvantages

- Usually labor intensive
- Thicker walls than in die casting

Typical Parts

- Industrial tool and motor housings, plumbing fixtures

Characteristics of Nonexpendable Molds

- Design flexibility, lending itself to specialized inserts and coring
- Dimensional stability to 0.040 inch of wall thickness
- High-volume applications with high repeatability
- Extremely tight tolerances

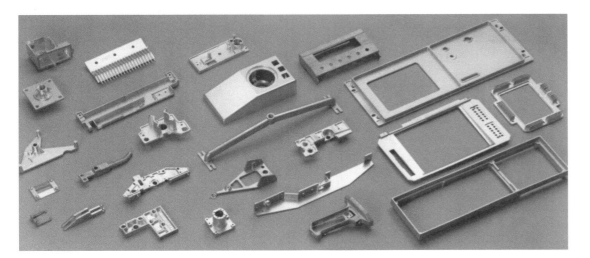

Figure 4–24 *Graphite mold castings. (Courtesy of Graphicast Inc.).*

Die Casting Molds

Die casting molds (dies) are machined in Type P tool steel. Molten aluminum, magnesium, or zinc alloys are injected into the water-cooled dies under high pressure. The dies open and the part is ejected. The flash is removed, usually by a trimming die, and finished. There are two types of machines: cold chamber and hot chamber.

The Equa Chair, designed by Don Chadwick and Bill Stumpf, uses several metal die castings (Figures 4–32, 4–33, and 4–34).

Figure 4–25 *Top-pour gravity fill of a graphite mold. (Courtesy of Graphicast Inc.).*

Figure 4–26 *Zinc part cast in a graphite mold (Courtesy Graphicast Inc.).*

Figure 4–27   *Gravity fill of an aluminum permanent mold (Courtesy of Talbot Associates Inc.).*

Spin and Centrifugal Casting

Spin casting is used for small parts and especially jewelry. The process is limited to low-melting-point metals such as precious metals, lead, tin, and zinc. Rubber molds can be used with very low melting point metals (Figures 4–35, 4–37, and 4–38).

Centrifugal casting is used for large symmetrical castings (pipe). Molten metal is spun in a drum mold at a high speed. During the process the highest-density metal is

forced to the outer wall, producing a pipe with fine grain of uniform density (Figure 4–36).

Continuous Casting

Continuous casting, or strand casting, is a primary process done at the time of smelting. Molten metal is poured through a cooler/die. The metal is pulled by rollers, which also controls straightness. Contours

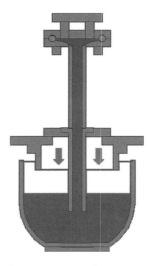

Figure 4–28   *Low-pressure casting process.*

Figure 4–29   *Vacuum (die) casting process (Courtesy Aurora Metals Division, Aurora Industries Inc.).*

Figure 4–30   *Vacuum (die) castings (Courtesy Aurora Metals Division, Aurora Industries Inc.).*

VACUUM DIE CASTING

Features

- Good density
- Precise detail

SPIN CASTING

Advantages

- Spin casting—low mold costs

Disadvantages

- Spin casting—limited to small parts

Typical Parts

- Jewelry, small electronic and industrial components

Figure 4–31   *Impeller. Low-pressure permanent mold (Courtesy of Talbot Associates Inc.).*

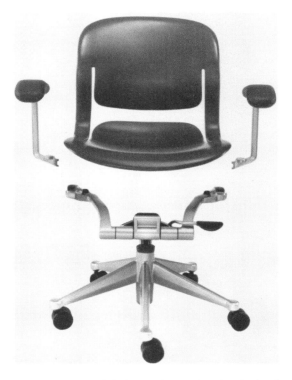

Figure 4–32   *Exploded view of Equa chair by Chadwick and Stumpf (Courtesy of herman miller inc.). photograph: Bill Sharpe*

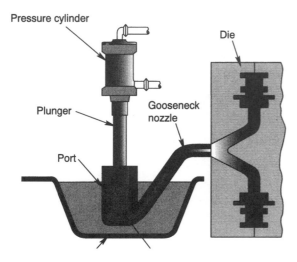

Figure 4–33 *Hot-chamber die-casting schematic (Courtesy of Casting Design & Applications).*

Figure 4–35 *Eight-cavity mold (Courtesy of Seybert Castings).*

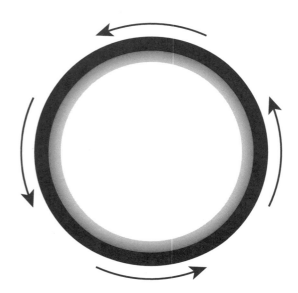

Figure 4–36 *Schematic of the centrifugal casting process. The mold is represented by black, metal in color. Highest density metal is forced to outer wall, with impurities at the inner wall.*

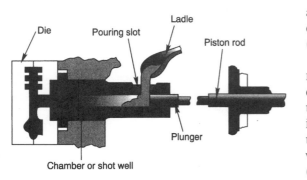

Figure 4–34 *Cold-chamber die-casting schematic. (Courtesy of Casting Design & Applications).*

are formed by the die-cored shapes (formed contours are limited to nonferrous alloys) (Figure 4–40).

The continuous casting process, originally developed for high-volume steel production, is done vertically and was designed to eliminate the costly and time-consuming ingot-casting and handling steps. New variations include continuous casting of sheet—which reduces some of the steps in rolling (Figure 4–39).

Continuous casting is now used to produce small produces such as the gear shown in Figure 4–41.

Metal Injection Molding

Metal injection molding (MIM) is a recent development that uses plastic injection-molding equipment (Figure 4–43). Metal

---

METAL INJECTION MOLDING

Advantages

- Small parts, but can be very complex

Disadvantages

- High volume only

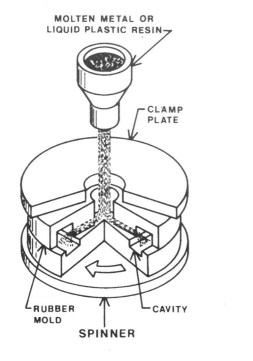

Figure 4–37 *Schematic drawing of spin-casting process (Courtesy of Seybert Castings).*

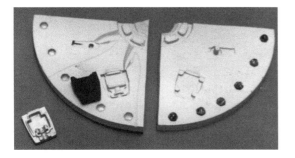

Figure 4–38 *Spin-cast plastic and zinc parts in a rubber mold (Courtesy of Talbot Associates Inc.).*

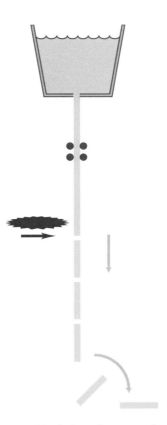

Figure 4–39 *Vertical continuous casting.*

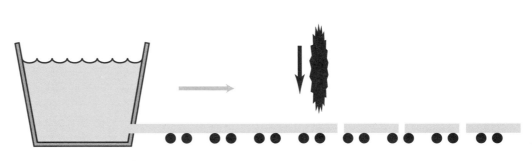

Figure 4–40 *Horizontal continuous casting.*

Figure 4–41 *Aluminum bronze continuous casting (Courtesy of Talbot Associates Inc.).*

Figure 4–42   *Metal injection-molded parts (Courtesy of Talbot Associates Inc.).*

powder is combined with a (plastic) binder material and is injected into the die. The part is ejected, and then sintered, which melts or dissolves the binder (Figure 4–42).

4.2   PLASTIC STATE FORMING

Plastic State Forming Chart (Figure 4–45)

Plastic state forming is a forming operation on a solid bar of metal at elevated temperature (but below critical or melt temperature). The objective of this process is not only to shape the metal but to control the grain structure so that the strength of the formed part is enhanced (calculated to counter expected forces). Some processes are relatively expensive, but it is possible to achieve superior performance not possible through other

Figure 4–43   *Detail of a plastic injection-molding machine (Courtesy of Husky).*

manufacturing processes. Enhanced properties can also be achieved through heat treatment following the forming operation. Extrusion, particularly direct extrusion, is relatively inexpensive and very versatile.

The value of plastic-state forming is shown in a simplified schematic (Figure 4–46) that demonstrates three possibilities of how to shape a bar in an "S" shape:

1. Casting in which the grain structure is random. If enough stress is applied to the S bar, a stress crack will soon develop along the grain boundaries. In

Mold Comparison Chart

Molds	Physical Considerations				Logistics		Costs	
	Usable Metals	Size Range (inches)	Min. Draft (inches)	Min. Section Thickness (inches)	Lead Time Samples (Weeks)	Lead Time Production (Weeks)	Tooling Cost (relative)	Part Cost (relative)
Expendable								
Sand	Most castable metals	ozs.–tons	noncore: 1–5° cores: 1–1.5°	ferrous: 1/4–3/8" nonferrous: 1/8–1/4"	2–10	2–4	$$$$$	$$$$
Resin Shell	Most castable metals	<500" sq.	external: 0–0.5° internal: 0.5–2°	ferrous: 1/8" nonferrous: 3/32"	12–16	6–10	$$	$$
Evaporative (Full)	Most castable metals	ozs.–tons	none		2–10	2–4	$$$$$	$$$$$
Plaster	Aluminum, brass, bronze, beryllium copper, zinc	<550" sq.	external: 0–0.5° internal: 0.5–2°	.07"	2–6	2–4	$$$$	$
Investment	Most castable metals	<150 lbs.	none	sm. areas: 0.03" lg. areas: 0.06"	5–16	4–12	$$$	$$
Ceramic	Most castable metals	5 lbs.–350 lbs.	0–0.5°	1/8"	3–8	2–8	$$$$	$
Ceramic Shell	Most castable metals	<150 lbs.	none	0.09"	5–16	4–12	$$$	$
NonExpendable								
Graphite	Zinc alloys	1 oz.–10 lbs 12" x 14" x 7"	external: 0.5° internal: 1°	0.09–0.125"	6–10	4	$$$$	$$$
Powdered Metal (PM)	Iron, iron alloys, copper bronze, brass, stainless steel, aluminum	ferrous: <20" sq. nonferrous: >20" sq.	none	0.03–0.09"	8–14	4–8	$$$	$$$$$
Permanent	Aluminum, zinc, some brass bronze, lead, gray iron	ferrous: <60 lbs. Al: <150 lbs. Cu bronze: <25 lbs.	outside: 0.5° inside: 1	ferrous: 1/2–1/4" Al: 1/8–3/16" Cu base: 0.09"	8–20	3–8	$$	$$$$
Die Casting	Aluminum, zinc, magnesium, some brass	less than 4' sq.	Al/Mg: 1–3° Zinc: 0.5–2° Brass: 2–5°	Al: 0.03–0.06" Mg: 0.03–0.045" Zn: 0.025–0.04"	12–22	8–10	$	$$$$$
Metal Injection Molding (MIM)	Primarily ferrous limited copper base	0.0005 lbs.–0.22 lbs.	0.25°	sm. areas: 0.015"	10–16	4–86	$$$	$

Figure 4–44 *Mold comparison chart based on information supplied by Talbot Associates.*

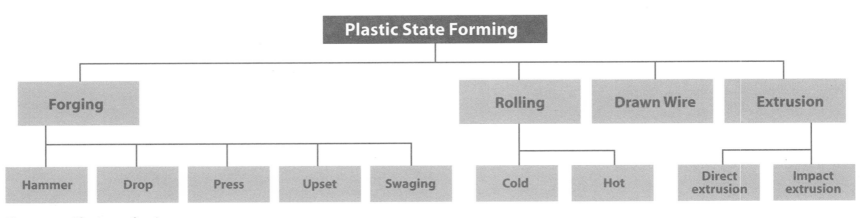

Figure 4–45 *Plastic state forming.*

Casting

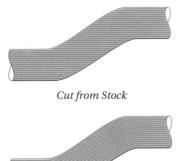

Cut from Stock

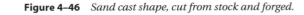

Forging

Figure 4–46 *Sand cast shape, cut from stock and forged.*

casting. If wall thickness is not uniform there will be stresses—called stress concentrations—that will enhance the potential for failure.

2. Cut from a rolled or wrought slab. The grain of the slab is horizontal and the cut is through the grain, which is poor in terms of stress. As a result, the potential for crack development along the grain boundaries is nearly as great as in casting.

3. Forging part, where the grain follows the shape. This grain structure is superior to the others in countering stress and is one of the main benefits of forging or of plastic state forming.

4.2.1 Rolling

Hot and Cold Rolling

The changes in grain are shown in rolling, which is a primary process. Industrial designers normally are not involved in primary manufacturing processes (except for direct extrusion, which is essentially a primary process), but it is important to understand how the grain is modified during the rolling process and that these changes are common in all plastic-state forming. There are two kinds of rolling—hot and cold. Cold rolling is not actually cold at all, but it is not as hot as hot rolling, which is done just below critical temperature. The process itself causes stress and friction, which generates heat, so the rollers must be water-cooled during the rolling process.

In hot rolling, a preheated bar or bloom passes between a series of rollers that

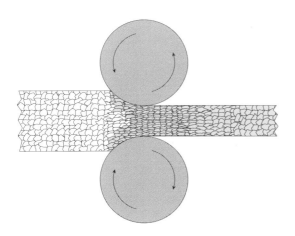

Figure 4–47 *Hot rolling (red indicates grain transformation).*

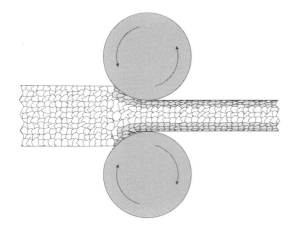

Figure 4–48 *Cold rolling (red indicates grain transformation).*

squeeze it, reducing and/or shaping it into a plate, sheet, or structural shape. The grains are crushed and elongated. During the recovery period the grains tend to regrow, yielding a coarse or rough surface (Figure 4–47).

In cold rolling, a previously hot-rolled sheet is further compressed by rollers (in a cold condition) that crush and elongate the grains. However during the reheating or annealing phase the grains are smaller, yielding a smooth, fine surface. This process improves the steel sheet but increases cost by 20 percent (Figure 4–48).

During steel making molten metal is cast into ingots or continuous cast and shaped into slabs, billets, or blooms, and then rolled to the shapes shown in Figures 4–47 and 4–48. These processes, called *primary processes,* produce the mill products that will then be formed into industrial and consumer products by secondary processes such as forming, cutting, and joining.

4.2.2   Forging and Swaging

Forging and Swaging

In *hammer forging* a bar is heated near but below critical temperature and then formed to its near-final shape by repeated blows of a hammer against an anvil—the method a blacksmith uses to shape metal (Figure 4–49).

The *drop forge* (closed die) process is similar to hammer forge, except that the upper die half is mounted in a large-mass hammer in a machine that raises the hammer (with the die) and drops it repeatedly on

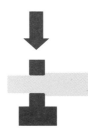

Figure 4–49 *Hammer forge operation on a rectangular bar*

a red-hot workpiece placed in the stationary half of the die secured to the anvil part of the machine.

In press forging, a heated bar is slowly pressed or squeezed between two opposing roller dies (Figure 4–50). Complex shapes can be forged using closed dies and side punches (Figure 4–54).

In upset forging, a punch flattens or reshapes the end of a rod as it is held in a stationary die. Upset forging is used to make

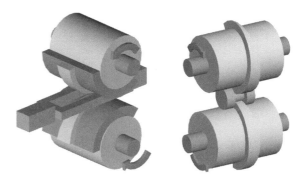

Figure 4–50 *Views of the roll-forging operation, also known as cross-rolling.*

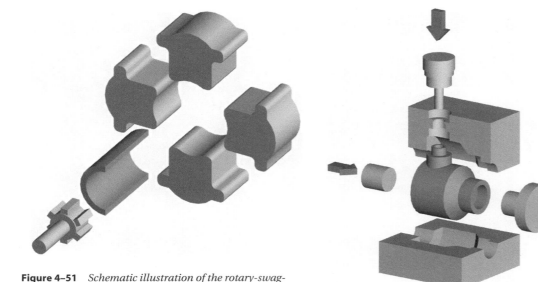

Figure 4–51   *Schematic illustration of the rotary-swaging process.*

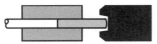

Figure 4–52   *Upset forging—head formed in punch.*

Figure 4–53   *Upset forging—head formed in die.*

Figure 4–54   *Forging a complex shape, including piercing, using side punches.*

nails, bolts, and similar products (Figures 4–52 and 4–53).

In *rotary swaging* (open die), a tube is squeezed onto a mandrel by dies to reshape its cross-sectional area (Figure 4–51).

4.2.3   Extrusions

Direct Extrusion

In *extrusion* a round heated billet is placed in a chamber of a large press and is forced through a die by a hydraulic ram, forming a long profile shape.

Shapes formed can be solid, semi-hollow, or hollow, as shown in the chart (Figures 4–55–4–57). Virtually any profile is possible

Types of Extrusions

 A solid symmetrical shape whose cross section is round

 A solid symmetrical shape with rounded or sharp corners

 A hollow symmetrical shape with a uniform wall

 Any extruded shape other than a hollow or semi-hollow extruded shape

 A shape whose cross section partially encloses a void

Figure 4–55   *Types of extrusions.*

Gap Width

 CLASS I
Equal Tongue Ratio

 CLASS II
Unequal Tongue Ratio

Minimum gap width is 0.030 inch.

Figure 4–56   *Class of extrusion.*

to meet a large variety of design requirements. Extrusions have revolutionized design and manufacturing of many products, in part because most extrusion material and dies are relatively inexpensive (Figures 4–58, 4–59, and 4–60).

Classes of Hollow Extrusions

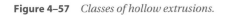

CLASS 1
Shape with a round void

CLASS 2
Shape with a single void
that is not round

CLASS 3
Shape with multiple
voids

Figure 4–57 *Classes of hollow extrusions.*

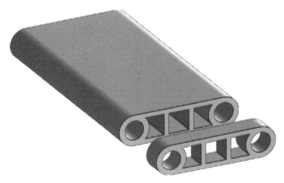

Figure 4–59 *Part made by cutting off a piece of an extrusion.*

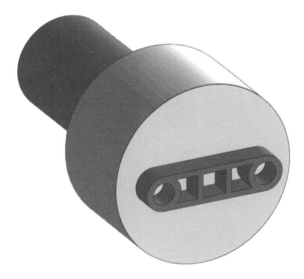

Figure 4–58 *Basic concept of the extrusion process.*

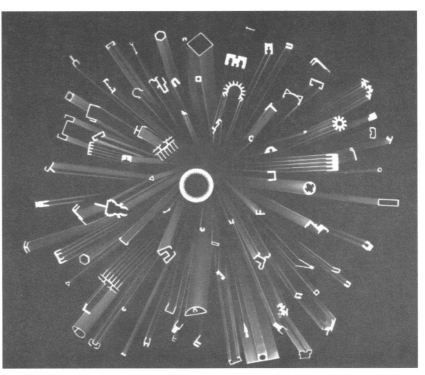

Figure 4–60 *An array of extrusions (Courtesy of Minalex).*

Figure 4–61 *Large-tonnage upright press. (Courtesy of Metal Impact Corporation.)*

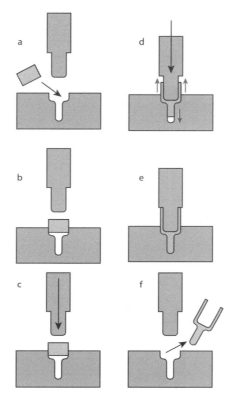

Figure 4–62 *Schematic drawing of impact extrusion, showing both forward and reverse extrusion.*

of short shapes including thin-walled symmetrical containers. The part is then ejected. There are three basic types of dies for impact extrusion: forward, reverse, and combination. Parts can be extruded in aluminum, copper, and brass alloys (Figure 4–63).

4.2.4 Drawn Wire

Drawn Wire

The *drawn wire process* is essentially the opposite of extrusion. A rod is made thinner when it is pulled successively through a series of constricting opening dies (Figure 4–64).

Impact Extrusions

In *impact extrusion* a large forage press (Figure 4–61) is used to form small to medium sized parts, with thin walls and no draft. A blank is placed in a die (steps a and b) and is struck by a plunger (step c), causing the material to become plastic. It is extruded upward (steps d and e) between the plunger and the die wall or forward, forming a variety

IMPACT EXTRUSION

Advantages

- No draft
- Varying wall thickness
- 5 inch diameter (D) up to 24 inches long
- Low tooling cost
- 100 + to high production
- Increased part strength
- Precision tolerances

Figure 4–63 *Aluminum impact extrusion parts (Courtesy of Metal Impact Corporation).*

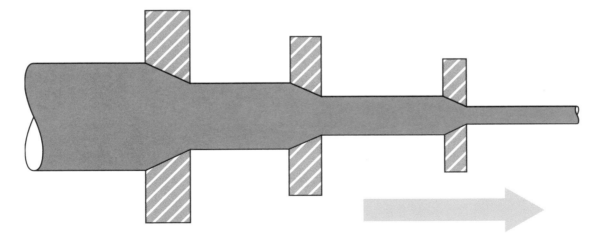

Figure 4–64 *Essential features of the drawn-wire process.*

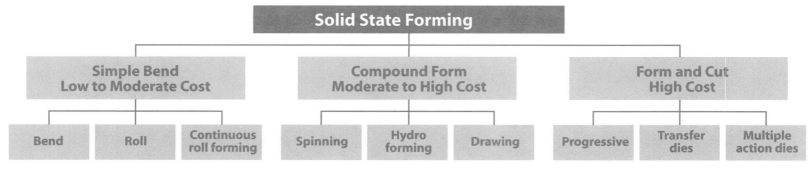

Figure 4–65 *Solid state forming.*

4.3 SOLID STATE FORMING

Solid state forming is the shaping of metal sheet, rod, wire, or tube, usually at room temperature. In some cases heating the metal may be required if it is thick, is not very ductile, or becomes work-hardened during forming. A sheet is normally defined as metal that is less than 0.25 inch thick (T). Anything 0.25 inch T or over is considered plate. Although there is some metal flow during most solid state processes, it is incidental—unlike plastic state forming, where grain-direction control is the objective. Nonetheless the mechanical properties are affected and there is some strength gain, which can be one design objective of the forming operation. During the forming process some metals can become brittle and may require annealing before the forming operation is continued. In bending sheet there is a rule of thumb wherein the radius of the bend is related to the thickness of the sheet—a 2T bend means that the radius should equal two times the thickness of the

sheet (= $2 \times T$). Bending with the grain should be avoided whenever possible. Rules are dependent on the "bendability" of the material and, to some extent, on the equipment used. These guidelines are provided by the supplier and/or handbooks.

Small but complex parts are sometimes formed by progressive, transfer, or multiple-action dies that cut as well as form the part, especially where there is high production and multiple actions with simple bends. In a very high volume operation, the process is often called *stamping,* but the term is also often used for sheet forming operations in general (Figure 4–65).

4.3.1 Simple Bends

Wire Forming

Because of their relatively low cost, high strength, and ability to take abuse, formed sheet, rod, wire, and tube are important to industrial designers, especially in automotive and transportation design and in a large array of enclosures for residential, industrial, med-

ical, and research equipment. Short-run cabinets of any size and nearly all large enclosures are more than likely made of sheet metal—usually aluminum or steel. Sheet metal is used in most large and small home appliances and enclosures, especially where high heat is generated, as in cookware, ovens, and lighting fixtures. It is also used for protective shrouds and fuel tanks for most lawn and garden equipment, where gasoline engines and rugged use are normal. Sheet metal, rod, wire, and tube are important in residential and office furniture and in commercial showcase and display fixtures. Other applications include recreational products, exercise and sports equipment, and virtually any product category where high strength, light weight, short lead times for tooling, and low cost are important design considerations.

Bending and forming wire requires special tooling but is an economical production process. Formed and spot-welded wire is strong and has applications in many industries. The wire chairs by Harry Betoria demonstrate the aesthetic possibilities of transparent, textured curved planes made of line (Figure 4–66).

Figure 4–66 *The Bertoia Collection, Bertoia Side Chair (Courtesy of Knoll.).*

Figure 4–67 *The Breuer Collection, Wassily Chair, (Courtesy of Knoll.).*

Tube Bending

Bending and forming tubes and other hollow sections requires an internal support called a *mandrel* to prevent buckling of tubes during the bending process (*see* Figure 4–68).

The classic 1927 Wassily chair set the standard for modern furniture (Figure 4–67). Perhaps inspired by Thonet, Breuer used steel tube instead of wood, thus eliminating Thonet's problem of splitting wood in a tight bend. Breuer had limits in bending too, which he turned into the aesthetic of the chair. The consistent bend radii give the design a sense of order and unity (Figure 4–69).

Bending Sheet Metal

Bending sheet metal along one plane is normally a fairly inexpensive operation that creates simple shapes and gives the sheet some rigidity and strength. A hand-operated brake—a common sheet-forming tool in many small shops—can handle limited

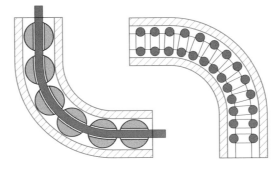

Figure 4–68 *Mandrels to prevent the tube from collapsing during bending .*

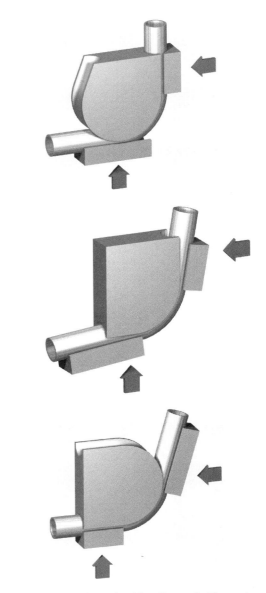

Figure 4–69 *Tube and rod bending tools. The stationary or moving die determines the radius of the bend, and the supporting followers move the tube or rod to make the bend.*

bending. The large sheet-forming machines, which are computer controlled, are capable of complex forming, but along only one axis for each bend. Conceptually it may be useful to think of one-axis sheet bending as being somewhat similar to bending paper. The piggy bank (Figure 4–71) with slide-out-tray is laser cut from stainless steel sheet and then formed using 14 bends on a press brake using an airbend or v-die bending tool (Figure 4–76 and 4–77).

A *brake* (wiping die) is an inexpensive bending tool often available in small model shops (Figure 4–70). It usually has a number of radius attachments that provide a variety of bending radii (r). A hand-operated version of these brakes is used for on-site bending of residential and commercial aluminum siding.

Roll bending sheet on one axis is an inexpensive operation (Figure 4–72). Hand-op-

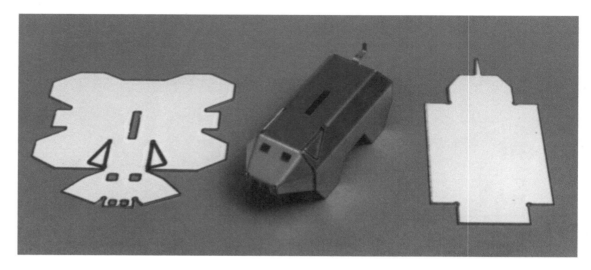

Figure 4–71 *Piggy bank laser cut from a stainless steel sheet and formed by a brake (Courtesy of Trumpf Inc.).*

erated machines with an adjustable roll provide a range of rolling radii (r). These machines are typically used in small model shops.

Air and V-Die Bending

Air bending, or three-point bending, is a moderately priced operation that uses only a punch into an opening rather than a die (Figure 4–76). The metal is supported by two

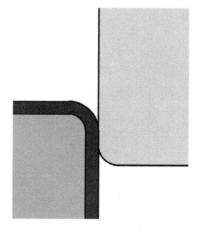

Figure 4–70 *Wiping die for simple bends.*

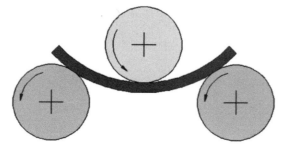

Figure 4–72 *Roll bending schematic.*

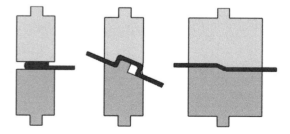

Figure 4–73 *Hem , offset, and joggle bends.*

points and hit by a punch (the third), which creates the bend. It is called air bending because there is air between the metal and the opening into which it has been forced. Although the elimination of the die reduces cost, it also reduces accuracy compared to v-die bending (Figures 4–74 and 4–75).

V-die bending is the most expensive bending operation because it uses a matched set of punch and die (or tool) and/or sophisticated computer control (Figure 4–77). The tool, which produces very accurate bends, is often designed for a particular application; and although it remains with the fabricator, the tool is proprietary and cannot be used for any other application without the owner's permission (Figure 4–73).

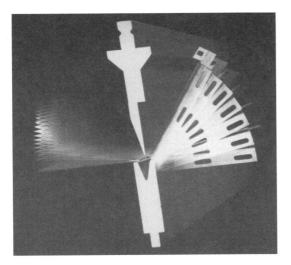

Figure 4–74 *Bending die with multiple exposure of the bending action (Courtesy of Trumpf Inc.).*

Figure 4–76 *Air bending.*

Continuous Roll Forming

Continuous roll forming is a high-speed process used to produce metal shapes that are somewhat analogous to extrusions except that the profile is limited to the original thickness of the sheet (Figure 4–78). Metal sheet from a coil is fed through a series of top and bottom rollers, gradually creating a fin-

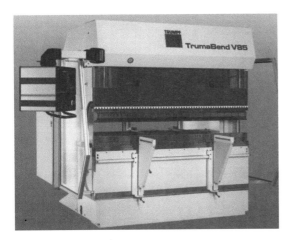

Figure 4–75 *TrumaBend V Series (Courtesy of Trumpf Inc.).*

Figure 4–77 *V-die bending.*

Advantages of Continuous Roll Forming

- Economical at high volume
- Almost any length

Disadvantages

- Uniform profile thickness required
- 5-foot to 10,000-foot minimum order

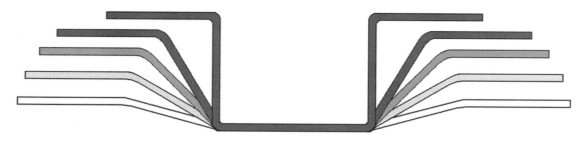

Figure 4–78 *Roll forming process.*

ished profile. Any thin ductile sheet metal can be formed by continuous roll forming, including galvanized and prepainted carbon steel, stainless and specialty steels, aluminum, brass, and bronze (Figures 4–79a and b).

4.3.2 Compound Bending

Spinning

Spinning is commonly used to produce symmetrical cuplike shapes or frisbee-shaped discs (Figure 4–82). The process is very interesting to see, and the transformation of the sheet into a final shape is almost unbelievable—even as it happens before your eyes. A

(a)   (b)

Figure 4–79 *Catalog and typical roll-formed parts* *(Courtesy of Johnson Bros. Metal Forming Co.).*

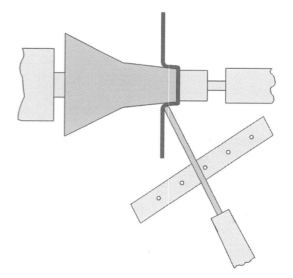

Figure 4–80 *Spinning schematic.*

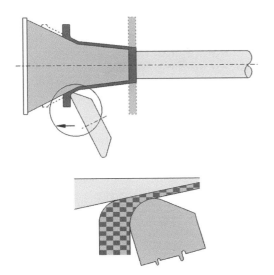

Figure 4–81 *Spinning details.*

forming tool forces the metal sheet onto a wooden or metal pattern as it spins on a special lathe (Figure 4–80). In Figure 4–81 the metal is shown being squeezed, causing some flow and resulting in a change in thickness. This is both good and bad: good because there is some gain in strength, bad because there is brittleness and other varying mechanical properties. Often the designer can take advantage of this condition. The process is labor intensive, but the dies are inexpensive. Spinning can be automated for high production but most likely cannot compete with drawing for very high volume production (Figure 4–83).

Hydroforming (Fluid Forming)

In *hydroforming*, a flexible membrane sealing a fluid-filled cavity allows a punch to shape the workpiece or blank. The fluid pressure eliminates the need for a matching die cavity (Figure 4–84).

Drawing and Deep Drawing

In *drawing*, sheet metal is formed into hollow shapes by a punch that forces the metal into a matching die cavity (Figure 4–85). In *deep drawing*, normally accomplished in successive steps, the depth of the hollow is two or more times the diameter (Figures 4–86 and 4–87).

4.3.3 Form and Cut

Stamping

Some sheet operations are forming as well as punching. The term *stamping* is often used to describe these operations, which are done either simultaneously or in sequence by the same machine—usually at a very rapid rate. In this case the forming is normally of a rather shallow depth, and although there is some "drawing," it is limited. A sheet-metal house may do both stamping and drawing, but these operations are normally considered separate and distinct. Stamping machinery uses progressive, transfer, and multiple-action dies in large production runs—usually of small parts (Figures 4–88 and 4–89).

A *simple die* performs one action, such as forming (bending) or punching (cutting),

Figure 4–82 *Spinning operator (Courtesy of AMALCO).*

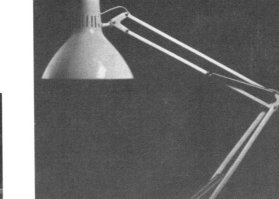

Figure 4–83 *Classic Luxo lamp originally designed using the spinning process (Courtesy of Luxo Corp.).*

Figure 4–84 *Hydroforming (Courtesy of AMALCO).*

Figure 4–86 *Drawing press (Courtesy of Belmet Products Inc.).*

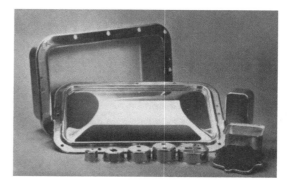

Figure 4–87 *Gauge, meter, and relay housings (Courtesy of Belmet Products Inc.).*

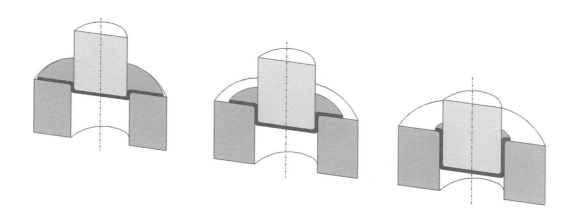

Figure 4–85 *Schematic of the drawing process.*

Figure 4–88 *Stampings (Courtesy of Peterson Manufacturing Co.).*

Figure 4–89 *Reverse drawn parts (Courtesy of Risdon Corp.).*

Figure 4–90 *Stampings (Courtesy of Bokers Inc.).*

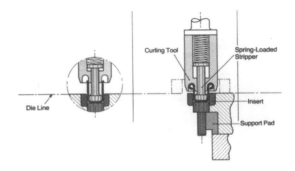

Figure 4–92 *Curling (Courtesy Risdon Corp.).*

at one time at one die. The part, if not complete, is then removed by hand or robot from the die to await the next process at another station (Figure 4–91).

A *compound die* performs two (or more) separate actions such as forming and punching at one time at one station. The part, if not complete, is then removed by hand or robot from the die to await the next process at another station.

A *progressive die* is designed to perform a series of successive punches and limited forming steps on a strip as it progresses to each station in one complex die. The parts are held by the strip skeleton or tabs until the last station, where the parts are separated from the strip. Because of the complexity of progressive dies, their cost tends to be high and they are limited to small, fairly flat but intricate high-production-rate parts (Figure 4–90).

A *transfer die* is designed to perform a series of successive punching and forming steps when the size and/or complexity of the part requires that it be separated from the strip. The part is moved from die to die by a

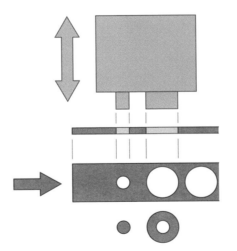

Figure 4–91 *This progressive die schematic drawing is of the blanking operation to make a simple washer. It demonstrates the concept clearly. Many progressive dies are more complex and also include cutting and bending operations.*

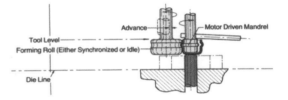

Figure 4–93 *Beading (Courtesy Risdon Corp.).*

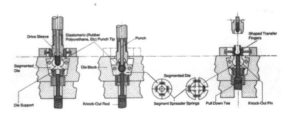

Figure 4–94 *Bulging using an elastomeric punch (Courtesy Risdon Corp.).*

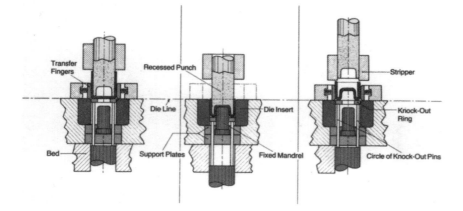

Figure 4–95 *Reverse drawing (Courtesy Risdon Corp.).*

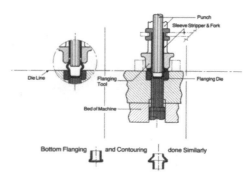

Figure 4–97 *Body flanging (Courtesy Risdon Corp.).*

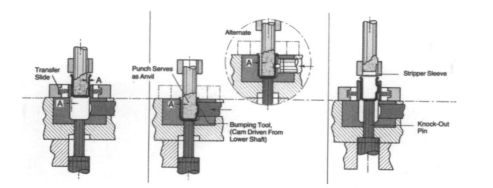

Figure 4–96 *Bumping (Courtesy Risdon Corp.).*

Figure 4–98 *Formed parts (Courtesy Risdon Corp.).*

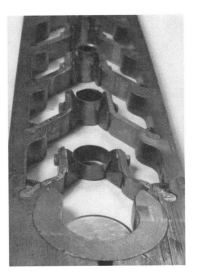

Figure 4–99 *Transfer yoke or fingers in a progressive die (Courtesy Risdon Corp.).*

transfer yoke or fingers to each successive die until the part is completed (Figure 4–99). Because of the complexity of transfer dies, their cost tends to be high, and they normally have a maximum diameter of 3.75 inches and a draw depth of 3.125 inches on fairly complex, high-production-rate parts. Specific operations include blanking, cupping, fluting, ironing or thinning, reverse drawing, bulging, curling, necking, body flanging, bottom/side piercing, marking, threading, beading, bumping, and knurling (Figures 4–92, 4–93, 4–94, 4–95, 4–96, 4–97 and 4–98).

In a *multiple-action die* the strip or sheet is held in place while dies above and below the sheet preform a series of forming steps. The dies work independently in a succession of separate steps. Parts produced by multiple-action dies tend to be fairly small and complex and are generally limited to forming operations, with a moderate to high production rate.

METAL CUTTING

In the Webster's College Edition Dictionary the seemingly simple word *cut* requires a half page of definitions. The definitions are characterized by a result or outcome, as in denoting penetration or incision; separation, removal, or division; or reduction, and the like. These are further divided to explain each category more precisely.

In manufacturing, the word *cutting* is equally complex, and care should be taken to use the proper term to describe the concept in each particular manufacturing group. Generally the exact term for a particular kind of cutting has evolved in relation to a manufacturing group, the shape of the material to be cut, and/or the required tolerance.

Sheet Metal

In the sheet metal industry the word *cut* is not used to describe processes, except to rough-cut, or size, sheet stock. But even in this case the process would normally be referred to as a *shear*. However the scrap is referred to as cut-offs (or drops). The sheet metal industry uses the word *blank* or *punch* to denote cutting a hole into a sheet or creating a shape.

Machining

In cutting into a block of metal (in the chip-forming processes), the word *machining* is used to describe the process, even though a specific cutter or cutting tool is used. The word *machining* is used because a special machine (which drives the cutting tool) is required to achieve a cut to a given precise tolerance. In the recent past, plus or minus 5 thousandths ($\pm$0.005) of an inch was considered normal. Today with computer control, plus or minus 5 ten-thousandths ($\pm$0.0005) of an inch is routine.

5.1 SHEET PUNCHING AND SHEARING

Sheet-metal punching or shearing is limited to sheet 0.25 inch thick (T) or less. Sheet metal is important in industrial design, especially in office products and equipment design, including computers, copiers, and a large array of industrial, medical, and research equipment. Short-run cabinets of any size, as well as almost all large enclosures, will most likely be sheet metal—usually aluminum or steel. Sheet metal is used in most large home appliances and enclosures where high heat is generated, as in gasoline engines, ovens, and lighting fixtures.

Computer numerical control (CNC) and programming advances have greatly improved accuracy, dramatically reduced costs and tool changing time, and have expanded the potential for design innovation. In the past a punch and die (tool) had to be designed and produced in order to punch a specially designed opening in sheet metal. The computer and laser/plasma-arc cutting technology has virtually eliminated that requirement, and turnaround time for parts is now normally a matter of days instead of weeks or months. These new technologies have improved quality and virtually eliminated errors. New advances in decorative and protective coatings have also contributed to the design potential of sheet metal.

The old punch and die technology has not been entirely eliminated by the new

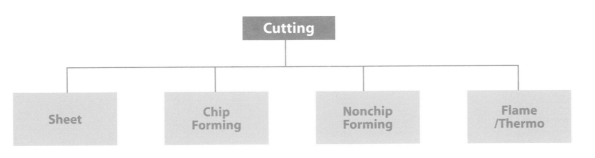

Figure 5–1 *Cutting.*

technologies. There is a continuing need for the older sheet-punching technologies for long runs, where a specially designed tool is the most cost-effective strategy in manufacturing parts (Figure 5–4).

Sheet-Metal Industry Terminology

In the sheet metal industry there is a tendency to be rather specific about each punching term that is used, even though there may be little difference among them. A good example is *punching* and *blanking,* which are almost identical except for the part that is discarded. A punch usually makes a hole in the sheet (Figure 5–2) whereas in blanking, the part is usually a larger part or shape that may have have holes punched in

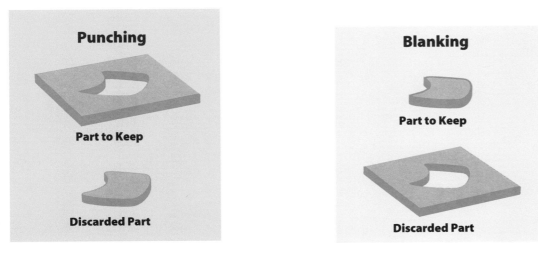

Figure 5–2 *Punch graphic.*

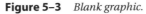

Figure 5–3 *Blank graphic.*

prior to being blanked out of the sheet stock (Figure 5–3).

Punching

The *turret punch* contains a turret with a variety of punches that can execute various sized holes nonstop (Figure 5–5). The tool change is very rapid, since same-size cuts are made on a sheet that is moved back and forth below the punch (*see* Figures 5–6 details 5–7 and 5–8).

Most sheet-metal punching is done on CNC sheet metal machining center with limited contouring and forming abilities. These machines are extremely accurate, very fast, and perform rapid tool changes. They have replaced the old method of designing a punch, called a blanking die, for cutting a specific configuration. Most punches are of standard geometry, and many hits are required to produce holes of varying shapes. Specific tools such as vents and electronic connector openings are still created for applications where the design is not likely to change and the volume is large enough to warrant the expense. A recent feature is the addition of thermal cutting using a laser or plasma-arc described in Section 5.3 (Figure 5–44).

Automated Sheet Handling and Punching

Newly developed are the automated sheet handling and punching centers (Figure 5–9).

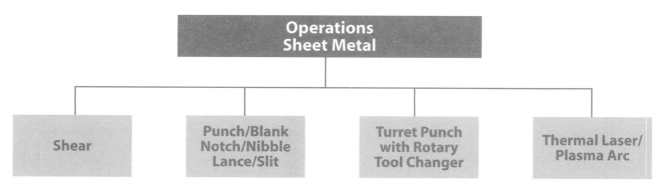

Figure 5–4 *Stamping and shearing—sheetmetal.*

Figure 5–5 *Usually hole patterns such as these vent slots are produced by one specific punch. The designer should find out what stock punches are available before specifying a pattern that may have to be ordered at a higher cost and cause a delay (Courtesy of Trumpf Inc.).*

Figure 5–6 *Trumatic 200, with features shown in Figure 5.7 (Courtesy of Trumpf Inc.).*

Figure 5–7 *Trap door to remove parts and scrap after punching (Courtesy of Trumpf Inc.).*

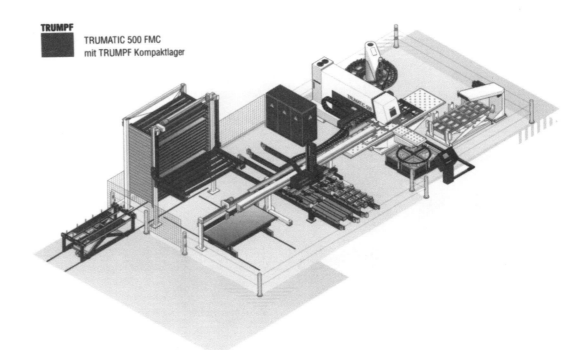

TRUMPF
TRUMATIC 500 FMC
mit TRUMPF Kompaktlager

Figure 5–9 *Sheet-handling system (Courtesy of Trumpf).*

Figure 5–8 *Punch detail (Courtesy of Trumpf Inc.).*

Shearing

Shear

The *shearing process* is a scissorlike action between a punch and a die. The punch or blade breaks the surface to initiate the shearing action. As seen in Figure 5–11, the quality of the cut depends on the "c" clearance. The process is a tearing action, and the edge has a residue, or burr, that is very sharp and must be removed or deburred. If the clearance is too large (as in Figure 5–12), the sheet will be distorted, have a large burr, and will be difficult to use for normal purposes (Figure 5–10).

Figure 5–10   *Shear (Courtesy of AMALCO).*

5.2   CHIP-FORMING CUTTING

In this section, "cutting" refers to the separation or reduction of a material by the removal of chips. Most materials can be cut by these processes, as long as the cutting tool (cutter) is harder than the workpiece or material to be cut.

When cutting achieves tolerances (of at least) ±0.005 inch, it is called *machining*. In machining, the workpiece and cutting tool are held in a precise relationship to achieve the desired cut within the required tolerance. The speed, feed, rate of cutting, and proper coolants/lubricants are important economical and tool-life considerations in machining. Machining is usually a secondary process that follows a forming process but normally precedes joining and finishing processes (Figures 5–13 and 5–14).

Turning

A *lathe* is used to turn symmetrical cylindrical solid and hollow shapes, as well as threads and similar forms, along the axis. In this process the workpiece, held in a chuck, rotates as a cutter, held in a tool assembly called a compound tool rest, controlled by an operator (Figure 5–15). The lathe is one of the oldest tools. Today turning centers are automated and fitted with turret heads with up to eight cutting tools each (Figure 5–16). There are special-purpose lathes for spinning and large-diameter parts.

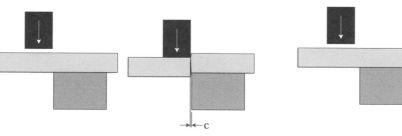

Figure 5–11   *The proper clearance (c) at the deformation zone in shearing.*

Figure 5–12   *Effect of improper clearance (c) at the deformation zone in shearing.*

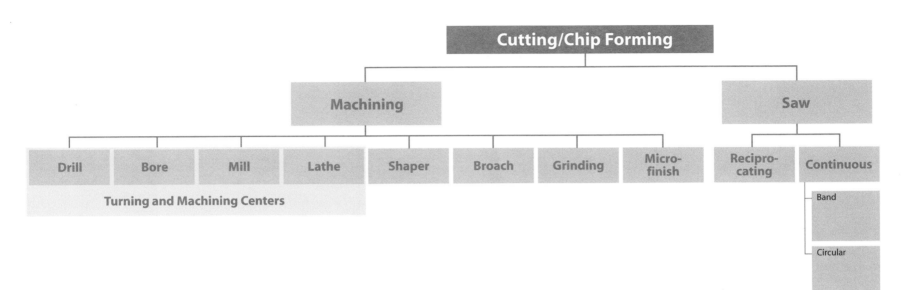

Figure 5–13 *Chip-forming cutting.*

Figure 5–14 *Chip forming cutting action of a tool is shown in this clever illustrtion by Steve Svancara taken from an ad by LMT•FETTE cutting tools. (Courtesy LMT•FETTE).*

Milling

A *vertical mill* looks like a drill, and in principle works a bit like one except that it has much more flexibility in its axis of cutting and workpiece movement. The head can be tilted in a number of positions (Figures 5–17 and 5–18).

A *horizontal mill* is somewhat similar to a vertical mill except that its cutting head is limited to horizontal cuts. These machines are no longer manufactured; they have been replaced by machining centers (Figures 5–19 and 5–20).

Shaper and Bore

A *boring machine* is used to finish cut circular internal profiles in hollow workpieces or on a hole made by casting or other processes, similar to the turning process (Figures 5–21 and 5–22). Boring bars are made with vibration-dampening capabilities. When used for a cannon barrell, the term *bore* refers to the process that gives it the finish cut, internal configuration, and internal diameter.

A *shaper* essentially scrapes the surface of a small part in a reciprocating movement.

Figure 5–15 *ROMI Engine Lathe (Courtesy of Bridgeport Machine).*

Figure 5–16 *A computer-controlled turning center. (Courtesy of Monarch Co.).*

Figure 5–17 *The classic Bridgeport milling machine (Courtesy of Bridgeport Machine).*

Shaping is basically planing and is used to finish-cut, not to make the primary cut. The process is not generally considered a high-production process (Figure 5–23).

Broach and Grinding

The basic *grinding operations* are surface, cylindrical, internal, and centerless grinding. The cutting tool is composed of hard abrasive grains bonded to a wheel in a random distribution. Each grain removes a small chip. The grinding process is a finishing operation, normally for bearing or sliding surfaces. Tolerances of +/−0.0002 inch are common (Figures 5–24 and 5–25).

A *broach* has multiple teeth that are used to finish-cut internal and external surfaces. It is in effect a long multitoothed cutting tool that looks like a large tooth file (Figure 5–27). It can, in one pass, produce cuts with a good surface finish and dimensional

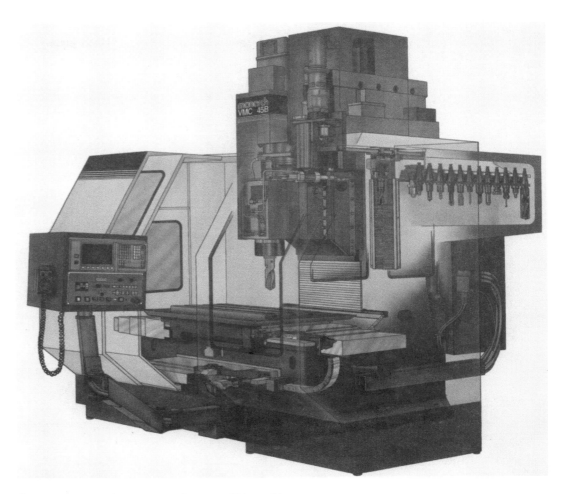

Figure 5–18 *Computer control of Bridgeport milling machine (Courtesy of Bridgeport Machine).*

Figure 5–19 *Machining center (Courtesy of Monarch).*

accuracy. The high cost of designing and developing a special broach can be justified only for high-quantity production (Figure 5–26).

Machining

The most important advancement is the *machining center,* which is now the dominant (standard) machining process owing to its speed and accuracy compared to those of individual processes. Whereas it used to take hours to set up the machine each time a part was moved, one fully automated machining center can cut five sides without moving the part. This reduces the total machining time to minutes or hours instead of days or weeks, at routine tolerances of plus or minus 5 ten-thousandths (±0.0005) of an inch.

Machining and Turning Centers

A machining center is designed to bring the cutting tools to the workpiece rather than vice versa. The major advantage is that a machining center eliminates the extensive set-up repositioning each time a part is moved. The old method increased the possibility of error and delayed the actual cutting time while the part was moved. These computer-controlled machines, with automated tool-changing capability, are designed to perform

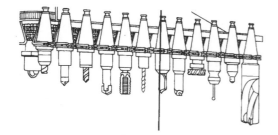

Figure 5–20 *Machining center cutlers (Courtesy Monarch).*

Figure 5–22 *Schematic illustration of a typical shaper cut (Courtesy IscarMetals, Inc.).*

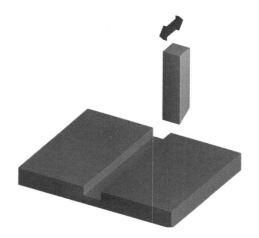

Figure 5–23 *Internal machining holder bar for blades (Courtesy IscarMetals, Inc.).*

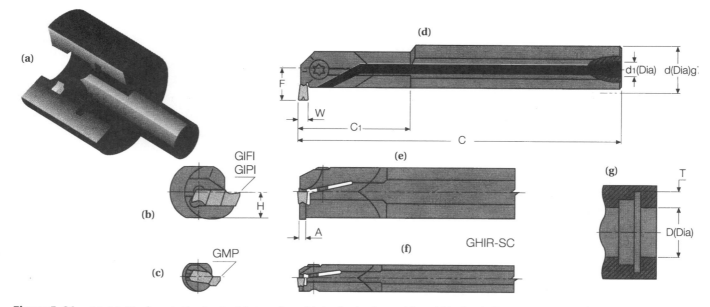

Figure 5–21 *(a)–(g). Single-point boring tool. Internal machining boring bars with carbide shank (Courtesy Iscar Metals, Inc.).*

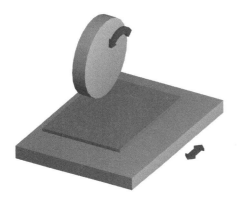

Figure 5–24 *Schematic of the grinding operation.*

Figure 5–26 *Parts finished cut by broaches (Courtesy of duMont Corporation).*

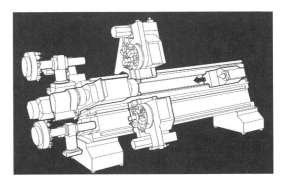

Figure 5–28 *A turning center schematic (Courtesy of The Monarch Machine Tool Co.).*

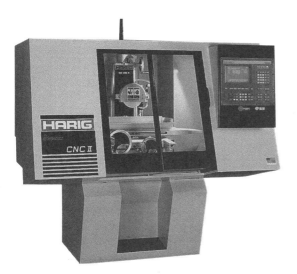

Figure 5–25 *Harig 618 CNC II Grinder (Courtesy of Bridgeport Machine).*

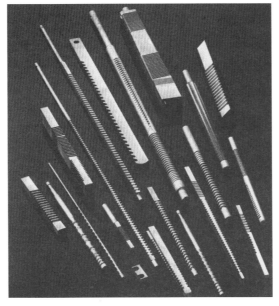

Figure 5–27 *Broaches (Courtesy of duMont Corporation).*

a variety of cutting operations on up to five surfaces without moving or repositioning (Figure 5–29).

Turning centers are also computer controlled and may have dual turrets with twin turret changers. A part-turning program can equip and exchange complete sets of tooling in less than 30 seconds, a job that formerly required one or more hours to change the tooling and chuck jaws. Some turning centers provide immediate on-machine access to as many as 48 turning (cutting) tools that can perform all operations on most parts. The largest machines are designed for maximum productivity on both spindles, whether turning both ends of a single part or machining two dissimilar parts simultaneously (Figure 5–28).

Drill/Saw

Drilling, one of the most common machining processes, employs the twist drill as its

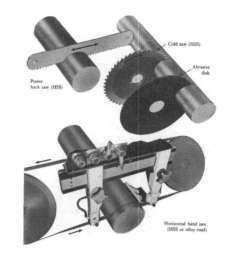

Figure 5–30   *Types of saw blades (Courtesy of DoAll).*

Figure 5–29   *A vertical machining center VMC 1000 (Courtesy of Bridgeport Machine).*

Figure 5–31   *20" vertical band saw (Courtesy of Powermatic).*

most common cutting tool. The twist drill is used to cut holes in a workpiece in one axis (Figure 5–32).

Sawing is often used to cut stock to length for other cutting operations. Most industrial machines are capable of cutting to ±0.005 inch and are essential manufacturing tools. The two basic types of sawing are reciprocating and circular. Circular is divided into a continuous band and the disc blade (Figure 5–30). The appropriate machine and cutting blade are chosen for their type and thickness or the shape of the material to be cut (Figure 5–31).

Figure 5–32   *Variable-speed drill press (Courtesy of Powermatic).*

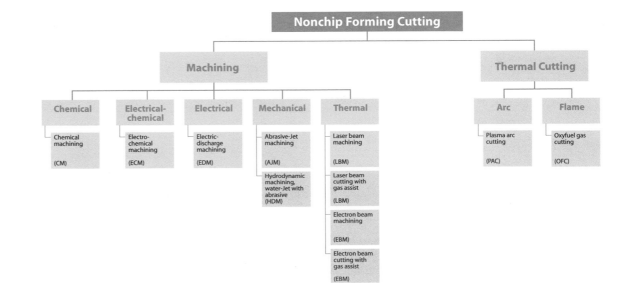

Figure 5–33   *Nonchip forming cutting.*

5.3   NONCHIP FORMING CUTTING

Nonchip forming (cutting) uses high-tech processes that are used extensively in the fabrication of electronic, scientific, and defense equipment. Tolerances of ±0.0005 inch are common.

The thermal cutting processes shown in Figure 5–33 are distinct from the machining processes in that they are generally used for bulk cutting, which is not normally considered machining. However these cutting processes can achieve tolerances of ±0.005 inch.

Chemical Machining/Milling (CM) and Electro-Chemical Machining (ECM)

In *chemical milling,* shallow cavities (up to 0.47 inches) are usually formed in parts for overall weight reduction (Figures 5–34 and 5–35). Selective attack by a chemical on the workpiece is controlled by masks or by partial immersion in the chemical (Figure 5–36). The associated tooling costs and equipment are low and the process is suitable for low production (Figure 5–37).

Electrochemical machining is essentially the reverse of electroplating; it removes large amounts of metal in complex and deep cavities. A conductive *salt solution* removes the material formed on the workpiece by electrochemical action, forming a cavity. The associated tooling and equipment costs are expensive, and power consumption is high. Tools are generally made of brass, copper, bronze, or stainless steel. The process is suitable for medium to high production.

Miscellaneous Machining

Electrical Discharge Machining (EDM)

In *electrical discharge machining* (EDM) metals are eroded by spark discharges. EDM, developed in the 1940s, uses a shaped tool

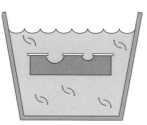

Figure 5–34 *Chemical machining schematic.*

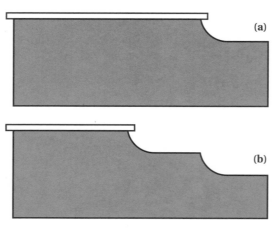

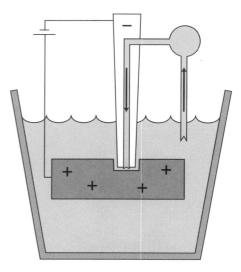

Figure 5–37 *Electrochemical machining process schematic .*

made of carbon. The workpiece, in a non-conductive fluid is connected to a power supply. A spark discharges through the fluid, removing a small amount of metal (Figure 5–41). The associated tooling and equipment costs are expensive but can be cost effective when compared to conventional milling, largely because errors are virtually eliminated. EDM is used extensively in producing injection and die-cast tooling (Figure 5–38). A recent development, wire EDM, uses a traveling wire as a cutter.

Figure 5–36 *(a)–(c). Stages in producing a profiled cavity by chemical machining.*

Figure 5–35 *Typical weight-reduction design by chemical machining.*

Abrasive-Jet Machining (AJM)

In AJM, clean dry air (or gas) with grit or abrasive powder is focused on the workpiece at velocities up to 1000 fps through a tungsten carbide or synthetic sapphire nozzle (Figure 5–39). AJM can cut any material with little heat, and it is operator safe. Very thin brittle materials can be cut without breakage, because there is little impact. The process is slow, however, and requires extensive dust collection.

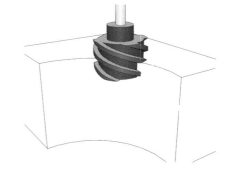

Figure 5–38 *Spiral cavity produced by an EDM rotating electrode tool. Drawing is based on a design for a Lego-type gear, designed and molded at the Stevens Institute in New Jersey.*

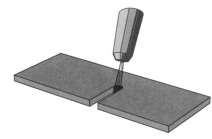

Figure 5–39 *Abrasive jet machining.*

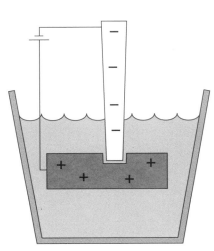

Figure 5–42 *Water jet cutting (Courtesy of Sikorsky).*

Hydrodynamic Machining (HDM)/Water-Jet Cutting with Abrasive

In HDM, pure water (with an abrasive) is shaped into a small coherent stream and fired into a material at velocities up to 3400 fps, resulting in clean, smooth cuts at a very fast rate (Figure 5–40). This process is used to cut virtually any material in any direction, without heat or particulate generation, and with little waste. Usually no finishing is required (Figure 5–42).

Figure 5–41 *Electrical discharge machining (EDM) process schematic .*

Thermal Machining

Laser Beam Machining (LBM)

In LBM a laser uses highly focused, high-density energy to melt and vaporize portions of the workpiece (Figure 5–44). Laser beam machining is used to machine metallic and nonmetallic materials, and for drilling holes as small as 0.0002 inch, with depth-to-diameter ratios of 50 to 1. LBM equipment is expensive and consumes much energy, but does not require a vacuum (Figure 5–43).

Electron Beam Machining (EBM)

The energy source for EBM is high-velocity electrons. Its applications are similar to those of LBM except that it requires a vacuum. EBM machines use high voltage to accelerate electrons up to 80 percent of the speed of light. They produce hazardous x-rays and the equipment is expensive (Figure 5–45).

Lasers and electron beam equipment are used for extremely accurate cutting. Surface finish is better and kerf width is narrower than that in other thermal cutting processes.

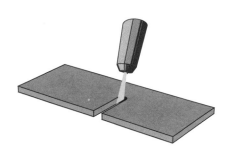

Figure 5–40 *Hydrodynamic machining process or water-jet machining.*

Figure 5–43 *Laser machining center (Courtesy of Bridgeport Machine).*

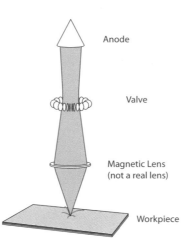

Anode

Valve

Magnetic Lens
(not a real lens)

Workpiece

Figure 5–45 *Electron beam schematic.*

5.4 FLAME/THERMAL CUTTING

Oxy-Acetylene and Plasma-Arc Cutting

In *oxygen-acetylene cutting,* acetylene and oxygen gases are mixed in a cutting attachment chamber and ignited using a special tip. As the metal is heated to a critical temperature, the flow of oxygen is increased, which oxidizes the metal and creates a cut through the plate (Figures 5–49 and 5–50).

Figure 5–44 *Laser concept drawing (Courtesy of Amada).*

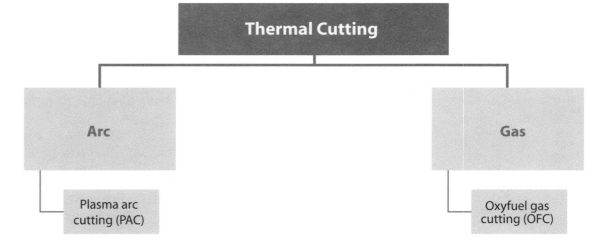

Thermal Cutting

Arc

Plasma arc cutting (PAC)

Gas

Oxyfuel gas cutting (OFC)

Figure 5–46 *Arc and gas cutting chart.*

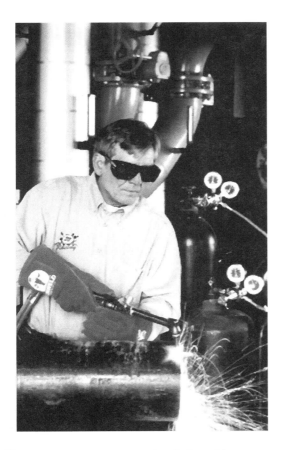

Figure 5–47 *Fame cutting of steel plate with oxyacetylene torch (Courtesy of ESAB Welding Products).*

Figure 5–48 *Plasma arc cutting (Courtesy of ESAB Welding Products).*

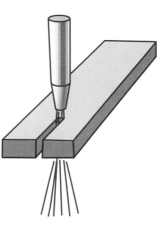

Figure 5–49 *Schematic of flame-cutting of steel plate with oxyacetylene torch.*

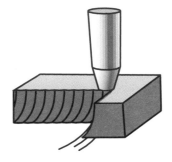

Figure 5–50 *Schematic of a cross section of flame-cut plate showing irregular drag lines.*

Steel plates up to 6 inches thick can be easily cut using this process. A disadvantage is the cumbersome tanks and awkward hoses required. An advantage is its portability, requiring no other power source (Figure 5–47).

Plasma-arc cutting (PAC) produces temperatures higher than those in the oxygen-acetylene process and is therefore more productive. It produces a smooth cut and is used to cut non-ferrous and stainless steel, can easily be automated, and has become the most popular method of thermal cutting. A real advantage over oxygen-acetylene cutting is that it is more compact and does not require cumbersome gas tanks and awkward hoses. It does require a high-voltage power source (Figure 5–48).

6

METAL JOINING

Almost all products are assemblies and the manufacturing process normally requires the joining of parts of various materials. The options that are available are shown in Figure 6–1. Each option has advantages and disadvantages, but all are expensive, and a final choice must be based on considerations such as joint strength/reliability, appearance, repair/maintenance requirements, and materials or parts to be joined. The best strategy is to minimize the need to assemble through creative redesign or, where applicable, design of the parts for robotic assembly—design for assembly (DFA).

Typically more than 50 percent of total production time is spent on assembly or mechanical fastening functions. Tolerances required for automatic assembly often exceed those required by the product. Standardization is always recommended to lower assembly costs.

Brazing, welding, and adhesives present various difficulties that slow assembly, and unless there is sufficient production, they are not economical to automate. In using mechanical fasteners, for example, the number of parts in a product is typically proportional to the cost of assembling that product. Mechanical fasteners usually represent less than 5 percent of the total in-place cost of the manufactured product, but assembly and fastening often account for the major cost of manufacturing a product.

It makes little sense to use different-sized machine screws and fasteners to save a few cents when the real cost is in accommodating and the supply of various-sized fasteners in assembly.

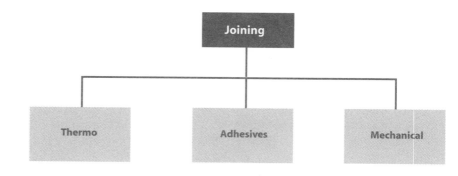

Figure 6–1 *Joining processes.*

Thermojoining

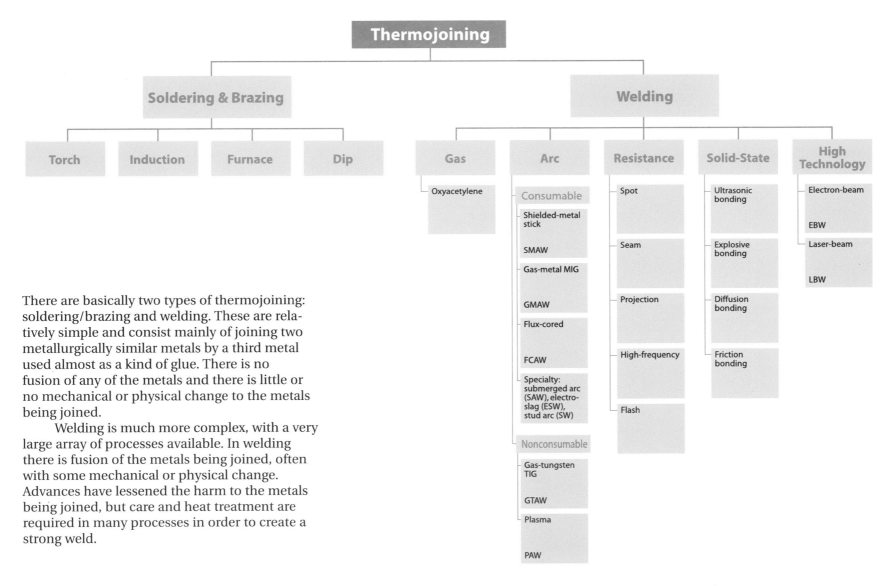

There are basically two types of thermojoining: soldering/brazing and welding. These are relatively simple and consist mainly of joining two metallurgically similar metals by a third metal used almost as a kind of glue. There is no fusion of any of the metals and there is little or no mechanical or physical change to the metals being joined.

Welding is much more complex, with a very large array of processes available. In welding there is fusion of the metals being joined, often with some mechanical or physical change. Advances have lessened the harm to the metals being joined, but care and heat treatment are required in many processes in order to create a strong weld.

Figure 6–2   *Thermojoining chart.*

6.1 SOLDERING and BRAZING

6.1.1 Soldering

Soldering is used primarily to conduct electric current and to seal cans and similar products. In this process a nonferrous filler metal called solder and a flux are used to join metals using temperatures below 850°F. The pieces to be joined must have higher melt temperatures than the solder and must be metallurgically compatible. When heated, the solder flows into the joint, which must be coated with a flux to prevent oxidation and allow the solder, as it cools, to bond the parts together (Figure 6–3).

Solder has little strength, so the joint must be designed to support a load. Soldering is best used when the joint is not under stress. Limited nonmetals—such as glass— can be soldered when pre-coated to accept the solder.

Solder Alloys

Tin-lead
Tin-lead-antimony
Tin-antimony
Tin-silver
Tin-zinc
Lead-silver
Cadmium-zinc
Zinc-aluminum

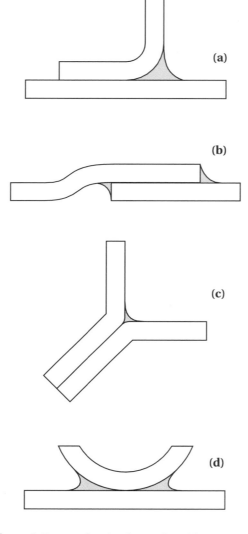

Figure 6–3   *(a)–(d). Joint designs for soldering.*

SOLDER/BRAZING

Advantages

- Dissimilar metals can be joined.
- Different thicknesses can be joined.
- Cast and wrought metals can be joined.
- Original mechanical properties are generally not seriously affected.

6.1.2 Brazing

Brazing is similar to soldering except that it is done at temperatures above 850°F (but below melt temperature). A nonferrous filler metal, called a brazing alloy, and a flux bond the two pieces, which must have higher melt temperatures than the brazing alloy and must be metallurgically compatible. When heated, the brazing alloy flows into the joint, which must be coated with a flux to prevent oxidation. As it cools, the brazing alloy bonds

BRAZING

Advantages

- Assemblies can be joined in a virtually stress-free condition.
- Complex assemblies can be joined in several steps by using filler metals with progressively lower melting temperatures.
- Brazed joints require little or no finishing other than flux removal.
- The joint is sealed and conductive.

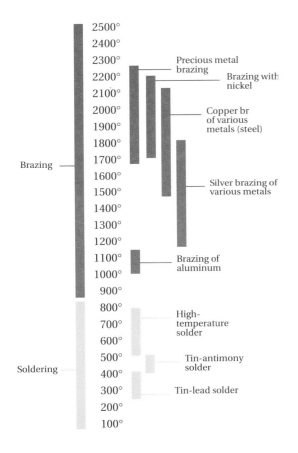

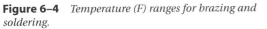

Figure 6–4 *Temperature (F) ranges for brazing and soldering.*

the materials. Brazing has more strength than soldering because some limited alloying occurs between the filler metal and the base metals at elevated temperatures; there is some intergranular penetration creating some atomic forces between the metals at the joint (Figure 6–4).

Filler Metals for Brazing (Fluxes are Sodium, Potassium and Lithium)

Base Metal	Temp. °C	Filler Metal
Aluminum alloys	570–620	Aluminum-silicon
Magnesium alloys	580–625	Magnesium-aluminum
Copper and alloys	700–925	Copper-phosphorus
Ferrous/nonferrous	620–1150	Silver/copper alloys
Iron/nickel-cobalt	900–1100	Gold
Stainless steels	925–1200	Nickel-silver

Torch Brazing

Torch brazing is common for most limited production. It is manual, versatile, and uses different mixes of gasses burning with a slightly reducing flame (Figure 6–6).

Induction Brazing

In induction brazing, an electrical coil is placed near the joint, providing the heat source. The process is normally automated and produces an accurate, uniform, and fast joint (Figure 6–5b).

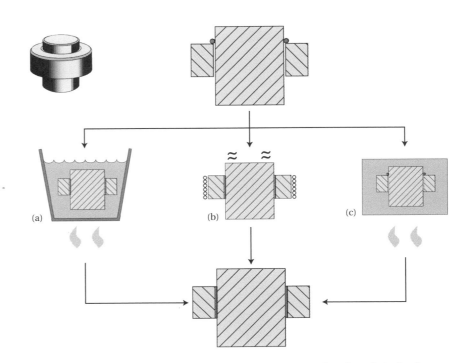

Figure 6–5 *Various forms of brazing: (a) dip brazing in a molten flux, (b) induction brazing, and (c) furnace brazing.*

Figure 6–6   *Torch brazing.*

Dip Brazing (Figure 6–6a)

This process is used to braze aluminum assemblies, which are jigged and then put into a molten salt bath that is the heat source.

Furnace Brazing (Figure 6–5c)

A hydrogen-atmosphere furnace is used to braze preassembled or self-jigging parts that can withstand the heat. No flux is necessary because there is no oxygen present in the furnace.

6.2   WELDING

6.2.1   Gas Welding

In *oxyacetylene welding,* oxygen and acetylene gases are mixed in a torch and ignited (Figure 6–8) to heat metal pieces to be joined above melt temperature so that they will flow together (Figure 6–7a). The pieces to be welded must be of a similar thickness, melt temperature, and metallurgy (Figure 6–7b). The high heat and welding changes the grain structure and causes stress as the welded joint cools (Figure 6–9). The stress can be relieved by heat treatment.

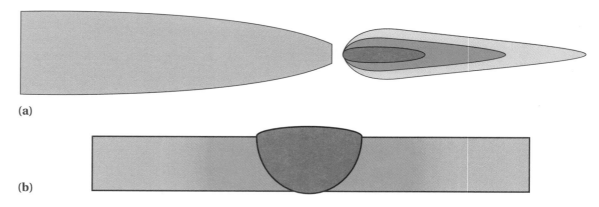

(a)

(b)

Figure 6–7   *Oxyacetylene flames. (a) By increasing the oxygen flow, the flame can be changed from a reducing to an oxydizing flame. (b) Oxyacetylene weld detail showing the fusion of two sheets (of similar size and metallurgy) with filler material, and the heat affected zone on either side. The mechanical properties have been affected and should be heat treated to restore uniform properties to the area.*

PUROX® W-300 and OXWELD® W-400 Welding Torches

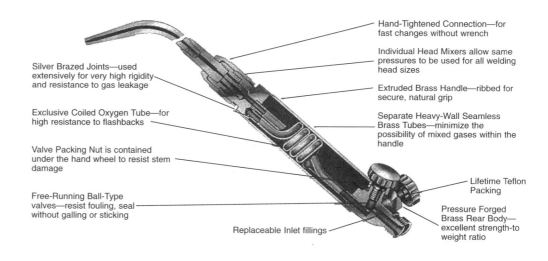

Silver Brazed Joints—used extensively for very high rigidity and resistance to gas leakage

Exclusive Coiled Oxygen Tube—for high resistance to flashbacks

Valve Packing Nut is contained under the hand wheel to resist stem damage

Free-Running Ball-Type valves—resist fouling, seal without galling or sticking

Replaceable Inlet fillings

Hand-Tightened Connection—for fast changes without wrench

Individual Head Mixers allow same pressures to be used for all welding head sizes

Extruded Brass Handle—ribbed for secure, natural grip

Separate Heavy-Wall Seamless Brass Tubes—minimize the possibility of mixed gases within the handle

Lifetime Teflon Packing

Pressure Forged Brass Rear Body—excellent strength-to weight ratio

Figure 6–8   *Sectional view of oxyacetylene welding torch (Courtesy ESAB Welding and Cutting Products).*

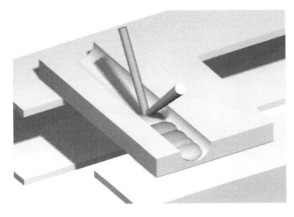

Figure 6–9 *View of a gas weld using a filler rod.*

6.2.2 Arc Welding

6.2.2.1 Arc Welding: Consumable

Shielded-Metal Arc Welding & Flux Core Arc Welding

Shielded-metal arc welding (SMAW), also known as stick welding, is the most common method of arc welding. An electrical arc is struck between the workpiece and a flux-covered electrode (Figure 6–13). The heat generated melts the metal to be welded and the flux, which protects the molten metal from oxidizing (Figure 6–15). As the stick is consumed, providing a filler metal to the weld, it must be replaced. This is time consuming and disruptive to the welding process, causing or increasing random stress in the welded joint. The melted flux or slag that collects at the weld must be removed by chipping before another pass is made over the weld. This low-cost process is versatile

and maneuverable but cannot be automated because of the limited length of the electrode (Figure 6–10).

Flux-cored arc welding (FCAW) grew out of stick welding and was developed to overcome the limitations of the original process. The electrode wire, which provides the filler metal to the weld, is wound on a reel, has a flux core, and is advanced automatically as it is consumed into the weld (Figure 6–14). Inert gas can be added as an option in situations where the flux is inadequate (Figure 6–12). GMAW and FCAW have advantages over SMAW in that they are continuous and can be automated (Figure 6–11).

Gas Metal Arc Welding

Gas metal arc welding (GMAW), also called metal inert gas (MIG) welding, is similar to FCAW but uses a bare wire electrode wound on a reel to conduct the arc. Instead of a flux core, the electrode is surrounded by inert gas

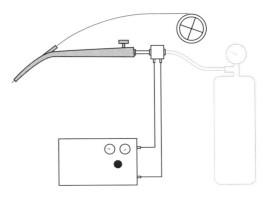

Figure 6–11 *Schematic of equipment for flux-cored arc-welding components with gas optional.*

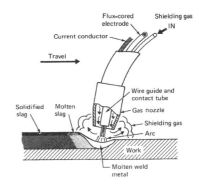

Figure 6–12 *Principles of flux-cored arc-welding process with optional gas (Courtesy of the Lincoln Electric Co.).*

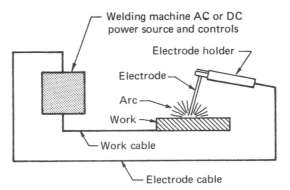

Figure 6–10 *Basic arc-welding circuit (Courtesy of the Lincoln Electric Co.).*

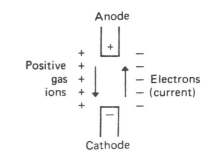

Figure 6–13 *Characteristics of the arc (Courtesy of the Lincoln Electric Co.).*

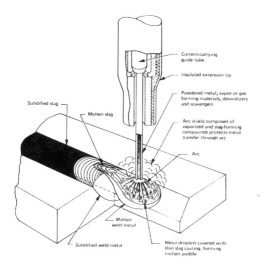

Figure 6–14 *Principles of flux-cored arc-welding process (Courtesy of the Lincoln Electric Co.).*

at the nozzle to keep oxygen from contaminating the weld. The wire electrode is advanced into the weld as the wire electrode is consumed. The process can be automated, but the real advantage is that there is no melted flux or slag to remove, providing an uncontaminated weld (Figure 6–18a). This process costs more and is less maneuverable than stick welding because of the required gas tanks (Figure 6–18b).

Submerged Arc Welding (SAW)

In *submerged arc welding* (SAW) a bare wire electrode strikes an arc that is submerged in the joint under a mound of granular flux (Figure 6–16). This process is used to weld plate metals from 2 to 8 inches thick with deep penetration and narrow beads in railroad-car, barge, and ship building; in pipe manufacture; in fabricating structural beams, girders, and columns; and in other applications that require long welds. The process produces extremely high current densities, and the flux blanket prevents the

rapid escape of heat and concentrates it in the welding zone.

Electroslag Welding (ESW)

ESW is an adaptation of the submerged welding process for joining thick materials in a vertical position. In this process, a granular flux is placed in the gap between vertical plates. Welding shoes move up the joint, welding the plates 1.5 to 15 inches thick (Figure 6–17).

Stud Arc Welding

In *stud arc welding*, a stud (electrode) is fused onto a metal surface with a stud-welding gun. When the trigger (switch) is pulled,

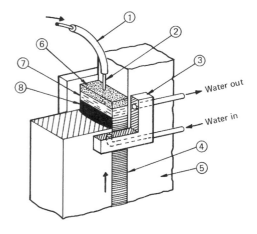

Figure 6–17 *Schematic sketch of a electro slag welding (1) electrode guide tube, (2) electrode, (3) water cooled copper shoes, (4) finished weld, (5) base metal, (6) molten slag, (7) molten weld metal, and (8) solidified weld metal (Courtesy of the Lincoln Electric Co.)*

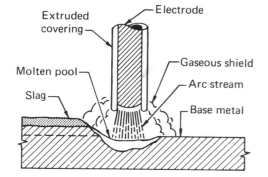

Figure 6–15 *How the arc and molten pool are shielded by a gaseous blanket from the stick electrode. (Courtesy of the Lincoln Electric Co.*

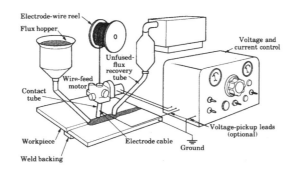

Figure 6–16 *Submerged arc-welding process (Courtesy of the Lincoln Electric Co.).*

(a)

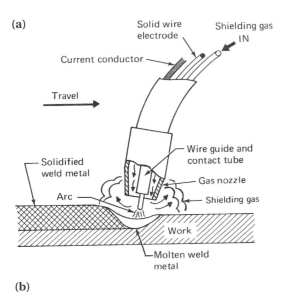

(b)

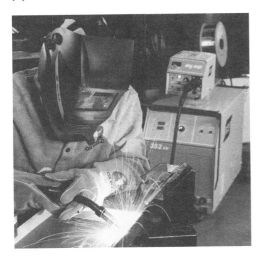

Figure 6–18 *(a) Principles of gas metal arc welding process (Courtesy of the Lincoln Electric Co.). (b) MIG or gas metal arc welding (Courtesy of ESAB Welding and Cutting Products).*

current flows between a stainless-steel or aluminum stud (held by the gun) and a metal surface, slightly melting both. Then the stud is pressed onto the surface, the metal cools, and gun is withdrawn (Figures 6–19 and 6–20).

6.2.2.2 Arc Welding: Nonconsumable

Gas-Tungsten Arc Welding

Gas-tungsten arc welding (GTAW), also called tungsten inert gas (TIG) welding, is somewhat like GMAW except that the electrode is made of tungsten, which has a very high melt temperature. Because it does not melt, it is not consumed during the welding process. A gas shield is used as a flux. A filler

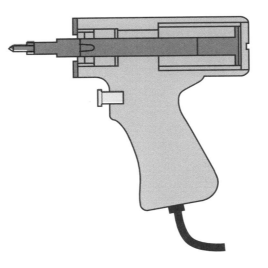

Figure 6–19 *Sectional view of a stud welding gun.*

rod is used, if needed, to supply molten metal to the weld (Figures 6–21 and 6–22).

Nearly all metals can be welded by GTAW, including most steels, aluminum alloys, magnesium alloys, copper, some brass and bronze, titanium, gold, and silver. The process can be adapted for high-quality welding of thin materials.

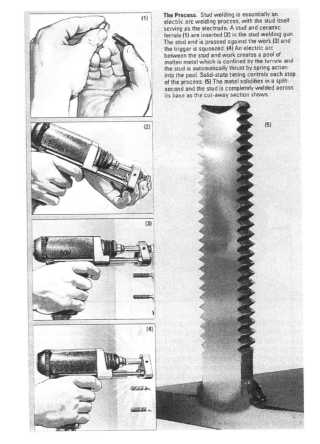

Figure 6–20 *Stud detail (Courtesy of TRW Nelson Stud Weld Division).*

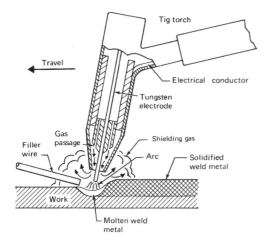

Figure 6–21 *Principles of gas tungsten-arc welding (Courtesy of the Lincoln Electric Co.).*

Figure 6–22 *TIG or gas tungsten-arc welding (Courtesy ESAB Welding Products).*

Plasma Arc Welding

Plasma arc welding (PAW) is a newer process that is used frequently as a substitute for GTAW. It offers greater welding speeds, better weld quality, and is less sensitive to process variables. The heat originates in an arc but is not diffused as in other processes. Instead, arc is constricted by being forced

PLASMA ARC WELDING

Advantages

- Reduced overall welding time
- Reduced joint preparation
- Uniform penetration
- More tolerance for joint mismatch

Disadvantages

- More complex process
- Two protective gases are required
- Complete gas shielding is difficult to obtain

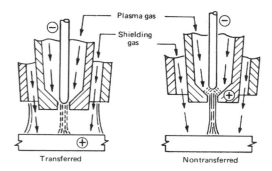

Figure 6–23 *Plasma arc welding. Transferred and nontransferred arcs. (Courtesy of the Lincoln Electric Co.)*

through a small orifice before reaching the workpiece. The current reaches 60,000°F, creating greater energy concentration, speed, and better arc stability (Figures 6–23 and 6–24).

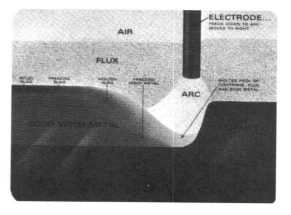

Figure 6–24 *Plasma arc welding schematic. (Courtesy of the Lincoln Electric Co.)*

6.2.3 Resistance Welding

Spot, Seam, Projection Welding

Resistance spot welding (RESW) is relatively simple, rapid, and economical. It is commonly used in sheet-metal fabrication, and widely used in the automotive industry. In this process metal sheets are clamped between two electrodes that conduct a measured current. Small depressions mar the joined sheets at the spots of contact. The pressure of the electrodes can be adjusted to reduce or eliminate the depression on the finish side (Figures 6–26 and 6–27).

Resistance steam welding (RSEW) is a variation of spot welding with rotating-wheel electrodes that produce continuous spot welds. Overlapping welds can produce a joint that is liquid/or gas-tight in products such as cans, containers, mufflers, and gas tanks (Figure 6–28).

In resistance projection welding (RPW), embossed dimples or projections are raised on the sheet and form contact points, localizing the heat produced by the current. The heat and pressure collapse the projections, joining the two sheets (Figure 6–25).

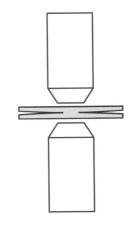

Figure 6–27 *Cross section of a spot weld.*

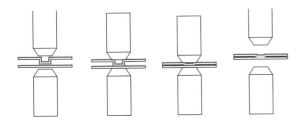

Figure 6–25 *Resistance projection welding sequence.*

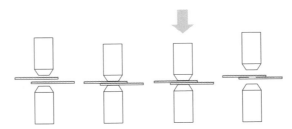

Figure 6–26 *Sequence in the resistance spot welding process.*

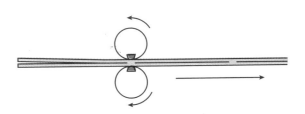

Figure 6–28 *Seam welding process.*

High-Frequency Welding

High-frequency welding is used to provide long, continuous welds for products such as seamed steel tubes and other seam-welded tubing. It uses a 450-kHz frequency to create an inductance that seam-welds tubes as they pass by the energy source, their sides squeezed together by rollers (Figure 6–32).

Flash welding is used for end joining of tubes, bandsaw blades, and other similar stock shapes. (It is common in model shops, where it is used to repair broken band saw blades.) To weld, the ends are spring clamped together and subjected to a 2000–5000 amp current to make the weld. The high resistance at the joint causes fusion, and the clamping force causes the plastic material to upset and join. (Figures 6–30 and 6–31).

Ultrasonic bonding is used for lap welding of thin sheet and wire and for sealing foil packaging. A high frequency of 10–75 kHz is transferred into mechanical vibrations that are transmitted by a transducer to the workpiece. The process is also commonly used to join plastics (*see* Section 11.0, page 204) (Figure 6–29).

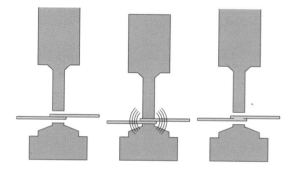

Figure 6–29 *Ultrasonic welding machine for lap welds.*

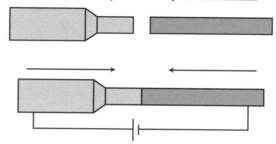

Figure 6–30 *Flash welding schematic. Parts to be joined must have similar cross section.*

Figure 6–31 *Part to be joined must be modified to have a similar cross section at the weld.*

Figure 6–32 *High-frequency welding of tubes.*

6.2.4   Solid State Welding

Explosive, Diffusion, and Friction Bonding

Explosive bonding is used to co-join dissimilar metals. The process uses an explosive of several million psi to clad slab and plate that can be metallurgically incompatible. Pressure is generated by the explosive, which is placed over the materials to be joined. The high energy of the explosive mechanically interlocks the two surfaces (Figures 6–33a and b).

Diffusion bonding is used to co-join dissimilar metals. Heat and pressure supplied by a press or static weights cause comingling of atoms. The temperature of the pieces joined during the process is one-half to one-third of their melt temperature (Figures 6–34a and b).

Friction bonding is used to join cylindrical parts. While rotating rapidly to create the heat necessary to join them, the ends of two pieces are forced against each other (Figures 6–35a, b, and c).

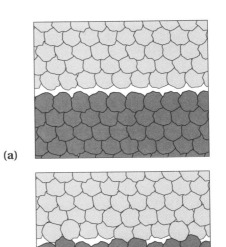

(a)

(b)

Figure 6–34   *(a)–(b). Diffusion bonding—using heat pressure to cojoin dissimilar metals.*

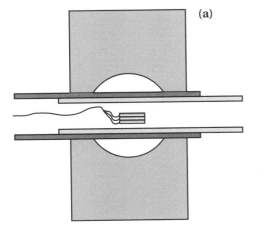

(a)

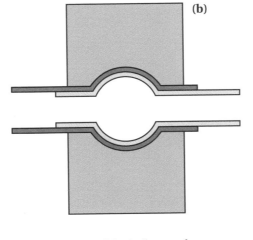

(b)

Figure 6–33   *(a)–(b). Explosion bonding uses an explosive charge to shape and bond dissimilar metals.*

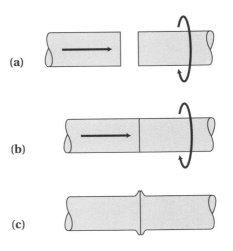

(a)

(b)

(c)

Figure 6–35   *(a)–(c). In friction welding one part is rotating as the other part is forced against it, causing heat. At a critical temperature the rotation is stopped and the bond is complete.*

6.2.5 High Technology Welding

Electron and Laser Beam Welding

In *electron beam welding* (EBW), high-velocity narrow-beam electrons are focused in a vacuum to generate enough heat to weld almost any metal and thickness, from foil to a 6-inch plate. No shielding gas or filler metal is required, and the process is capable of making high-quality welds with near parallel sides in a small heat-affected zone (Figure 6–39). The electron beam can be projected up to several meters. The automated computer-controlled equipment costs exceed $1 million.

The *laser beam welding* (LBW) process uses a focused high-power coherent light beam directed, shaped, and focused precisely on the workpiece. It is suitable for welding narrow and deep joints. LBW can be used on a variety of materials up to 1 inch thick, and it can be done in otherwise inaccessible locations. The automated computer-controlled equipment costs $$\frac{1}{2}$ to $1 million (Figures 6–36, 6–37 and 6–38).

Advantages of LBW over EBW

- No vacuum required
- The beams do not generate x-rays
- Better weld quality
- Less incomplete fusion, spatter, and porosity

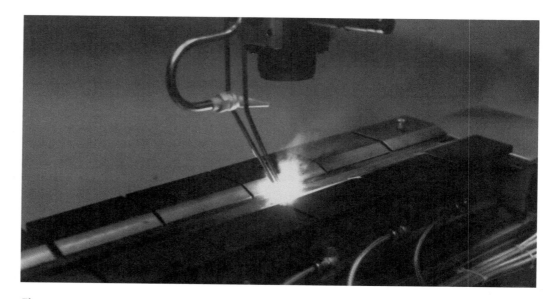

Figure 6–36   *Nd: YAG Laser welding. (Courtesy of Trumpf Inc.)*

Figure 6–37   *Haas-Yag laser (Courtesy of Trumpf Inc.).*

Figure 6–38   *Gillette Sensor razor. The Gillette Sensor razor has two narrow blades with twenty-two pinpoint welds (0.5 mm dia.) made by a Nd:YAG laser with a fiber optic delivery.*

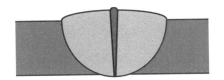

Figure 6–39 *Comparing the EBM and LBM weld beads to conventional welding, it is clear that the bead and heat-affected zone is much smaller, causing less stress.*

6.3 ADHESIVES (FIGURE 6–40)

Synthetic organic adhesives are important in manufacturing, and are often used for load-bearing applications, in joining thin materials, and for invisible joints. Adhesives must have the following characteristics: strength; toughness; and resistance to fluids, chemicals, and environmental degradation, including heat and moisture. A good joint should be designed to withstand shear, compressive, and tensile forces. The joint should not be subjected to a peeling force. One common application of adhesives in product design is attaching labels and membrane-switchs on operating panels.

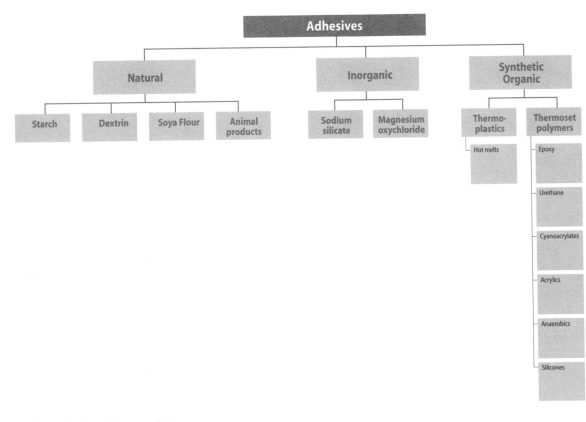

Figure 6–40 *Adhesives chart.*

Advantages of Adhesives

- Inherently smooth
- Join thin or fragile parts
- Do not deface exposed surfaces
- Do not disturb contours
- Distribute stress uniformly
- Join dissimilar materials w/differences in thermal expansion
- Provide corrosion protection
- Seal against liquids and gases
- Impart mechanical dampening

Disadvantages of Adhesives

- Have limited shelf life
- Have numerous and varied formulations
- Entail complicated control, assembly, and testing
- Destructive testing only
- May require highly skilled personnel
- May require oven cure
- Two-part systems limit time used
- Batch-to-batch variations
- Thorough cleaning required
- Require joined surface area preparation

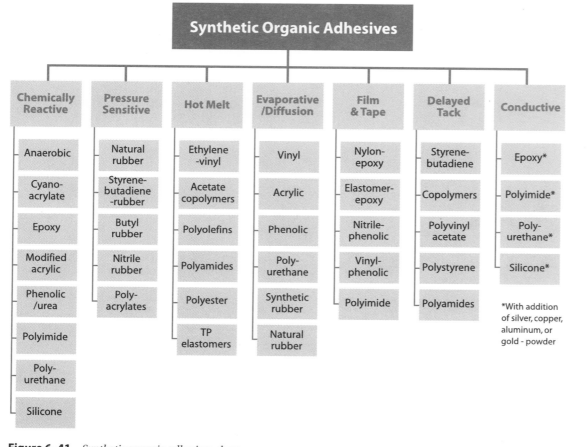

Figure 6–41 *Synthetic organic adhesives chart.*

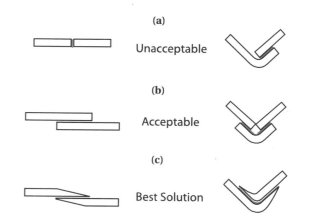

Figure 6–42 *(a)–(c). Adhesive joints require a large contact area. Suggested examples are shown in Figure 6–43.*

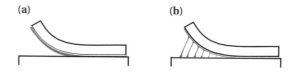

Figure 6–43 *(a) behavior of a brittle adhesive (b) characteristic behavior of a tough adhesive.*

Adhesives must have one or more of the following properties:

- Strength (shear/peel)
- Toughness
- Resistance to fluids and chemicals and to environmental degradation, including heat and moisture

- The capability to coat the interface to be bonded

Joints can be designed to withstand

- Shear forces
- Compressive forces
- Tensile forces

However, they should not be subjected to peeling forces (Figure 6–42 a, b, and c, and 6–43 a and b).

6.4 MECHANICAL FASTENERS

Mechanical fasteners are used during the assembly phase of production and are often a significant part of the cost. The best strategy is to minimize the need to assemble through creative redesign or, where applicable, to design the parts for robotic assembly—Design for Assembly (DFA). In using mechanical fasteners, the number of parts in a product is typically proportional to the cost of assembling that product. Whereas mechanical fasteners usually represent less than 5 percent of the total in-place cost of the manufactured product, assembly and fastening often account for the majority of the manufacturing cost.

Typically more than 50 percent of total production time is spent on the assembly or mechanical-fastening function. Tolerances required for automatic assembly may exceed those required by the product.

Standardization is always recommended to lower assembly costs. It makes little sense to use different-sized machine screws and fasteners to save a few cents when the real cost is in accommodating and supplying various-sized fasteners in assembly.

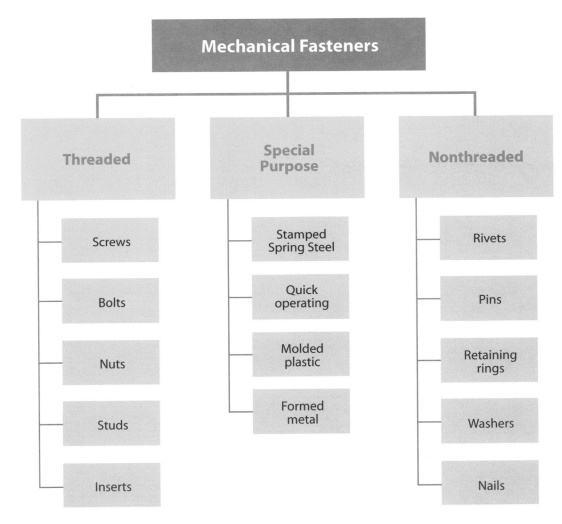

Figure 6–44   *Mechanical fasteners chart.*

Threaded Fasteners

Threaded fasteners are the most common fasteners used in assembly. Often times, the part can be drilled-and-taped to accept a machine screw. If the metal is too soft to withstand the expected high tensile and torque stresses, a thread insert or threaded stud can be used (Figure 6–45a—The equivalent for thermoset plastics is also shown). Fasteners for insertion into sheet metal are also commonly used—these are called *pems* for the Penn Engineering and Manufacturing Company, which was one of the first to develop them (Figure 6–45b).

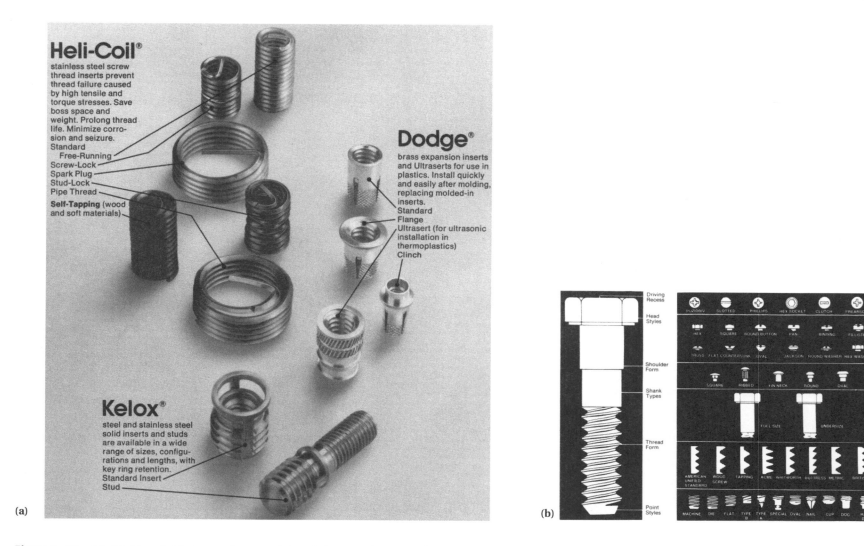

Figure 6–45   *(a) –(b). Threaded fasteners—inserts and threaded inserts (Courtesy Helicoil).*

Screws

Wood
Metal
Bolts
Machine
Lag

Nuts

Locking
Free-running
Single-thread

Studs

Tap end
Tap both ends
Continuous-thread

Inserts

Wire thread
Threadserts
Self-tapping

Non-Threaded Fasteners

Non-threaded fasteners are often invisible because they are usually held by friction within the fastener assembly. The most common, which is normally visible, is the washer.

Rivets

Blind
Tubular

(a)

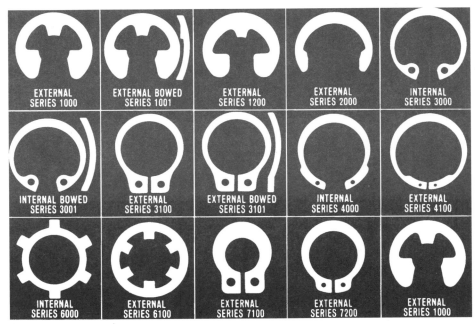

(b)

Figure 6–46 *(a) Eyelets. (Courtesy Stimpson Co. Inc.). (b) Retaining rings (Courtesy Industrial Retaining Ring Co.).*

Pins

Dowel
Taper
Clovis
Cotter
Spiral-wrapped
Slotted tube

Retaining Rings

Stamped
Wire-formed
Spiral-wound

Washers

Flat
Conical
Helical
Tooth lock
Spring

Special Purpose Fasteners

Special purpose fasteners range from paper clips to door locks and hinges. The range of special purpose fasteners is virtually unlimited; because they are normally economical to manufacture they can be made to order (Figures 6–47 a through d and 6–48 a and b).

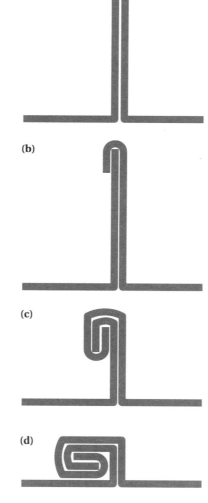

(a)

(b)

(c)

(d)

Figure 6–47 *(a)–(d). Schematic of a formed metal joint.*

(a)

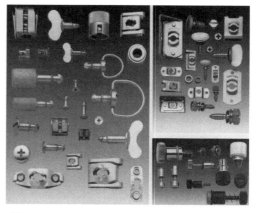

(b)

Figure 6–48 *(a) Special-purpose fasteners (Courtesy EATON Corporation, Engineered Fasteners Division). (b) Special-purpose 1/4-turn fasteners (Courtesy Southco Inc.).*

Stamped Steel Spring

Clips
Dart
Shaped
Cable/tube
Stud clips
Push-on
Finger-interlock
Round
Flange
Wire twist

Quick Operating

Lever-actuated
Slide action
Lift-and-turn
Magnetic
Push-pull
Push-push
Turn-operated
Plastic
Burdock
Velcro
Formed metal
Multi-function
Metal crimp

7 APPEARANCE FINISHING AND COATING

The finishes section is expanded and reorganized to be useful to industrial designers rather than according to a traditional practice. To be absolutely true to the organization of this volume, finishing is treated as a forming, cutting, or joining operation. Because finishing is rather unique and plays a major role in industrial design, it deserves a bit more attention.

Finishing is important because appearance is one of the prime responsibilities of the industrial designer, and appearance—form and finish—is a determining aspect of a product. Appearance can play a deciding factor in the success or failure of a product in the consumer as well as in industrial markets. Finish is a key aspect of appearance, but the protective and functional aspects of a finish are also important. The available options must be chosen using the same kind of cost-benefit analysis used in all design decisions. Aspects such as cost, compatibility, color, gloss, texture, and durability must be considered. The final choice should not be made after the product has been designed. The finish is one of the factors that must be taken into account at the very beginning of the product design process (Figure 7–1).

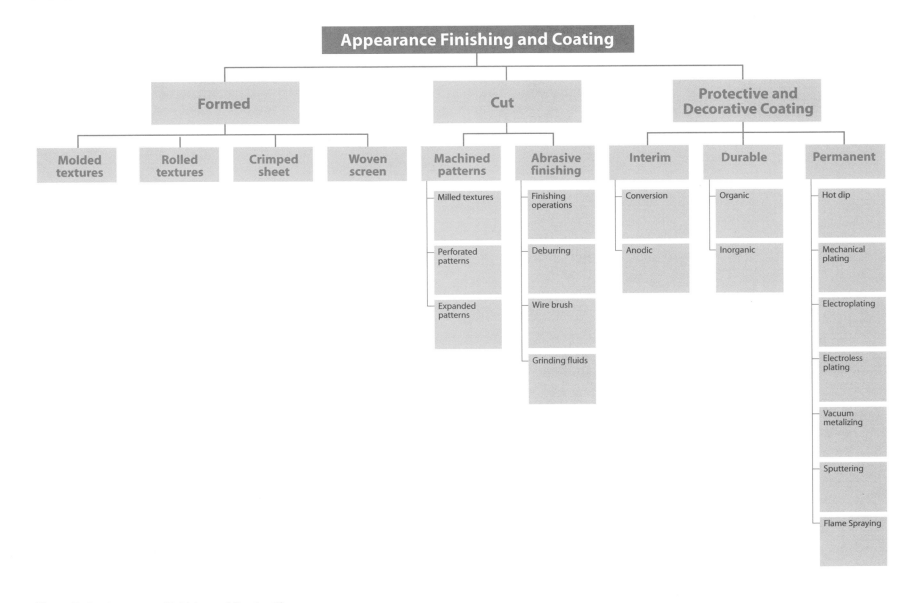

Figure 7–1 *Appearance Finishing and Coating Chart.*

7.1 FORMING TEXTURES/ MOLDED IN

Molded Textures

Texture plays an important role in design. Texture can improve product appearance, increase utility—as in improved grip and mar and scratch resistance—and decrease the reject rate by masking minor flaws, such as sink marks. Textures can be molded in during casting. The depth of the texture will increase the draft angle required, so there may be some negative aspects to consider. The rule of thumb for molding textures with an undercut is that the angle should be 1–1½° for every 0.001 inch of depth (Figures 7–2 and 7–3).

Letraset patterns, an excellent source of textures, can be adapted to molded texture design (Figure 7–4).

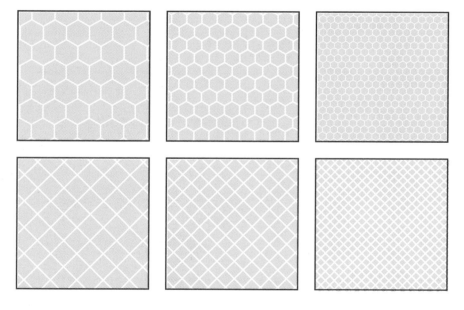

Figure 7–2 *Texture patterns.*

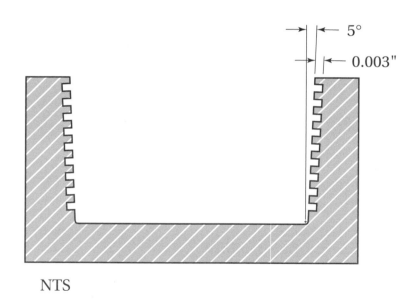

NTS

Figure 7–3 *Texture and undercut detail.*

7.1.1 Formed Textures

Rolled and Crimped Patterns

Rolled Patterns

Mill finish plate is available in a number of patterns. The most popular, Diamond Plate, is used for stair treads and on inclined planes to provide traction. Patterns are rolled in the sheet at the rolling mill (Figure 7–5).

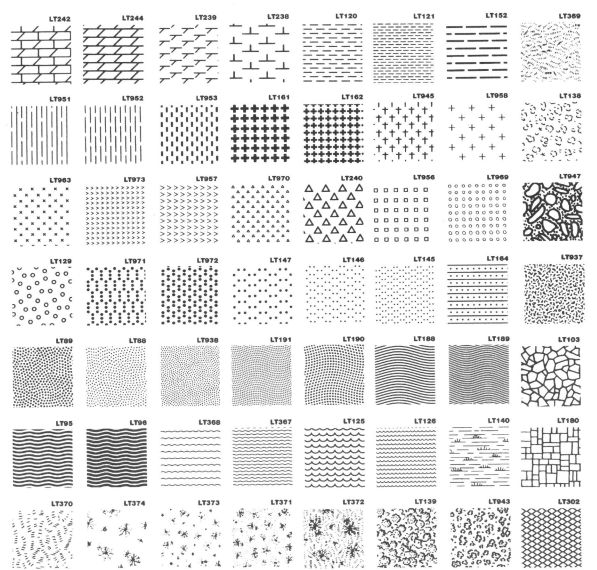

Figure 7–4 *Letraset patterns (Courtesy Letraset).*

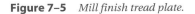

Figure 7–5 *Mill finish tread plate.*

Crimped Metals

Textures can be formed by crimping preplated sheets 0.020 to 0.036 inch thick, creating sparkling highlights of jewel-like prisms. Crimping provides extra strength and rigidity, often allowing a lighter gauge to be used (Figures 7–6 and 7–7).

7.1.2   Formed Sheet Metal Patterns

Formed Patterns

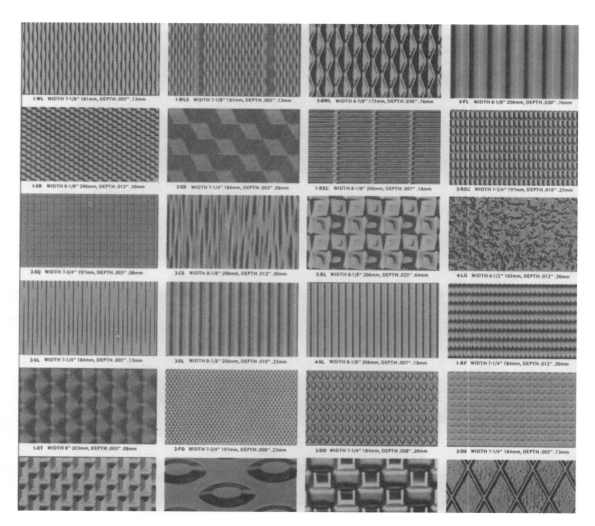

Figure 7–7   *Deep-textured metals (Courtesy Rigidized Metals Corp.).*

Figure 7–6   *Crimped metals (Courtesy American Nickeloid Company).*

Woven Wire Cloth

Woven wire cloth or screen has a variety of uses, including baskets, fabricated parts for filtration, laboratory test sieves, vent covers for heated air, as well as for protecting open areas and windows (Figure 7–8a and b). Perforated and expanded metals also offer a variety of textures and increased part strength, and provide the designer with unique and economical part design opportunities (Figures 7–9, 7–10, 7–11, and 7–12).

(b)

(a)

Figure 7–8   *(a)–(b) Woven wire cloth (Courtesy Newark Wire Cloth Co.).*

7.2 MECHANICAL/ CHEMICAL

Perforated and Expanded Metal Patterns

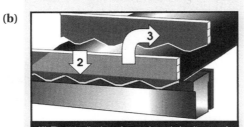

Figure 7–9 *Perforated Patterns.*

(a)

(1) Sheet or plate is advanced beyond the face of the bottom die an amount equal to the strand width before flattening.

(b)

(2) The top die then descends and simultaneously slits and cold forms an entire row of half diamonds.
(3) The top die then ascends and moves one half-diamond right as the base sheet or plate moves forward one strand width.

(c)

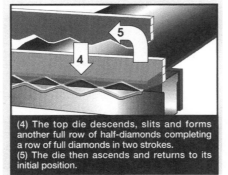

(4) The top die descends, slits and forms another full row of half-diamonds completing a row of full diamonds in two strokes.
(5) The die then ascends and returns to its initial position.

Figure 7–10 *(a), (b), and (c). Five-step process in manufacturing expanded metal (Courtesy of Metalex).*

Figure 7–11 *Manufacturing expanded metal (Courtesy of Metalex).*

Figure 7–12 *Expanded metal products (Courtesy of Metalex).*

Honing, Superfinishing, Lapping, Wirebrush and Coated Abrasives

Honing is a fine finishing process for the interior surfaces of round holes. A rotating mandrel with aluminum or silicon-carbide strips moving in a reciprocating action produces a cross-hatched pattern (Figure 7–14).

Superfinishing is a similar process except that it is used to finish the external surface on cylindrical parts (Figure 7–13).

Lapping is a very fine finishing operation on flat or cylindrical surfaces, such as an injection molding tool. Laps are made of metal, leather, or cloth, usually with embedded abrasive particles. Tolerances of 0.000015 inch can be achieved on flat or curved surfaces such as spherical objects and lenses.

Coated abrasives such as sandpaper and emery cloth (sheets, discs, or belts) can be used in finishing metallic and nonmetallic surfaces. The surface finish depends primarily on the grain size of the abrasive (Figure 7–15).

In *wire brushing,* a part or sheet is held against a circular wire brush rotating at a high speed, producing very fine to rough textures on the surface. Each industry group has its own brushed texture designations.

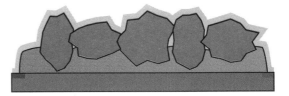

Figure 7–15   *Structure of a coated abrasive.*

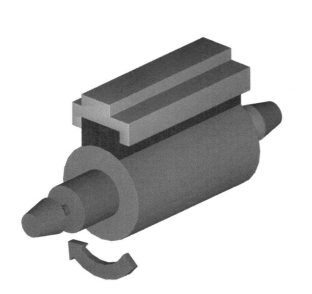

Figure 7–13   *Illustration of the superfinishing process.*

Figure 7–14   *Illustration of a honing tool.*

Shot Blasting

In shot blasting or sand blasting, a high velocity air jet propels abrasive particles on to the workpiece giving it a mat finish (Figures 7–16 a and b, and 7–17).

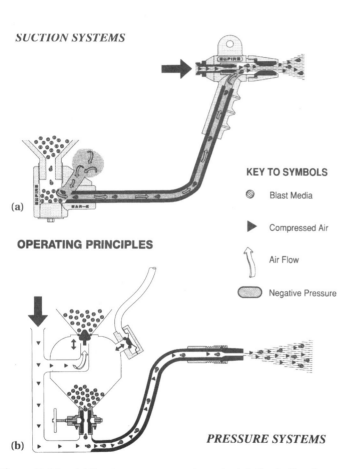

SUCTION SYSTEMS

(a)

OPERATING PRINCIPLES

KEY TO SYMBOLS

◉ Blast Media

▶ Compressed Air

⇧ Air Flow

⬭ Negative Pressure

(b)

PRESSURE SYSTEMS

Figure 7–16 *(a) Suction system operating principle for the Empire ProFinish sand blast finishing system (b) Pressure system operating principle for the Empire ProFinish sand blast finishing system. (Courtesy of Empire Abrasive Co.).*

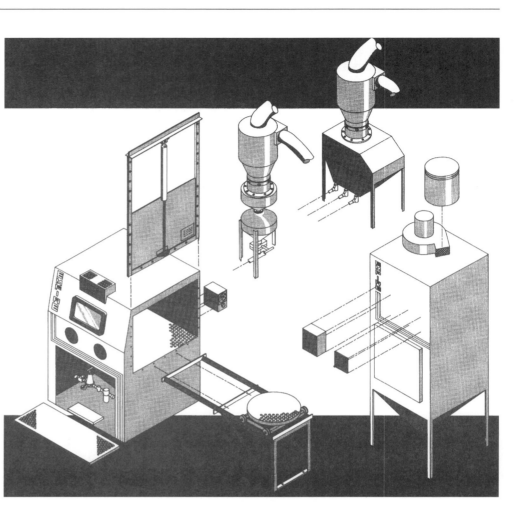

Figure 7–17 *Modular equipment for the ProFinish sand blast-finishing system (Courtesy of Empire Abrasive Co.).*

Various Finishing Processes

Deburring

Burrs are razor-like thin triangular ridges created when a sheet is sheared, or a casting or forged part is cleaned by a trimming shear. Machining produces a burr along the tool path. Burrs may interfere with assembly, can cause jamming and misalignment during assembly, or can strip wires, causing short circuits in electrical components. Burrs on sheets or parts can cause severe cuts during handling. Burrs are removed by files and by special deburring tools. Designing chamfers on part edges will eliminate the need for expensive deburring.

Vibratory and barrel finishing is a batch-type operation used to improve the surface finish and remove burrs from large numbers of small parts. Specially shaped abrasive pellets are tumbled with the parts to be deburred (Figure 7–18).

Grinding fluids reduce wear and lower power consumption. They also prevent temperature elevation in the workpiece and improve the finish and dimensional accuracy of the part.

Polishing

Polishing and *buffing*—using a fine abrasive and a soft, smearing material—produce a lustrous finish. Polishing disks or belts are made of fabric, leather, or felt embedded with an abrasive. Fine powders of aluminum oxide or diamond are used for metals. Buffing is a similar process except that a stick abrasive compound is used to provide the cutting medium.

Electropolishing, the reverse of electroplating, can produce mirror-like surfaces because there is no mechanical contact with the workpiece. In this process, an electrolyte attacks projections and peaks on the surface, resulting in a smooth surface. Electropolishing is suitable for irregular shapes (Figure 7–19).

Figure 7–18 *Ceramic pellets used in barrel and vibratory finishing.*

Figure 7–19   *Polished and plated metals (Courtesy American Nickeloid Company).*

7.3   COATINGS

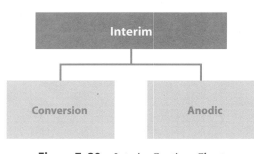

Figure 7–20   *Interim Coatings Chart*

Interim Coatings

In *conversion coating* or *chemical reaction painting,* phosphates or chromates create corrosion protection and a decorative finish. It is also a good primer for paints. Phosphates are used for coating steel, whereas chromates are used for coating aluminum, copper, zinc, and magnesium. Coatings can be applied by electrodipping, spraying, or brushing.

Anodic coating, or *anodizing,* is an oxidation process that converts the surface of aluminum and magnesium to an oxide layer, providing a decorative finish and corrosion protection. The workpiece is immersed in an acid bath, resulting in chemical adsorption of oxygen and black, red, bronze, gold, or blue organic dyes produce decorative surface films.

Anodizing is used to color and protect architectural products, automotive trim, cookware, furniture, and sporting equipment (Figure 7–20).

7.3.1   Paint/Coatings

Coatings

Powder organic coatings are applied by fluidized bed coating or electrostatic spraying.

In *fluidized bed coating*, a heated part is submerged in a bed of dry plastic powder made fluid by air pressure.

In *electrostatic spraying*, dry paint particles pick up a static positive charge and are sprayed over a grounded negative workpiece

Liquid Organic Paints are Applied by

- Dipping
- Brushing
- Rolling
- Flow coating
- Tumbling
- Centrifuging
- Spraying
- Electrostatic atomization (Figures 7–22 and 7–23)

that attracts the positively charged particles. Only surfaces with an opposite charge will be coated, resulting in a 10 percent loss of paint compared to as much as a 70 percent loss of paint in conventional spraying (Figure 7–24).

Inorganic coatings are powders made of alumina-borosilicate glass, coloring oxides, and other metal oxides that are highly wear-resistant porcelain enamels when fused by heat to metallic surfaces. Typical porcelain-enameled products are cookware, chemical processing equipment, and signs.

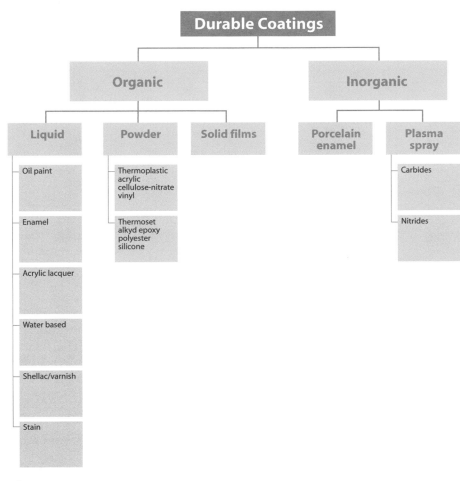

Figure 7–21   *Durable Coating Chart.*

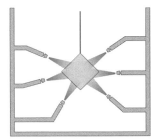

Figure 7–22   *Flow coating.*

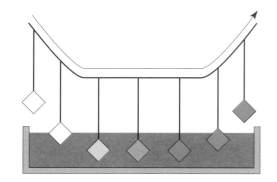

Figure 7–23 *Dip coating.*

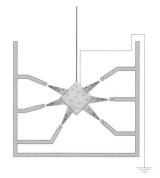

Figure 7–24 *Electrostatic spraying.*

Permanent Finishing

In hot dipping, iron or steel is dipped into a bath of molten zinc, tin, or aluminum, providing long-term corrosion resistance for steel products such as plumbing pipes and accessories and highway structures. The process is also used as a protective base coat for automotive chassis and subassemblies (Figure 7–26).

(a)

(b)

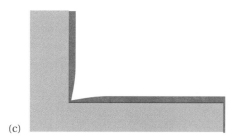

(c)

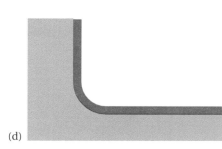

(d)

Figure 7–25 *(a) Nonuniform coatings in electroplated parts. Avoid sharp outside corners. (b) Uniform coating. (c) Nonuniform coatings in electroplated parts. Avoid sharp inside corners. (d) Uniform coating.*

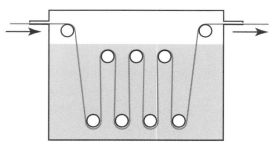

Figure 7–26 *Continuous hot dipping of galvanized sheet.*

In *mechanical plating,* fine metal particles are compacted onto a base metal surface by impacting them with glass, ceramic, or porcelain beads.

In *electroplating,* a workpiece is plated with chromium, nickel, cadmium, copper, zinc, or tin while suspended in an electrolyte solution. Silver, platinum, or gold is used to plate jewelry and defense and space electronics. ABS, polypropylene, polysulfone, polycarbonate, polyester, and nylon can be plated if an electroless nickel base plate is used. Most metals can be plated. Size is not a limitation, but complex shapes may have varying plating thicknesses. Chrome plating requires a base plate of copper, then nickel, and finally a layer of chromium.

In *electroless plating,* a chemical reaction of nickel chloride and sodium hypophosphite provides excellent wear and corrosion resistance.

In *vacuum metalizing* (vacuum plating), plating metal is evaporated at high temperatures in a vacuum and deposited on the

(a)

(b)

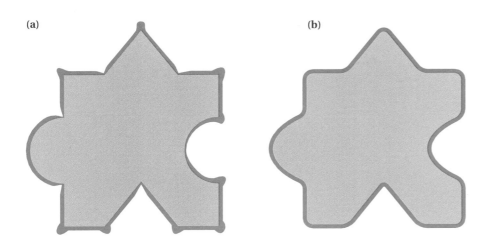

Figure 7–27 *(a) and (b) Avoid sharp inside and outside corners.*

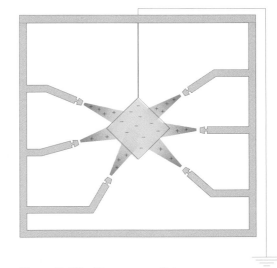

Figure 7–28 *Vacuum metalizing.*

part. This process can provide a uniform coating on complex parts. Typical uses are in electronics, optics, and in decorative applications such as jewelry (Figure 7–28).

In *sputtering*, inert gas is ionized by an electric field. The coating material is bombarded by positive ions, causing its atoms to sputter and then condense on the workpiece.

Flame spraying (thermal spraying/metallizing) is a process that developed out of powdered metal technology. A metal rod, wire, or powder is melted in a stream of oxyacetylene flame, electric arc, or plasma arc, and sprayed onto a preheated surface. This process is in essence a casting process because the metal is melted to a liquid state for spraying. Applications include steel structures, storage tanks, and tank cars coated with zinc or aluminum for corrosion resis-

tance. Other metalizing applications include the rebuilding of worn bearing surfaces. Ceramic coatings are used for high-temperature and electrical-resistance applications (Figure 7–29).

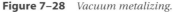
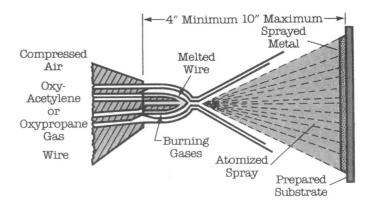

Figure 7–29 *Thermal spraying (Courtesy GE Plastics).*

PLASTICS

The term *plastic* is widely accepted in describing resins or polymers that are built from hydrogen, carbon, nitrogen, oxygen, fluorine, silicon, sulfur, and chlorine atoms, derived mostly from oil. It has become a cliché to refer to the film "The Graduate," wherein the term *plastic* became part of everyday language in the scene where Mr. Robinson whispers the word to the Graduate. It may be a bit more subtle, but for some the defining moment of the film was when Mrs. Robinson showed her stockings, creating an intense interest that may have resulted in field research and the discovery that stockings were made of nylon—the first engineering thermoplastic!

As discussed in 3.1 properties, plastic is used to describe how a material acts. Plastic means that a permanent change in shape takes place when a material is subjected to a load. "Plastic materials" were so named because their shape is easily changed with very little heat (unlike metals, which require much higher heat). Although plastic is used to describe these materials, the general term *plastic* is not used to discuss a specific material. The chemical name or trade name must be used in order to request information on specific materials, which are more specifically referred to as resins or polymers. Some of the chemical names are difficult to remember. Most designers and engineers refer to these materials by their trade names. In designing a part or product, specific performance demands are placed on the resin used, requiring certain mechanical and physical properties in order to meet the expected demands. Just as metal alloys have been tailored to meet specific demands, resins are often blended to provide required enhanced design performance.

It is not easy to organize resins, because they occur in families. Within each family, specific resins or blends are often combinations that may span two or more families. One of the most popular materials is Acrylonitrile Butadiene Styrene (ABS), which belongs in the styrene family but is a "terpolymer" that includes butadiene and acrylonitrile. To make matters more complex, ABS is often alloyed with other resins such as PVC or polycarbonate. And if that is not complex enough, many commercial forms are most often reinforced, primarily with glass fiber, to achieve even greater performance, or they are specially formulated for a specific manufacturing process.

Resins are usually organized alphabetically. This may be convenient but does little to help in gaining a comprehensive understanding of resins.

Section 9.0 organizes resins first into the major subdivision of thermosets and thermoplastics, and then into their family groups, arranged generally by increasing cost.* The trade name and supplier are also given, along with features, properties, and typical uses.

The information and drawings in Sections 8.0 and 8.1 are based on information from *Engineering Polymers Material Selection, A Design Guide,* by Bayer Corporation, and are reprinted with their kind permission.

---

*The cost fluctuates according to volume and other market forces. Most materials have reinforcements and other additives that increase costs.

Plastics: Origins and Definitions

To understand plastic materials or resins, it is necessary to understand polymers, the building blocks of plastics. Derived from the Greek term for many parts, *polymers* is used to describe materials that are large molecules composed of many repeating units that have been chemically bonded into long chains. Silk, cotton, and wool are examples of natural polymers. In the last 40 years, the chemical industry has developed a plethora of synthetic polymers to satisfy the material needs for a diversity of products: paints, coatings, fibers, films, elastomers, and structural plastics are examples. Literally thousands of materials can be grouped as plas-

tics, although the term today is typically reserved for polymeric materials, excluding fibers, that can be molded or formed into solid or semi-solid objects. Polymerization is the process of chemically bonding monomer building blocks to form large molecules. Commercial polymer molecules are usually thousands of repeating units long.

Thermoplastics and Thermosets

How a polymer network responds to heat determines whether a plastic falls into one of two broad categories: thermoplastics or thermosets. Thermoplastics soften and melt when heated and harden when cooled. Because of this behavior, these resins can be injection molded, extruded, or formed via other molding techniques. This behavior also allows production scrap to be reground and reused.

Unlike thermoplastics, thermosets form cross links—interconnections between neighboring polymer molecules that limit chain movement. This network of polymer chains tends to degrade, rather than soften, when exposed to excessive heat. Recent advances in recycling have provided new methods for reusing some thermoset materials.

Because they do not melt, thermosets are processed differently from thermoplastics. Heat will further polymerize some thermosets, such as phenolic resin, which cures when injected into a hot mold. Other thermosets—RIM polyurethanes, for example—rely on a controlled chemical reaction between components after they pass through a mixing head into the mold. A third type of thermoset—silicon is an example—cures as volatiles in the resin evaporate.

Although thermosets generally require longer cycle times and more secondary operations than thermoplastics—such as deflashing and trimming—they usually have less mold shrinkage and exhibit superior chemical and heat resistance.

Crystalline and Amorphous Polymers

Thermoplastics are further classified by their crystallinity—the degree of order within the polymer's overall structure. As a crystalline resin cools from the melt, polymer chains fold or align into highly ordered crystalline structures (*see* Figure 8–1). In general, polymer chains with bulky side groups cannot form crystalline configurations.

The degree of crystallinity depends on both the polymer and the processing technique. Because of their molecular structure, some polymers such as polyethylene crystallize quickly and reach high levels of crystallinity. Others, such as PET polyester, re-

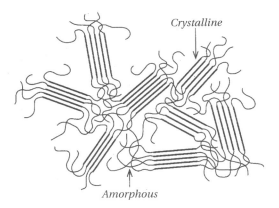

Figure 8–1   *Amorphous and Crystalline Structure (Drawing Courtesy of Bayer Corporation).*

quire longer times in a hot mold to crystallize. If cooled quickly, PET polyester remains amorphous in the final product, as in beverage bottles. Crystalline thermoplastics must be heated above the resin's crystalline-melt temperature for extrusion and injection molding.

Amorphous polymers—ones with little or no crystallinity—have random chain entanglements and lack a discrete melting point. As they are exposed to heat these polymers soften and become more fluidlike, allowing the polymer chains to slide past one another. As the polymer cools, chain movement diminishes and the polymer's viscosity increases. Generally, the higher a polymer's glass transition temperature, the better it will perform at elevated temperatures. As a rule, transparent plastics are amorphous rather than crystalline. The most common transparent thermoplastics include acrylic, polycarbonate, and polystyrene.

Crystalline and amorphous plastics have differences in several characteristics. The force required to generate flow in amorphous materials diminishes slowly as the temperature rises above the glass transition temperature. Conversely, in crystalline resins the force requirements diminish quickly as the material is heated above its crystalline-melt temperature. Because of these easier flow characteristics, crystalline resins have an advantage in filling thin-walled sections. Additionally, these resins generally have superior chemical resistance, greater stability at elevated temperatures, and better creep resistance. Amorphous plastics typically exhibit greater impact strength, less mold shrinkage, and less final-part warping than their crystalline counterparts. End-use re-

quirements usually dictate whether an amorphous or crystalline resin is preferred.

Blends

Blending two or more polymers offers yet another method of tailoring resins for specific applications. Because blends are only physical mixtures, the resulting polymer usually has physical and mechanical properties that lie somewhere between the values of its constituent materials. For instance, an automotive bumper made from a blend of polycarbonate resin and a thermoplastic polyurethane elastomer gains rigidity from the polycarbonate resin and retains most of the flexibility and paintability of the polyurethane elastomer. For business machine housings, a blend of polycarbonate and ABS resins offers the enhanced performance of polycarbonate flame retardance and UV stability at a lower cost.

Occasionally, blended polymers have properties that exceed those of their constituents. For instance, blends of polycarbonate resin and PET polyester, originally created to augment the chemical resistance of polycarbonate, actually have fatigue resistance and low-temperature impact resistance superior to those of either of the individual polymers.

Copolymers and Terpolymers

Unlike blends, or physical mixtures of different polymers, copolymers such as acetyl resin, styrene acrylonitrile (SAN), and styrene butadiene contain repeating units from two polymers within their molecular chain structure. In terpolymers—polymers with three different repeating units—individual components can also be tailored to offer a wide range of properties. An example is

ABS, a terpolymer containing repeating units of acrylonitrile, butadiene, and styrene.

Molecular Weight

A polymer's molecular weight—the sum of the weights of individual atoms that make up a molecule—indicates the average length of the bulk polymer chains. Low-molecular-weight polyethylene chains have backbones as small as 1000 carbon atoms long. Ultra-high-molecular-weight polyethylene chains, on the other hand, can have a half-million carbon atoms along their length. Many plastics such as polycarbonate, for instance, are available in a variety of chain lengths, or different molecular-weight grades. These resins can also be classified by an indirect viscosity value, rather than molecular weight. Within a resin family, higher-molecular-weight grades have higher viscosities.

Selecting the correct molecular weight for injection-molding applications generally involves a balance between filling ease and material performance. If an application has thin-walled sections, a lower-molecular-weight/lower-viscosity grade offers better flow. For normal wall thicknesses, these resins also offer faster mold-cycle times and fewer molded-in stresses. The stiffer-flowing, high-molecular-weight resins offer the ultimate material performance, because they are tougher and more resistant to chemical and environmental attack.

Fillers and Reinforcements

Often, fibrous materials, such as glass or carbon fibers, are added to resins to create reinforced grades with enhanced properties. For example, adding 30 percent short glass fibers by weight to nylon 6 improves creep resistance and increases stiffness by 300 percent. These glass-reinforced plastics usually suffer some loss of impact strength and ultimate elongation, and are more prone to warping because of the relatively large difference in mold shrinkage between the flow and cross-flow directions.

Plastics with nonfibrous fillers such as spheres or powders generally exhibit higher stiffness characteristics than unfilled resins, but not as high as those in glass-reinforced grades. Resins with particulate fillers are less likely to warp and show a decrease in mold shrinkage. Particulate fillers typically reduce shrinkage by a percentage roughly equal to the volume percentage of filler in the polymer—an advantage in tight-tolerance molding. When considering plastics with different amounts of filler or reinforcement, you should compare the cost per volume rather than the cost per pound. Most fillers increase the material density; therefore, increasing filler content usually reduces the number of parts that can be molded per pound.

Shrinkage

As a molded part cools and solidifies it usually becomes smaller than its mold cavity. Shrinkage characteristics affect molding costs and determine a part's dimensional tolerance limit. Materials with low levels of isotropic shrinkage typically provide greater dimensional control—an important consideration in tight-tolerance parts. The exact amount of this mold shrinkage depends primarily on the particular resin or system used. For instance, semi-crystalline thermoplastics generally show higher levels of shrinkage than amorphous thermoplastics because of the volume reduction during crystallization.

Other factors—including part geometry, wall thickness, processing, use and type of fillers, and gate location—also affect shrinkage. For instance:

- Holes, ribs, and similar part features restrain shrinking while the part is in the mold and tend to lower overall shrinkage.
- Shrinkage generally increases with wall thickness and decreases with higher filling and packing pressures.
- Areas near the filling gate tend to shrink less than areas farther away.
- Particulate fillers, such as minerals and glass spheres, tend to reduce shrinkage uniformly in all directions.
- Fibrous fillers, such as glass or carbon fibers, decrease shrinkage primarily in the direction of flow.
- Fiber-filled parts often shrink two to three times more in the cross-flow versus the flow direction.

Post-mold shrinkage—additional shrinking that may appear long after molding—often occurs in parts that were processed to reduce initial shrinkage and later are exposed to elevated temperatures. Over time, molded-in stresses will relax, resulting in a size reduction. Elevated temperatures can also lead to solid-state crystallization and additional shrinkage in some semi-crystalline materials.

Additives

Additives encompass a wide range of substances that aid processing or add value to the final product, including antioxidants, viscosity modifiers, processing aids, flame retardants, dyes and pigments, and UV stabilizers. Found in virtually all plastics, most additives are incorporated into a resin family by the supplier as part of a proprietary package. Additives are specified to maximize performance. For example, standard polycarbonate resin grades containing additives improve internal mold release, UV stabilization, and flame retardance; and nylon grades containing additives improve impact performance. Additives often determine the success or failure of a resin or system in a particular application.

Combustion Modifiers

Combustion modifiers are added to polymers to help retard burning in molded parts. Generally required for electrical and medical-housing applications, combustion modifiers and amounts vary with the inherent flammability of the base polymer. Flammability results are based on small-scale laboratory tests. The printed ratings are for comparison purposes only; they may not accurately represent the hazard present under actual fire conditions.

Release Agents

External release agents are lubricants, liquids or powders, that coat a mold cavity to facilitate part removal.

Blowing Agents

Used in foamed thermoplastic and polyurethane materials, blowing agents produce gas by chemical or thermal action, or both. When heated to a specific temperature, these ingredients volatilize to yield a large volume of gas that creates cells in foamed plastics.

Catalysts

Catalysts are substances that initiate or change the rate of a chemical reaction, do not undergo a permanent change in composition, or become part of the molecular structure of the final product.

Before listing the plastics, it may be useful to review some of the properties and behavior characteristics that are important considerations in selecting specific polymers.

8.1 PROPERTIES OF MOLDED POLYMERS

Introduction

Molded resins offer a wide range of physical and mechanical properties, as well as some unusual mechanical behaviors. Changes in the polymer repeat units, chain length, crystallinity, or level of cross-linking can yield materials with properties ranging from strong to weak, brittle to tough, or stiff to elastic. Under certain conditions, such as elevated temperatures and/or long-term loading, resins behave quite differently from other engineering materials. The following is a brief summary of selected properties and behaviors.

Viscoelastic Behaviors

Viscoelasticity

Plastics have a dual nature, displaying characteristics of both a viscous liquid and a springlike elastomer. These traits are known as *viscoelasticity*. This duality accounts for many of the peculiar mechanical properties found in plastics. Under mild loading conditions—such as short-term loading with low

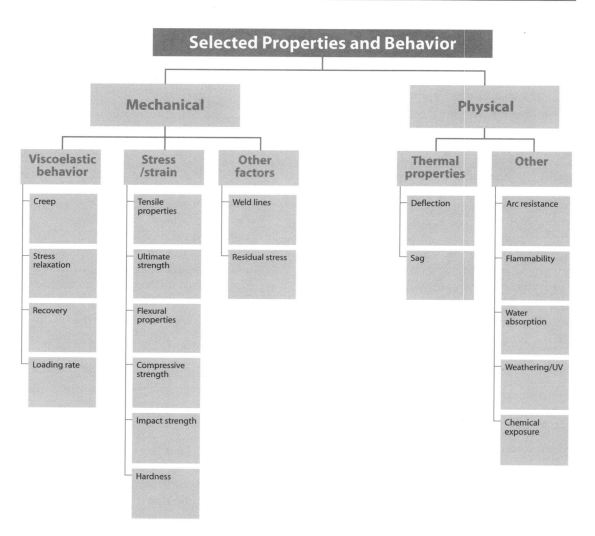

Figure 8–2 *Selected properties and behavior.*

deflections and small loads at room temperatures—plastics usually respond like a spring, returning to their original shape after the load is removed. No energy is lost or dissipated during this purely elastic behavior: Stress versus strain remains a linear function. Increasing the applied load adds a proportional increase to the part's deflection.

Many resins exhibit a viscous behavior under long-term heavy loads or elevated temperatures. While still solid, resins will deform and flow much the same as very high-viscosity liquids. To understand this viscous behavior, it is important to understand strain and stress. Strain is measured in percent elongation; stress is measured in load per area. Typical viscous behavior for tensile loading shows that strain resulting from a constant applied stress increases with time. This time-and-temperature-dependent behavior occurs because the polymer chains in the part slip and do not return to their original position when the load is removed.

The Voigt-Maxwell model of springs and dashpots illustrates these viscoelastic characteristics (*see* Figure 8–3). The spring in the Maxwell model represents the instantaneous response to loading and linear recovery when the load is removed. The dashpot connected to the spring simulates the permanent deformation that occurs over time. The Voigt model shows the slow deformation recovery after the load is removed. Although not a practical model for structural design use, the Voigt-Maxwell model offers a unique way to visualize viscoelastic characteristics.

Creep

One of the most important consequences of plastics' viscoelastic behavior—creep—is the

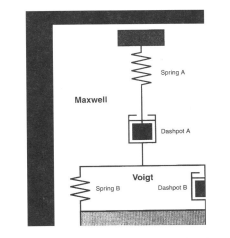

Figure 8–3 *Voight-Maxwell Test (Drawing Courtesy of Bayer Corporation).*

deformation that occurs over time when a material is subjected to constant stress at a constant temperature. Under these conditions, the polymer chains slowly slip past one another. Because some of this slippage is permanent, only a portion of the creep deformation can be recovered when the load is removed. The tensile test in Figure 8–4 clearly demonstrates creep. A weight hung from a plastic tensile bar will cause initial deformation d, increasing the bar's length. Over an extended period of time, the weight causes more elongation, or creep, c.

Stress Relaxation

Another viscoelastic phenomenon, stress relaxation, is defined as the gradual decrease in stress at constant strain and temperature. Because of the same polymer-chain slippage found in creep, stress relaxation occurs in simple tension, as well as in parts subjected

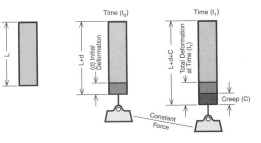

Figure 8–4 *Creep drawing (Courtesy Bayer Corporation).*

to multiaxial tension, bending, shear, and compression. The degree of stress relaxation depends on a variety of factors, including load duration, temperature, and types of stress and strain.

Figure 8–5 shows that a large weight initially produces elongation ~d and a strain, d/L (L = original length). To maintain the same elongation and strain in the test bar over time, less weight is needed because of stress relaxation.

In the creep example (Figure 8–4), elongation continues as the weight remains constant. In the stress-relaxation example (Fig-

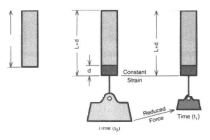

Figure 8–5 *Stress relaxation (Drawing Courtesy Bayer Corporation).*

ure 8–5), the weight is reduced to maintain the elongation.

In parts that will be subjected to a constant strain, stress relaxation should be accounted for. A typical press fit, such as a metal insert in a plastic boss, relies on stresses from the imposed strain of an interference fit to hold the insert in place. However, polymer-chain slippage can relax these stresses and reduce the insert-retention strength over time.

Stress/Strain

Tensile Properties

Tensile properties, important in structural design, are used to compare the relative strength and stiffness of plastics. The standard tensile tests for rigid thermoplastics (ASTM D 638 and ISO 527) or soft plastics and elastomeric materials (ASTM D 412) involve clamping a standard molded tensile bar into the test device (*see* Figure 8–6 and 8–7).

Tensile stress-strain curves graphically illustrate transitional points in a resin 5 stress-strain behavior (*see* Figure 8–8). Point A, the proportional limit for the material, shows the end of the region in which the resin exhibits linear stress-strain behavior. Point B is the material's elastic limit, or the point after which the part will be permanently deformed even after the load is removed. Applications that cannot tolerate any permanent deformation must stay below the elastic limit. Point C, the yield point, marks the beginning of the region in which ductile plastics continue to deform without a corresponding increase in stress. Elongation at yield gives the upper limit for applications that can tolerate the

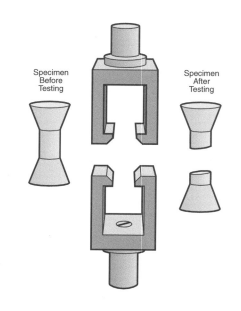

Figure 8–4 *Tensile strength for structural foam materials (Drawing Courtesy Bayer Corporation).*

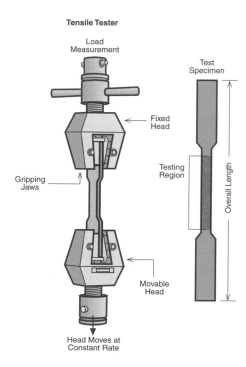

Figure 8–3 *Tensile strength (Drawing Courtesy Bayer Corporation).*

small permanent deformations that occur between the elastic limit and yield point, but not the larger deformations occurring during yield. Point D, the break point, shows the strain value at which the test bar breaks. These five transitional points, important in plastics part design, are the basis for several common tensile properties.

Ultimate Strength

Ultimate strength measures the highest stress value during the tensile test. This value should be used in general strength comparisons, rather than in actual calculations. Ulti-

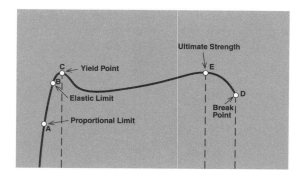

Figure 8–5 *Stress strain curve (Courtesy Bayer Corporation).*

mate strength is usually the stress level at the breaking point in brittle materials. For ductile materials it is often the value at yield or a value slightly before the breaking point (Figure 8–8).

Flexural Properties

Flexural properties relate to a plastic's ability to bend or resist bending under load. In the tests for most flexural properties (ASTM D 790 and ISO 178), a test bar placed across two supports is deflected in the middle at a constant rate, usually 2 mm/mm for glass-reinforced materials and 20 mm/mm for unfilled plastics (see Figure 8–9). Standard beam equations can be used to convert the force-versus-deflection data into an outer-fiber, stress-versus-strain curve.

Compressive Strength

Compressive strength, the opposite of tensile strength, is measured on a test specimen that is compressed (Figure 8–12).

Impact Tests

Impact Tests

Impact strength, a part's ability to absorb and dissipate energy, varies with the part's shape, thickness, and temperature. Variables such as part geometry, stress concentration points, molding stresses, and impact speed

reduce the accuracy of general test data for quantitative calculations. The most common tests are the ASTM D 1822 or ISO 8256; (Figure 8–11); and the Izod impact test (ASTM D 256, D 4812, or ISO 180), and the Charpy impact test (ISO 179) (Figure 8–10). These tests use notched samples to test the impact strength of materials.

Hardness Test

The hardness test is used to determine and compare the indention resistance of materials. The most common tests are the Rockwell

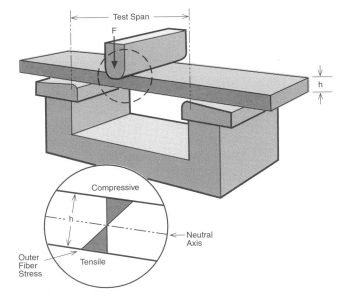

Figure 8–9 *Flexural properties test (Courtesy Bayer Corporation).*

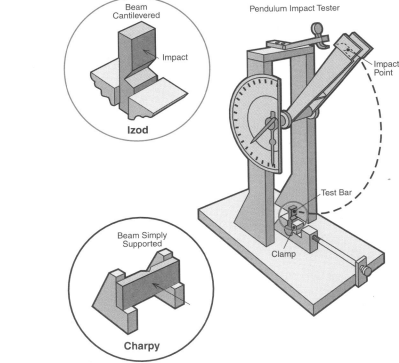

Figure 8–10 *Izod and Charpy Tests (Drawing Courtesy Bayer Corporation).*

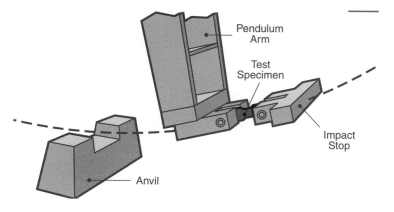

Figure 8–11 *ASTM D 1822 or ISO 8256 impact strength test (Drawing Courtesy Bayer Corporation).*

Hardness test (ASTM D 785 or ISO 2039-2) and the Durometer test (ASTM 2240 or ISO868—Shore A for soft materials and Shore D for hard materials). In these tests an indentor is forced against the surface of a material, and the amount of surface penetration is measured and can be used for comparison purposes (Figure 8–13).

Other Factors

Factors Affecting Mechanical Properties

Weld Lines

The hairline grooves on the surface of a molded part where flow fronts join during filling—called weld lines or knit lines—cause potential cosmetic flaws and reduced mechanical performance (*see* Figure 8–14). Because few polymer chains cross the boundary when the flow fronts butt, the tensile and impact strength in the weld-line area is reduced. The resulting notches on the weld line also act as stress concentrators, further

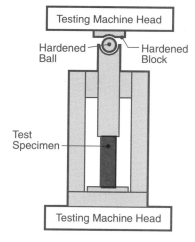

Figure 8–12 *Compression test (Drawing Courtesy Bayer Corporation).*

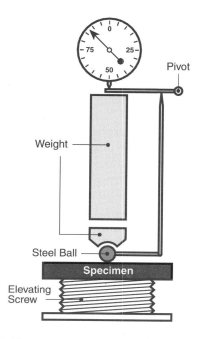

Figure 8–13 *Hardness test (Drawing Courtesy Bayer Corporation).*

reducing impact strength. If the flow fronts are covered with a film from additives or a layer of impurities, they may not bind properly, which again can reduce impact and tensile strength. Weld-line strength in thermoplastics varies with specific resin and processing parameters, such as flow-front temperature, distance from the gate, filling pressure, and level of packing. Resins can suffer more than a 50 percent loss of tensile strength at the weld line.

Residual Stress

Molding factors—such as uneven part cooling, differential material shrinkage, or frozen-in flow stresses—cause undesirable

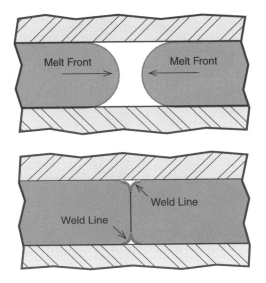

Figure 8–14   *Weld line (Drawing Courtesy Bayer Corporation).*

Ultimate Strength

As a molten thermoplastic fills a mold, its polymer chains tend to align with the direction of the flow (*see* Figure 8–16). Part thickness and a variety of processing variables—injection speed, mold temperature, melt temperature, and hold pressure—determine how much of this flow orientation remains in the solidified part. Most molded parts retain enough orientation to show small but noticeable differences in material properties between the flow and cross-flow directions at any location. Generally, mechanical properties in the cross-flow direction are lower than those in the flow direction. Directional differences can affect mechanical performance in parts whose polymer chains align uniformly along or across structural features. The glass fibers in outer layers of glass-reinforced plastics tend to align in the direction of flow, resulting in higher tensile strength

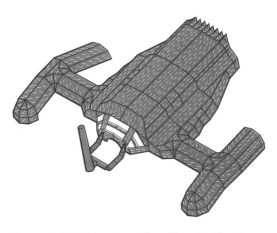

Figure 8–16   *Direction of flow (Drawing Courtesy Bayer Corporation).*

and stiffness in this direction. They also exhibit greater resistance to shear forces acting across the fibers. Generally, fiber-filled materials have much higher shrinkage in the cross-flow than in the flow direction. Cross-flow shrinkage can be as much as two to three times greater.

Physical Properties

Thermal Behavior

Deflection Temperature Under Load (DTUL)

DTUL values are used to compare the elevated temperature performance of materials under load at stated test conditions. In the ASTM D648 test for DTUL, the center of a test bar resting on supports is loaded to a specified stress. The temperature of the test chamber rises at 2°C per minute until the applied load causes the bar to deflect an additional 0.010 inch (Figure 8–17).

residual stresses in molded thermoplastics (*see* Figure 8–15). High levels of residual stress can adversely affect certain mechanical properties, as well as chemical resistance and dimensional stability. When molded-in tensile stresses on a part's surface are exceptionally high, as in parts where the geometry has extremely thin walls or dramatic thickness variations, impact and tensile strength can be reduced. Avoid high-stress features, because the molded-in stresses and their ultimate effect on mechanical performance can be difficult to predict. Certain stress-analysis techniques, such as solvent-stress testing, locate areas of high residual stress, but only after the mold has been built and mechanical problems may have developed.

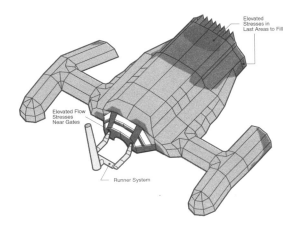

Figure 8–15   *Mold fill (Drawing Courtesy Bayer Corporation).*

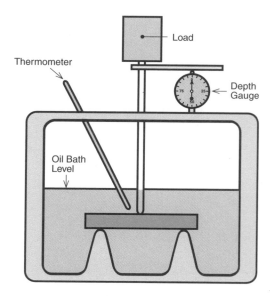

Figure 8–17 *Deflection test (Drawing Courtesy Bayer Corporation).*

Heat (High-Temperature) Sag

Heat sag is an important factor for parts that will be painted and baked or exposed to elevated temperatures. The ASTM D 3769 tests heat sag in solid and foamed polyurethane materials (Figure 8–18). One end of a painted sample is clamped into a fixture. After 5 minutes, measurements are compared with those after a 1-hour exposure at a given temperature. Test results are for comparison purposes only, and may not match actual conditions.

Other

Arc Resistance

Arc resistance measures the number of seconds a plastic specimen's surface will resist

forming a continuous conductive path while being exposed to a high-voltage electric arc. Burning, carbonization, heating to incandescence, or a breakdown in the material's surface usually determine the failure point. In the standard tests (UL 746 A and ASTM D 495), electrodes intermittently emit an arc on the specimen surface with increasing severity until the specimen fails (see Figure 8–19).

Flammability

Except for a few resins that are inherently flame retardant, most require an additive to meet higher flame-resistance ratings. Because these additives can add to the material cost, cause a variety of molding problems, and result in lower mechanical properties, it is wise to avoid overspecifying the degree of flame resistance required.

The vertical-flame test subjects the lower end of a sample to two applications of a 19-mm-high blue flame from a Bunsen burner for a duration of 10 seconds each (see Figure 8–20). The horizontal test applies a 25-mm flame from a Bunsen burner to the free end of a test specimen for 30 seconds (see Figure 8–21). The flame-class criteria for

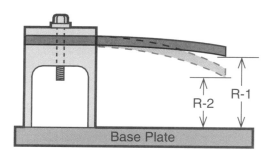

Figure 8–18 *Sag test (Drawing Courtesy Bayer Corporation).*

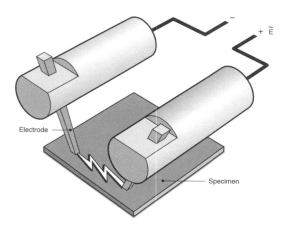

Figure 8–19 *Arc resistance (Drawing Courtesy Bayer Corporation).*

the test results are listed in Tables in Figures 8–22 and 8–23). Rigid foam polyurethane systems for building materials should be tested to ASTM F 84. Other end-use tests for doors, windows, and walls are performed to specific industry standards. Flammability standards for a variety of electrical products are listed in UL 746 C. To avoid costly tests to prove conformance to this standard, consider resins that have been pretested and meet the indicated requirements.

Water Absorption

Many resins are hygroscopic: Over time they absorb water. Too much moisture in a thermoplastic resin during molding can degrade the plastic and diminish mechanical performance. Water absorbed after molding can harm mechanical properties in certain resins under specific conditions. Through a process called hydrolysis, water in the resin severs the polymer chains, reduces molecular weight, and decreases mechanical proper-

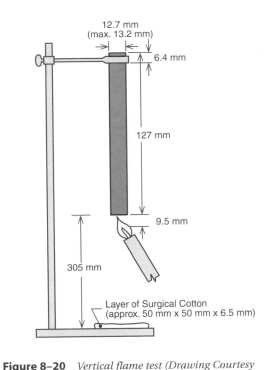

Figure 8–20 *Vertical flame test (Drawing Courtesy Bayer Corporation).*

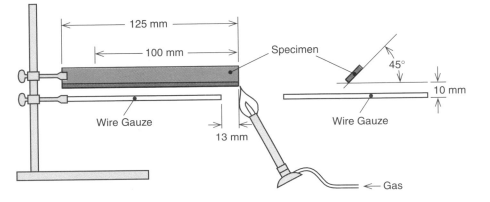

Figure 8–21 *Horizontal test (Drawing Courtesy Bayer Corporation).*

Table 7-2	Vertical Burning Test for UL Flammability Classifications 94V-0, 94V-1, 94V-2		
		Flammability Classification	
Test Criteria	94V-0	94V-1	94V-2
Flaming combustion time after each application of flame	≤ 10 s	≤ 30 s	≤ 30 s
Total flaming combustion time for each set of 5 specimens (10 flame applications)	≤ 50 s	≤ 250 s	≤ 250 s
Flaming or glowing combustion up to the holding clamp	no	no	no
Duration of glowing combustion after second removal of test flame	≤ 30 s	≤ 60 s	≤ 60 s
Ignition of surgical cotton by dripping flaming particles	no	no	yes

Figure 8–22 *Vertical flame table (Courtesy Bayer Corporation).*

Table 7-3	Horizontal Burning Test for Flammability Classification 94HB	
Specimen Thickness	Burning Rate	
≥ 1/8 in	≤ 1–1-1/2 in/min	
≥ 1/8 in	≤ 3 in/min	

or material ceases to burn before flame reaches the second reference mark

ties. Longer exposure times at elevated temperatures and/or loads worsen hydrolytic attack. When designing parts for prolonged exposure to water or high humidity, check available data on hydrolytic degradation.

Weathering and UV Radiation

The effects of outdoor weather—particularly ultraviolet (UV) radiation—on appearance and properties can range from a simple color shift to severe material embrittlement. After several years in direct sun, most resins show reduced impact resistance, lower overall mechanical performance, and a change in appearance.

Weatherability varies with polymer type. Many resin grades are available with UV-absorbing additives to boost weatherability. Generally the higher-molecular-weight grades of a resin fare better than lower-molecular-weight grades with comparable additives. Also, some colors tend to weather better than others.

Chemical Exposure

The effects of chemical exposure on a specific resin can range from minor mechanical-property changes to immediate catastrophic failure. The degree of chemical attack depends on a number of factors: The type of resin, the chemical in contact, chemical concentration, temperature, exposure time, and stress level in the molded part are a few of the more common ones. Some plastics can be vulnerable to attack from families of chemicals, such as strong acids or organic solvents. In other instances, a resin may be vulnerable to a specific or seemingly harmless chemical. Verify a material's resistance to all the chemicals to which it will be exposed during processing, assembling, and final use.

Simple changes is the stress level, such as a decrease in the bend radius, can cause part failure when exposed to chemicals (Figure 8–24).

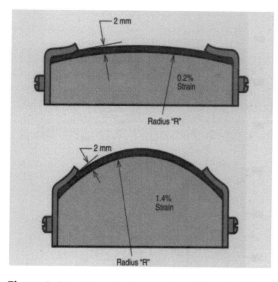

Figure 8–24 *Stress level comparison (Drawing Courtesy Bayer Corporation).*

8.2 THERMOSETS

Introduction

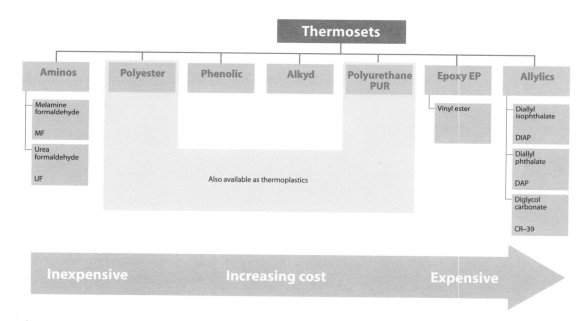

Figure 8–25 *Thermosets.*

Aminos and Polyesters

Melamine (Amino)

Fiberite: ICI Fiberite

Properties:

- Water-white, transparent, or opaque colors
- Will not impart taste or odor to foods
- Excellent electrical insulation characteristics
- Flammability ratings of 94V-0
- Extended exposure above 170°F will affect color
- Exposure at 300°F may cause a color change or blistering in less than 1 hour
- Hard, rigid, abrasion resistant
- High resistance to deformation under load

Urea (Amino)

Properties:

- Below –70°F becomes brittle, electrical properties are not affected
- Supplied as liquid or dry resins

Uses:

- Molding compounds, laminating resins, wood adhesives, coatings
- Wet-strength paper resins, textile-treating resins

Polyester*

Premi-Glas: Premix	Durez: Occidental
Cyglas: CYTEC	MR resins: Aristech
Arpol/Hetron: Ashland	Glastic: Glastic
QC resins: Quantum	Haysite: Haysite

Characteristics:

- Polyester and alkyd molding compounds are based on unsaturated polyester resin systems
- Polyesters have a high monomer level
- Alkyds have lower monomer level
- Properties depend on type, compounding, processing
- "Fiberglass" glass-fiber-reinforced formulations

Uses:

- Boats
- Fishing rods
- Automobile body panels
- Hand lay-up-spray-up for small to moderate quantities of large parts
- Compression molding with SMCs—preforms for high-volume production of moderate-sized parts with intricate details
- Cold-press molding for smaller components
- Pultrusion for constant-section shapes

---

*Also available as a thermoplastic

Bulk-molding compounds (BMCs) are mixtures of polyester resin/short-glass fibers/filler and catalyst
- Supplied in bulk form or extruded rope

Sheet-molding compounds (SMCs) consist of polyester resin/long-glass fibers/catalyst and additives
- Supplied in rolls between polyethylene carrier films

- Resin-transfer molding for low-pressure intermediate production
- Suited for automated production

Phenolics and Alkyds

Phenolics

Fiberite: ICI Fiberite	Valite: Lockport Thermosets
Duerz: Occidental	Plaslok: Plaslok
Plenco: Plastics	Resinoid: Resoid Engineering
Rogers: Rogers	

Characteristics:

- Low cost (workhorse of the thermosets)
- High-performance engineering plastic
- Compounds contain organic and inorganic reinforcing fibers and fillers
- Molding compounds have superior heat resistance

Properties:

- High heat-deflection temperature
- Excellent moldability with dimensional stability
- Limited to black or brown
- Good electrical properties and flame resistance
- Good water and chemical resistance

Uses:

- Bonding, impregnating materials
- Usually formulated to provide special properties

Alkyd

Durez: Occidental   Glaskyd: CYTEC
Plenco: Plastics   Cosmic: Cosmic
                                    Engineering
Rogers: Rogers

Characteristics:

- Based on unsaturated polyester-type resins combined with cross-linking monomers, catalysts, reinforcements, lubricants, or fillers
- Supplied as bulk-molding compounds (BMCs) or sheet-molding compounds (SMCs)

Properties:

- Low-moisture absorption, excellent dimensional stability
- Outstanding electrical characteristics (most compounds)

- Some can be used to 350°F
- Dimensional stability/properties over a wide temperature range
- Some grades are UL-rated at 94V-0
- Others 94HB to V-0

Uses:

- Military switch-gear
- Electrical-terminal strips
- Relay and transformer housings bases
- Radio and TV components
- Electrical appliance housings and components

Polyurethane

Polyurethane

Texin and Desmopan: Estane: BF Good-
  Bayer   rich
Cablon-flex: Cabot   Pellethane: Dow

Characteristics:

- Wide variations of forms and physical and mechanical properties

Properties:

- Outstanding flex life and cut resistance
- Up to 20 times more abrasion resistant than metals
- Elastomeric forms: soft and flexible or firm and rigid
- Natural color of RIM urethane is tan

Flexible Foams

Properties:

- Can be pigmented to any color but turn yellow when exposed to air and light
- Some hold up to 40 times their weight of water
- Polyether types are not affected by high-temperature aging, wet or dry
- UV exposure produces brittleness and reduces properties

Uses:

- Air filters and gasketing
- Clothing interliners
- Sound-absorbing elements

Polyether Types

Properties:

- Higher mechanical properties, good oil resistance

Uses:

- Vehicle seats, bedding, carpet underlay
- Furniture upholstering, packaging

Elastomeric foam uses:

- Automotive bumpers, fascia, fenders
- Other exterior body panels

Semirigid uses:

- Athletic protective gear
- Automotive crash-protection

- Horn buttons, sun visors, arm rests

Rigid Foams

Characteristics:

- Low water absorption
- Properties vary with density and formulation

Uses:

- Insulation for refrigerators
- Refrigerated trucks and railroad cars
- Cold-storage warehouses and process tanks, flotation devices
- Structural and decorative furniture components
- Sheathing, roof insulation for buildings

Rigid Structural Foams

Uses:

- Housings for computer systems
- Chair shells, furniture drawers
- Sports equipment

Integral-Skin Foam

Properties:

- Range from soft/flexible to impact-absorbing grades

Uses:

- Structural parts
- Coatings are recommended for UV protection

Epoxy and Vinyl Ester

Epoxy

Lytex: Quantum Composites
Cosmic: Cosmic
E-260H TEM: ICI Fiberite
Rogers: Rogers
E-8354M TEM: ICI Fiberite

Properties:

- Extremely low shrinkage during polymerization
- Variety of combinations of epoxy resins and reinforcements provides a wide latitude of properties in molded parts
- Excellent electrical/thermal/chemical resistance
- Excellent adhesions in structural applications (one- or two-part systems)
- Hard, rigid, relatively brittle
- Excellent dimensional stability over a broad temperature range to 450°F (fiber-reinforced to 500°F for brief periods)

Uses:

- Appliances
- Automotive
- Marine
- Industrial (paints)
- Coatings and decorative top coats
- Industrial switchgear
- Semiconductor encapsulation
- Printed circuit boards
- Aerospace components

Vinyl Ester

Ashland
Interplastic
Reichhold
Dow
Owens-Corning

Characteristics:

- Derived from epoxy

Properties:

- Anti-corrosion
- Anti-heat

Allyl

Allyl

Durez: Occidental
Rogers: Rogers
Diallyl isophthalate (DAIP)
Cosmic: Cosmic
Diallyl phthalate (DAP)

Characteristics:

- Used as cross-linking agents for unsaturated polyester compounds
- Reinforced with fibers (glass/polyester/acrylic)
- Glass fiber provides maximum mechanical properties
- Acrylic fiber provides the best electrical properties
- Polyester fiber improves impact resistance and strength (in thin sections)
- Prepregs (preimpregnated glass cloth) contain no toxic additives
- Long storage stability, ease of handling and fabrication

Properties:

- Colorless or range of colors
- Good flame resistance
- Will not corrode copper or plated inserts and contacts
- Good electrical properties to 370°F for DAP (400°F for DAIP)
- Excellent dimensional stability
- Excellent resistance to moisture/chemicals/liquid oxygen
- No odor, low toxicity
- Long-term retention of electrical-insulation characteristics

Uses:

- Radomes, printed circuit boards
- Aircraft parts, tube, ducts

8.3 THERMOPLASTICS

Introduction

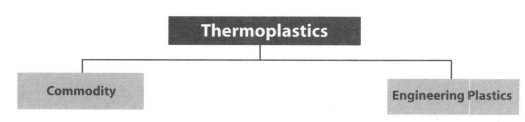

Figure 8–26 *Thermoplastics.*

In the following organization of thermoplastic polymers, commodity plastics are those that are generally priced below $1 per pound. Some of the polymers placed within these families of materials have higher performance characteristics and can compete with higher-priced polymers. Their price, however, is higher because of their better performance and because they are often alloyed with higher-priced polymers. Because of the very large volume of these materials their price is generally very competitive with the higher-performing polymers.

The mid-priced polymers generally range from over $1 per pound to about $5 per pound. This group also contains higher-preforming polymers and are usually blended or alloyed with higher-priced polymers.

The high-performance "engineering plastics" are selected because they normally preform very well at high temperatures and under high stress. These materials can cost up to $12 per pound or more and often are difficult and/or costly to process. They generally have very good burn resistance or are self-extinguishing with low smoke and fume characteristics.

Commodity Thermoplastics

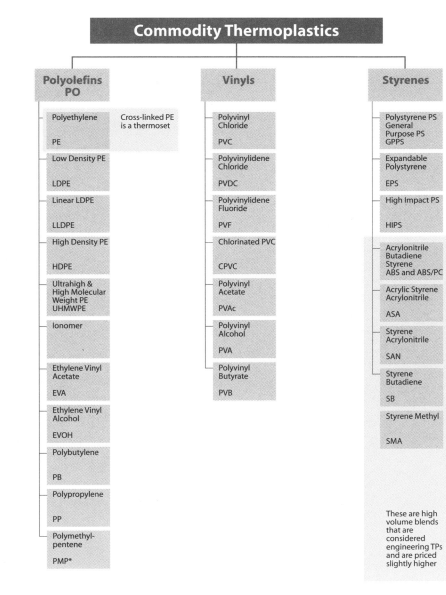

Figure 8–27 *Commodity thermoplastics.*

Polyolefins

Polyethylene (PE)

Amoco: Amoco	DFDA: Union Carbide
Chevron: Chevron	Anathon: DuPont
Tenite: Eastman	Escorene: Exxon
Fina: Fina	Hostalen: Hoechst
Marlex: Phillips	Celanese
Rexene: Rexene	Petrothene: Quantum
Union Carbide	Fortiflex: Solvay
Neopolen: BASF	Westlake

Properties:

- Range from low-impact strength to nearly unbreakable
- Good clarity to opaque
- Service temperatures range from –40 to 200° F
- Near-zero moisture absorption
- Excellent chemical resistance and electrical properties
- Low coefficient of friction

(There is also a cross-linked polyethylene—a special grade that is essentially a thermoset with outstanding heat resistance and strength.)

Low-Density PE (LDPE)

Properties:

- Good toughness
- Flexibility
- Low-temperature impact resistance
- Good resistance to chemical attack

Uses:

- Blow-molded containers and toys
- Hot-melt adhesives
- Injection-molded housewares
- Paperboard coatings
- Wire insulation
- Clear film with low heat resistance
- Half of LDPE production is used for packaging applications: industrial bags, shrink bundling, soft goods, produce and garment bags
- Rotation-molded large agricultural tanks, chemical shipping containers, and tote boxes

Linear Low-Density Polyethylene (LLDPE)

Uses:

- Grocery and industrial trash bags, liners, heavy-duty shipping bags
- Mainly in film applications, suitable for injection, rotational, and blow molding

Resin Production Facts

- Polyolefins account for the largest volume of all resins in world production
- Polyethylene accounts for 31% of all polyolefin production
- Polypropylene accounts for 14% of all polyolefin production
- Polyolefins account for 45% of world plastic production (110 million metric tons in 1994)

Properties:

- Mechanical properties significantly higher than LDPE/HDPE
- Excellent impact/tear/heat-seal strengths/environmental stress-crack resistance

High-Density PE (HDPE)

Properties:

- Mechanical properties significantly higher than LDPE/MDPE
- Excellent rigidity and tensile strength, low impact strength

Uses:

- Film products to large blow-molded industrial containers (meets DoT and OSHA specs)
- Largest market is blow-molded containers for milk, fruit juices, water, detergents, household, and industrial liquids
- Molded housewares, industrial pails, food containers, tote boxes, structural-foam housings
- Extruded water- and gas-distribution pipe (highest strength rating for PE pipe), wire insulation

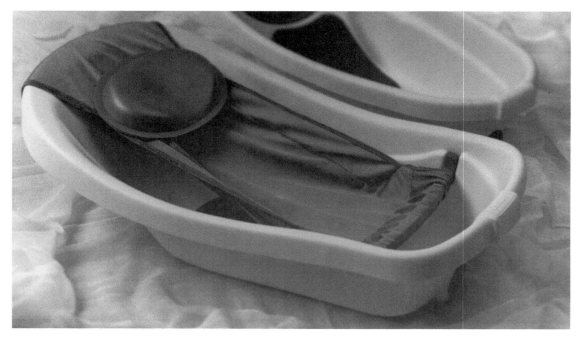

Figure 8–28 *Polyethylene infant washing basins (Courtesy Anderson Design).*

- Rotationally molded large and complex-shaped products such as fuel tanks, trash containers, dump carts, pallets, agricultural tanks, highway barriers, and water and waste tanks for recreational vehicles
- Extruded sheet applications include pool liners, truck-bed liners, outdoor leisure products, merchandise bags, trash bags, and grocery bags

High-Molecular-Weight-PE HDPE (HMW-HDPE)

Characteristics:

- Outstanding toughness and durability at low temperatures.

Ultra-high-molecular-weight PE (UHMWPE)

Characteristics:

- Difficult to process—methods include compression molding, ram extrusion, and warm forging

Properties:

- Outstanding abrasion resistance
- Low coefficient of friction
- High impact strength
- Does not break in impact-strength tests using standard notched specimens
- Excellent chemical resistance
- Maximum service temperature is 200°F

Ionomer

Properties:

- Extremely tough
- High tensile and impact strengths
- Excellent abrasion resistance
- Optical clarity
- Good adhesion to metal foils
- High impact strength
- Cut resistance

Uses:

- Used in food packaging
- Heat-seal layer in composite structures
- Injection-molded athletic soles with metal cleats insert-molded
- Ski boot and ice skate shells, wrestling mats
- Foam boat bumpers and navigation buoys
- Thermal insulation for pipes, covers for hot-water storage tanks
- Foam-molded bumper guards
- License-plate holders

Ethylene-Vinyl Acetate: EVA Copolymers

Geon: Geon	TempRite: BF Goodrich
Oxyblend: Occidental	Pilovic: Goodyear
Vista: Vista	Westlake: Westlake
Dural: Alpha CandP	Alpha: AlphaGary
Bolatron: GenCorp	Maclin: Maclin
Kohinor	Rimtec: Rimtec

Characteristics:

- Derived from LDPE technology
- Near elastomeric materials in softness and flexibility
- Competitive with plasticized PVC and rubber

Properties:

- Pastels to deep hues, good clarity and gloss
- Barrier properties, little or no odor
- Adhesive properties
- Resistant to UV radiation
- FDA approval for direct contact with foods
- Electrical properties are not as good as LDPE, competitive with rubber and vinyl
- Retains toughness and flexibility at low temperatures
- Good stress-crack resistance

Uses:

- Tube for medical equipment, beverage-vending, milk-packaging, and beer-dispensing equipment
- Molded appliance bumpers
- Blow-molded bellows, seals, gaskets
- Hot-melt adhesives

Polybutylene PB

Duroflex: Shell

Characteristics:

- Semicrystalline, rubberlike with very low molded-in stress

Properties:

- Superior resistance to creep and stress cracking
- Films have high tear resistance, toughness, and flexibility
- Chemical and electrical properties are similar to those of PE/PP

Uses:

- Pipe, packaging
- Hot-melt adhesives and sealants
- Film industrial refuse bags that resist bursting, puncturing, and tearing

Polypropylene (PP)

Amoco: Amoco	Tenite: Eastman
Escorene: Exxon	Fina: Fina
Marlex: Phillips	Petrothene: Quantum
Shell: Shell/Rexene	Fortslene: Solvay

Properties:

- Moderate strength
- Semitranslucent or milky white with excellent colorability
- Low density
- Good balance of thermal, chemical, and electrical properties

- Special, HMW, rubber-modified grades have increased toughness
- Limited heat resistance, UL-rated at 248°F for continuous service
- Resists chemical attack and staining
- Unaffected by aqueous solutions of inorganic salts, mineral acids, and bases
- Unstable in the presence of oxidative conditions and UV radiation

Polymethylpentene (PMP)

Characteristics:

- Moderately crystalline

Properties:

- Short-time heat resistance to 400°F
- Low specific gravity
- Transparent (crystalline and amorphous phases have the same index of refraction)
- Light-transmission value of 90%

Uses:

- Molded containers for quick-frozen foods that can be heated later in the same container
- Hot-liquid level indicators, transparent plumbing
- Coffeemaker bowls
- Medical syringes, laboratory ware
- Light diffusers
- Electrical and electronic applications, wire coatings
- Components for microwave equipment

Vinyls

Polyvinyl Chloride (PVC)

Geon: Geon	Vista: Vista
Westlake: Westlake	Dural: Alpha C&P
Temprite: BF Goodrich	Boltaron: GenCorp
Maclin: Maclin	Kohinor: Rimtec
Alpha: Alpha Gary	Oxy & Oxyblend: Occidental

Characteristics:

- The "poor man's engineering plastic"
- Can be compounded to be flexible or rigid, opaque or transparent, high or low modulus
- Foams can be open or closed cell, elastomeric or rigid
- Water-white or clear in rigid compounds or pigmented to most colors

Properties (no single compound is typical):

- Alloying improves impact resistance, tear strength, resilience, heat-deflection temperature
- Low combustibility, high resistance to ignition
- Self-extinguishing with good corrosion and stain resistance
- Attacked by aromatic solvents, ketones, naphthalenes, chloride, acetate, acrylate esters
- Not recommended for continuous use >140°F

Uses:

- Transparent, nontoxic, tough enough for mineral-water bottles
- Pressure pipe for water distribution
- Flexible compounds: used for baby pants and imitation suede
- Used for thermal and electrical insulation
- Coatings applied by fluidized-bed and electrostatic powder-coating methods
- Dip molding and coatings

Styrenes

Polystyrene (PS)

General Purpose Polystyrene (GPPS)

Dylite: ARCO	Styropor: BASF
Cabot: Cabot	Amoco: Amoco
Fina: Fina	Novacor: Novacor
Fiberstran: DSM	Thermocomp: LNP

Characteristics:

- Amorphous
- Low-cost, competitive with higher-priced resins
- Family includes ABS, SAN, SMA, and ASA copolymers with similar structural characteristics

Properties:

- Good heat resistance and hardness
- Sparkling clarity and excellent colorability
- Ease of processing

Expandable PS (EPS)

Characteristics:

- A specialized form used to make low-density foam shapes or blocks

Properties (unmodified PS):

- Unaffected by most foods, drinks, and household fluids
- Attacked by citrus-fruit-rind oil, gasoline, turpentine, and lacquer thinner
- Rigid and brittle
- Moderate strength, increased significantly by blending with polybutadiene (others)

High-Impact PS (HIPS)

Styrene Copolymers

Styrene Maleic Anhydride (SMA)

Characteristics:

- Higher heat resistance than ABS families
- Available in crystal-clear or a wide range of transparent, translucent, and opaque colors

Properties:

- Heat resistance is 20° to 50°F (greater than PS, SAN, or ABS)
- Glass-fiber reinforcement improves thermal properties, rigidity, flexural properties, dimensional stability, and impact strength

- Crystal-clear, impact-modified grades meet FDA/DoA requirements
- Flammability rating is UL94 HB

Uses:

- Appliance panels and knobs
- Automotive: instrument panels and nameplates
- Housewares and food processors
- Disposable beverage glasses
- Toys
- Medical instruments
- Communications and business equipment lenses
- Decorative packaging

Acrylonitrile Butadiene Styrene (ABS)

Cycolac: GE	Lustran: Monsanto
Thermocomp: LNP	Fiberfil and Fiberstran: (DSM)

Characteristics:

- Amorphous
- Medium-priced
- Good heat resistance and flame retardance
- Platability

Properties:

- Translucent to opaque
- Hard, rigid, and tough
- Available with different levels of impact strength

ABS/PC Alloys

- Better balance of heat and impact properties
- Reinforced grades contain up to 40% glass fibers

Acrylic-Styrene-Acrylonitrile (ASA) Polymers

Luran: BASF   Geloy: GE
Centrex: Monsanto

Characteristics:

- Amorphous
- Mechanical properties similar to those of ABS
- Less affected by outdoor weathering

Properties:

- High gloss
- Natural color is off white, colors are available
- Good chemical and heat resistance
- Better resistance to environmental-stress cracking than ABS
- Available with UL94-HB classification
- High impact strength at low temperatures

Uses:

- Appliance panels and knobs
- Camper tops, instrument panels, and nameplates
- Housewares and toys
- Medical instruments
- Communications and business equipment

Styrene Acrylonitrile (SAN)

Lustran: Monsanto   Fiberstran: DSM
Thermocomp: LNP   Luran: BASF

Characteristics:

- Copolymer—no butadiene

Properties

- High heat and chemical resistance
- Has electrical characteristics
- General-purpose grades are adequate for some outdoor applications
- Sunlight causes color change and reduces surface gloss without coating protection
- Unaffected by water, salts, most inorganic acids, food acids, and alkalies
- FDA acceptance dependent on pigmentation
- Good impact and abrasion resistance
- Dimensional stability
- Low-temperature properties
- Surface hardness and rigidity
- Can accommodate snap-fit assembly requirements

Mid-Priced Engineering Thermoplastics

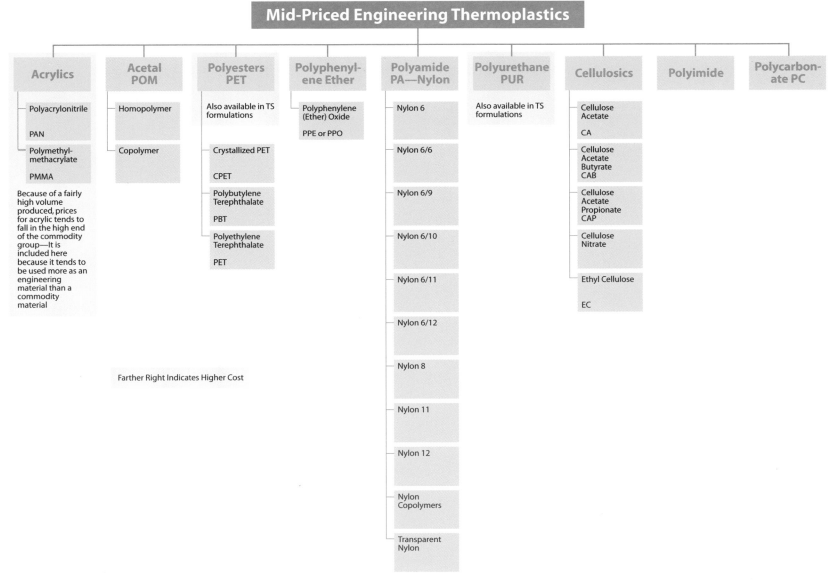

Figure 8–29 *Mid-priced engineering thermoplastics.*

Acrylics

Acrylics

Plexiglas: Atohas   Acrylite: Cyro
Lucite: DuPont   Perspex: ICI
Optix: Plaskolite

Characteristics:

- Crystal clarity
- Outstanding weatherability
- General-purpose, ultraviolet-absorbing mirrored, super-thermoforming, cementable grades with various surface finishes and in transparent, translucent, and opaque colors

Properties:

- 92% transmittance, used in lens or optical applications to transmit and control light
- Superior weather resistance
- Good dimensional stability
- Unaffected by exposure to the elements, salt spray, or corrosive atmospheres
- Withstands fluorescent lamps without darkening or deteriorating
- Discolors when exposed to high-intensity UV light
- Special formulations resist UV emission from mercury and soldium-vapor lamps
- Short-term loading, long-term service
- Tensile stresses limited to avoid crazing and surface cracking
- Fairly good scratch resistant; however normal maintenance/cleaning operations will scratch/abrade them

- Special abrasion-resistant sheets available, most formulated for long-term outdoor durability and to filter ultraviolet energy
- Special molecular orientation improves crack resistance (used for jet-aircraft cabin windows)

Uses:

- Camera lenses
- Appliance panels and knobs
- Camper tops, parking and taillights, dials
- Housewares and toys
- Medical instruments

Acetals

Acetal

Characteristics:

- Crystalline

Properties:

- Strong
- Rigid
- Good moisture, heat, and solvent resistance
- FDA approval for contact with food to 250°F
- National Sanitation Foundation approval for potable water to 180°F

Homopolymer

Delrin: DuPont

Properties:

- High tensile strength, stiffness, resilience, and fatigue endurance
- Moderate toughness under repeated impact
- High resistance to organic solvents
- Excellent dimensional stability
- Low coefficient of friction
- Outstanding abrasion resistance
- General-purpose resins for environmental conditions
- UV-stabilized grades for long-term exposure to weather
- Not recommended for prolonged exposure to strong acids or bases

Uses:

- Automotive: fuel-system, seat belt components, steering-column supports, and window brackets
- Plumbing: shower heads, ballcocks, and faucet cartridges
- Consumer: garden sprayers, lighter bodies, zippers, and telephones
- Industrial: impellers, conveyor plates, gears, sprockets, and springs

Copolymers

Ultraform: BASF
Celcon (terpolymer): Hoechst Celanese

Properties:

- High tensile and flexural strength, fatigue resistance, and hardness
- Natural translucent white and colors
- Some electroplatable, UV-resistant grades
- Glass-reinforced, low-wear, impact-modified, and low-warpage grades

Uses:

- Automotive: fuel-system, seat belt components, supports, and brackets
- Plumbing: faucet valves, stems, and pumps
- Industrial: impellers, plates, and gears
- FDA approval for: food conveyors, milk pumps, coffee spigots, and filter housings

Polyesters and Polyphenylenes

Polyesters (PBT and PET)

Petra: Allied Signal
Ultradur: BASF
Valox and Xenoy: GE
Texapol: Texapol
Pocan and Petlon: Albis
Eastman: Eastman
Celanex: Hoechst Celanese
Thermofil: Thermofil

Characteristics:

- Crystalline
- High molecular weight
- Excellent balance of properties
- Available in unreinforced molding resins and glass-reinforced grades

Properties:

- Unreinforced and glass-filled grades UL 94HB/5V
- Excellent resistance to a broad range of chemicals at room temperature
- Attacked by strong acids and bases
- High creep resistance with low moisture absorption
- Excellent dimensional stability
- Exceptional impact strength, notch sensitive
- Film is tough, durable, and dimensionally stable
- Can be metallized, embossed, slit, die cut, and laminated
- Available in crystal clear, white, opaque, and translucent forms
- Glassy smooth, matte, antistatic, adhesion-promoting, and/or heat-sealable surfaces

Uses:

- Consumer products
- Soft drink and food containers
- Automotive products
- Electrical and electronic products
- Industrial products

Polyphenylene (Ether) Oxide (PPE or PPO)

Fiberfil: DSM
Noryl: GE
Thermofil: Thermofil

Characteristics:

- Compatible with PS (often combined)
- Often alloyed with nylon

Properties:

- Low water absorbtion
- High dimensional stability
- Excellent dielectric properties

Uses:

- Housings for appliances and business machines
- Automobile instrument panels and seat backs
- Fluid-handling equipment
- Large blow-molded structural parts
- When alloyed with nylon, used for injection-molded automobile fenders

Polyamides

Polyamides (Nylons)

Adell: Adell
Capron: Allied Signal
Durethan: Bayer
Zytel: DuPont
Celanese: Hoechst Celanese
Maranyl: ICI
NYCOA: Nylon Corp.
Texalon: Texapol
Nypel: BASF
Fiberstran: LNP
Plaslube: Polymers Int.
Albis: Albis
Ashiene: Ashley
CRI: Custom Resins
Grilon: EMS
Vestamid: Huls
Vydyne: Monsanto
Aklun: A. Schulman
Wellamid: Wellman
Ultramid: DSM
Fiberfil: MRC
Nylatron: Thermofil

Characteristics:

- Excellent fatigue resistance
- Low coefficient of friction
- Good toughness, resists fuels, oils, and chemicals
- Semi-crystalline
- First thermoplastic engineering resin
- Originally developed as high-strength textile fibers

Properties (vary widely):

- Inert to biological attack
- Adequate electrical properties
- All absorb moisture
- Type 4/6: high crystallinity with high strength and stiffness
- High heat-deflection temperature (HDT)
- High fatigue, wear, and creep resistance
- Type 6: tougher and more flexible than type 6/6
- Type 6/6: higher heat and abrasion resistance, strength, stiffness, and hardness than type 6
- Type 6/12: absorbs less moisture, maintains mechanical and electrical properties in high-humidity environments with lower strength, stiffness, and use temperatures at higher cost
- Types 11 and 12: lower moisture absorption with superior resistance to fuels, hydraulic oils, and most automotive fluids

Uses:

- Bearings and wear surfaces
- Automotive: instrument panel gears, underhood components such as cooling fans, wire connectors, radiator and other tanks
- Hydraulic and air conditioning equipment
- Journal bearings, cams, sheaves, wear plates

Polyurethanes and Cellulosics

Polyurethane (PU)

Texin and Desmopan: Estane: BF Goodrich
   Bayer   Pellethane: Dow
Cablon-Flex: Cabot

Characteristics:

- Wide variations in forms and physical and mechanical properties
- Outstanding flex life and cut resistance
- Up to 20 times more abrasion resistant than metals
- Elastomeric forms: soft and flexible or firm and rigid

Properties:

- Excellent abrasion resistance
- Excellent resistance to fuels and oils
- High tensile and tear strength
- High elasticity and resilience
- Good vibration dampening

Uses:

- Automotive: cams, gears, mechanical parts, exterior and side body moldings
- Sports equipment: golf balls, ski-goggle frames, and ski boots
- Other: screens, ID tags, seals, hoses, caster wheels, buckets, catheters, and connectors

Cellulose Acetate

Tenite: Eastman/CA700, Albis/CA/GP, Rotuba Cellulose Acetate Butyrate
Tenite: Eastman/B900, Albus

Characteristics:

- Available as film (cellophane) or fiber (rayon)
- Chemically modified to produce thermoplastics
- Available in a wide range of transparent, translucent, or opaque colors

Ethyl Cellulose

Characteristics:

- Light amber in uncolored formulations

Properties:

- Low specific heat, thermal conductivity gives a pleasant feel
- Not suitable for outdoor use

- Cellulosics are made from cellulose derived from wood pulp or cotton linters

- Most formulations have a 94HB flammability classification
- Formulations are available for contact with food
- Tough at very low temperatures

Uses:

- Eyewear frames, pen barrels and caps, toys, marine products, fuel-filter bowls, toothbrushes, cosmetic containers, face and safety shields
- Blister packaging for food and other products
- Outdoor signs, window well covers and skylights, sprinklers
- Helmets, rollers, slides, flashlights, and tool handles

Polyimides and Polycarbonates

Polyimide

Vespel: DuPont

Characteristics:

- TP
- Highest heat and fire resistance

Properties:

- Can be used in air continuously to 500°F
- Intermittent exposure ranges from cyrogenic to 900°F

- Near zero creep
- Good wear resistance

Uses:

- Jet-engine bushings, gear pump gaskets, valve seals, and rings
- High-speed computer printer parts
- Thin-film products, enamel, adhesives, and coatings

Polycarbonates

Calibre: Dow   Lexan: GE
Makrolon   APEC HT: Bayer
Naxell: MRC   Fiberstan: DSM
Thermofil: Thermofil

Characteristics:

- Exceptional toughness over a wide temperature range
- Amorphous

Properties:

- Water-clear and transparent
- Heat and flame resistant
- Affected by greases, oils, acids
- Room-temperature water has no effect
- Continuous exposure in hot (65°C) water causes gradual embrittlement
- Boiling water has little effect on dimensions

- Excellent toughness
- Superior impact resistance
- Dimensional stability
- Humidity has little effect on dimensions or properties

Special grades include:

- Flame-retardant formulations
- Grades that meet FDA regulations for food-contact or medical applications
- Grades used for blow-molding
- Weather and UV resistance
- Glass reinforcement
- EMI/RFI/ESD-shielding
- Structural-foam applications

Uses:

- Transportation: lighting components, instrument panels, and aircraft canopies
- Consumer: tool housings, food containers, appliances, bottles, and film
- Business equipment: computer and printer housings, audio discs, and data storage discs
- Medical: diagnostic, cardiovascular and intravenous devices; drug-delivery systems; and packaging
- Other: meter covers, telephone components, lighting diffusers, and lenses

High Performance Thermoplastics

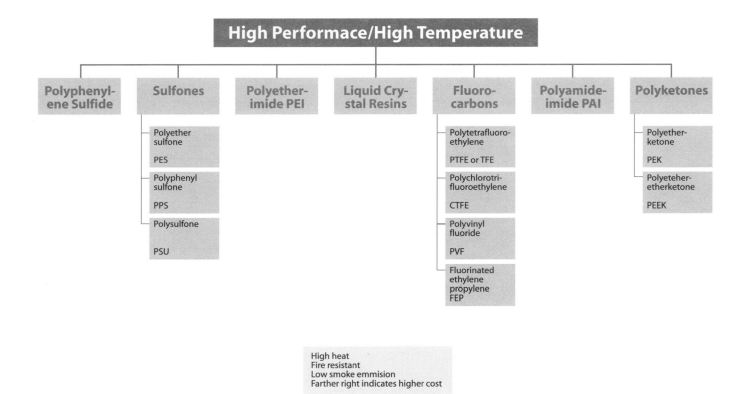

Figure 8–30   *High performance/high temperature.*

Polyphenylene Sulfide (PPS)

Fortron: Hoechst Celanese   Ryton: Phillips
Tedur: Albis   Fiberfil: DSM
Thermocomp: LNP

Characteristics:

- Recommended for mechanical and electronic applications requiring high mechanical strength, impact resistance, and insulating characteristics

Properties:

- Broad chemical resistance
- No known solvent below 400°F
- Inherent flame resistance and retardance
- Excellent stability at very high temperatures
- UL temperature index is 200 to 240°C/UL 94V-0/5
- Outstanding high-temperature stability
- Dimensional reliability
- Wide range of injection-molding grades are available
- Crystalline moldings have optimum dimensional stability
- Amorphous moldings have optimum mechanical strength at room temperature

Uses:

- Computers and communications equipment
- Industrial: chemical and petroleum-processing equipment
- Automotive: connectors and components
- Aircraft: interior panels and seats

Sulfone Polymers

Polyethersulfone (PES)

Ultrason E: BASF

Polyarylsulfone (PAS)

Radel: Amoco

Polysulfone (PSU)

Udel: Amoco   Ultrason S: BASF

Characteristics:

- Noted for high heat-deflection temperatures
- Outstanding dimensional stability
- Highest performance processible on conventional machinery
- Amorphous

Properties:

- Outstanding high-temperature stability
- Natural color is transparent light amber
- Available in opaque colors
- Only thermoplastic that remains transparent at 400°F
- Continuous use in air or steam at rated temperature will not cloud or craze
- Outstanding heat resistance
- Service temperature limited by heat-deflection temperature of 345 to 400°F
- Good electrical properties at elevated temperatures
- PSU—320°F/rated V-2
- PES—355°F/rated V-0 per UL94
- Absorbs ultraviolet rays, poor weather resistance
- Extremely tough, will not break in standard impact tests
- Exceptionally low creep at elevated temperatures and under continuous load
- Excellent dimensional stability
- Excellent for precision-molded parts

Uses:

- Hair-dryer grilles, hot water valves, business machine parts, automotive electrical parts, and medical instruments (respiration and filtration membranes, implants)
- Food: steamable pans, coffeemakers, hot-water beverage dispensers, and microwave cookware

Polyetherimide (PEI)

Ultem: GE (available in sheet)

Characteristics:

- Amorphous

Properties:

- Unreinforced grade is transparent
- Standard and custom colors are available

- UL listed 94V-0 at 0.016 inch and 94-5V at 0.075 inch without additives
- Limiting oxygen index 47% (among the highest of ETP)
- Inherent flame resistance
- Low-smoke evolution
- Chemical resistant under varied conditions of stress and temperatures
- Good resistance to UV radiation
- Suitable for short-term and repeated steam exposure
- Excellent electrical properties
- Stable over a range of temperatures and frequencies
- High heat resistance, strength, and modulus
- Maintains properties at elevated temperatures
- Notch sensitive (avoid sharp corners)
- Stress concentrations should be minimized
- Excellent processibility
- Ductile for snap fit

Uses:

- Electronic: close-tolerance connectors, chip carriers, and wiring devices
- Aircraft: jet engine parts, seating, wall and window components, electrical and mechanical parts
- High temperature: wire coating, coils, fuseblocks, and flexible circuitry

Liquid Crystal Polymers (LCPs)

Zenite: Dupont

Characteristics:

- Aromatic copolyesters
- High-heat/high-cost polymer
- Based on polyester

Properties:

- High temperature resistance
- High strength
- Thermal stability
- UL 94 V-0

Uses:

- High-performance microminiature connectors for computers and communications equipment
- Cellular phones
- Pagers
- Conventional and microwave cookware

Fluorocarbons

Polytetrafluoroethylene (PTFE)

Algoflon: Ausmont   Teflon: DuPont
Fulon: ICI   Hostaflon: Hoechst
                     Celanese

Characteristics:

- Crystalline
- Extremely inert
- Opaque

- Malleable
- Amorphous above 648°F (returns to original state when cooled)

Properties:

- Chemically inert
- High- and low-temperature stability
- Excellent electrical properties
- Low friction
- Transparent
- Intractable
- Fracture if severely deformed

Uses:

- Powders for compression molding
- Ram extrusion
- Lubricated extrusion
- Aqueous dispersions for dip coating and impregnation

Polychlorotrifluoroethylene (PCTFE)

Acion: Allied Signal   KelF81: 3M

Characteristics:

- Chemical inertness
- Thermal stability
- Good electrical properties
- Nothing adheres readily to them
- Absorb practically no moisture
- Usable from 400 to −400°F

Polyvinylidene Fluoride (PVDF)

Hylar: Ausimont   Kynar: Elf Atochem N.A.
Solef: Solvey

Characteristics:

- Toughest of the fluoroplastic resins
- Excellent resistance to stress fatigue, abrasion, and cold flow

Uses:

- Powders or dispersions for corrosion-resistant coatings
- Used to insulate wire, computer and electrical cable, and electronic equipment
- Heat-shrinkable tubing for resistors and diodes
- Encapsulate soldered joints

Fluorinated Ethylene Propylene (FEP)

Teflon: DuPont

Characteristics:

- Copolymer of TFE and hexafluoropropylene

Properties:

- Good toughness
- Excellent dimensional stability
- Can be molded by conventional TP processing equipment

Uses:

- Pipe lining for chemical-processing equipment
- Wire and cable applications
- Glazing in solar reflectors

Polyamide-imides

Torlon: Amoco

Characteristics:

- Extremely resistant to flame with very low smoke generation

Properties:

- Excellent dimensional stability
- High tensile and compressive strength at high temperature
- Good impact resistance
- Structural integrity in continuous use to 500°F
- Unfilled grade is rated 94V-0
- Exceeds requirements for flammability, smoke density, and toxic gas emission
- Injection moldable (requires postcuring)

Uses:

- Automotive: power-train, valve stems and retainers, piston rings, and timing gears
- Aerospace: brackets, bushings, housings, stand-offs, and fasteners
- Business machines: high-heat applications, wear, picker fingers, and gears
- Electronic: sockets, switches, and relays

Polyketones—Partially Crystalline

Kadel: Amoco   Ultrapek (PAEK): BSAF
Areton (PEKK):   Hostatec: Hoechst
   DuPont   Celanese
Victrex (PEK
   PEEK): ICI

Characteristics:

- Stronger and more rigid than most TPs

Properties:

- Used at high temperatures
- Excellent resistance to burning with very low flame spread (V-0 per UL94)
- Extremely low smoke density
- Excellent chemical resistance
- Affected by UV radiation
- Low coefficients of friction
- Very high fatigue strength and wear rates
- High strength, tough
- Impact resistant over a wide range of temperatures

Uses:

- Powder
- Wire coatings for high-performance applications
- Pump impellers
- Electrical connectors
- Seals

9 RESIN FORMING PROCESSES

Thermosets

Thermoset		Physical Considerations		Logistics				Costs
		Min./Nonomal Wall Thickness	Nonomal/Max. Part Size	Cores /Side Action	Inserts	Pressure Required	Surface Finish, Finishing Required /Problems	Tooling
Open Mold	Hand Lay-up	0.25" / 0.50"	Unlimited	None	Molded in	Open mold: no pressure	Mold side gives polished finish with sharp features	$
	Spray-up	0.25" / 0.50"	Unlimited	None	Molded in	Open mold: no pressure	Polished finish with sharp features	$
Closed Mold	Compression Molding	<0.350 Non-uniform wall common	With BMC With SMC limited only by press	Cores are common Side action not recommended	Molded in but limited	2000–10,000 psi +700 psi for each inch of depth	Polished finish with sharp features	$ $
	Transfer Molding	Less varied with nonuniform wall possible with fine detail	1 lb. maximum	Common	Molded in Unlimited	2000–6000 psi	Polished finish with sharp features	$ $ $
	Resin Transfer Molding	+0.25	Unlimited	Common	Molded in Fragile inserts possible	25–50 psi	Good surface	$
	RIM-Reaction Injection Molding	0.25 / 0.50 Nonuniform wall common	Large parts	Not applicable	Molded in	Up to 3500 psi In mold pressure is 50 psi	Class A finish for bottom only Painting required	$
	RRIM-Reinforced Reaction	+0.50	Large parts	Not applicable	Molded in	Up to 3500 psi In mold pressure is 50 psi	Good surface May require finishing & paint	$
	SRIM-Structural Reinforced Reaction Injection	+0.50	Large structural parts	Not applicable	Molded in	Up to 3500 psi In mold pressure is 50 psi	Good surface May require finishing & paint	$
	Foam Molding	Unlimited	Unlimited	Not applicable	Not applicable	Pressure varies according to density	Not applicable	$

Figure 9–1 *Forming processes comparison chart for thermosets.*

Thermoplastics

Thermo-plastic	Physical Considerations		Logistics				Costs
	Min./Nonomal Wall Thickness	Nonomal/Max. Part Size	Cores /Side Action	Inserts	Pressure Required (CF=Clamping Force)	Surface Finish, Finishing Required /Problems	Tooling
Open Mold — Vacuum Forming (with mechanical assist)	Varies somewhat, nonuniform wall	Limited by machine size	None	After molding	Vacuum	Good finish away from tool, soft to good features	$ $
Open Mold — Pressure Forming (with vacuum assist) and Twin Sheet	Varies somewhat, nonuniform wall	Usually limited to one foot cubed	None	After molding	50–80 psi (+ vacuum)	Very good tool side, sharp features	$ $
Closed Mold — Rotational Molding	0.016"–0.25" uniform wall, variation possible	Hollow shapes 1" cube to 6' × 6' × 12'	None	Molded in or after molding	No pressure used	Good finish, good features	$ $
Closed Mold — Injection Blow Molding	0.015" uniform wall	Mostly bottles, globes and containers not usally > one ft. cubed	None	Molded threads or none	One ton psi CF, 80–120 psi	Good finish	$ $ $
Closed Mold — Extrusion Blow Molding	Varies with nonuniform wall possible	Limited by tool size	Side action possible	Molded in possible but ususally after molding	50–120 psi	Good finish, sharp features	$ $ $
Closed Mold — Gas Assist Injection Molding	0.125" uniform wall with no transition to 0.250" rib	Large parts to 4' × 4' × 3"	Common	After molding	One ton psi CF	Polished finish, sharp features, gloss variation	$ $ $
Closed Mold — Counter Pressure Structural Foam Injection Molding	0.220" uniform wall	Large parts to 4' × 4' × 24"	Common	After molding	Half ton psi CF	Good finish, painting usually required, sharp features, knit lines	$ $ $
Closed Mold — Low-Pressure Structural Foam Injection Molding	0.250" uniform wall preferred	Large parts to 4' × 8' × 24"	Common	After molding	Quarter ton psi CF	Swirl finish, painting required	$ $ $
Closed Mold — Injection Molding	0.05"–0.125 uniform wall required	Typically limited but large parts possible	Common	After molding	One ton psi CF	Polished finish, sharp features, sink marks, warping potential	$ $ $

Figure 9–2 *Forming processes comparison chart for thermoplastics.*

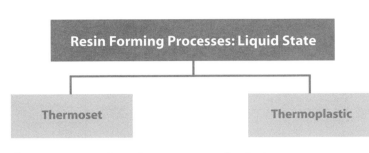

Figure 9–3 *Liquid state forming processes for plastics.*

Liquid-state forming processes for plastics are analogous to metal-casting processes. In liquid-state forming processes, heated resins become fluid as they enter the mold or are mixed (often under pressure) in the mold. In some processes the resin never appears as a liquid, but is transformed into a finished part in the tool. Thermosets are often in a dough-like mixture when they are placed by hand in the mold.

Thermoplastics do not actually become liquid, but rather become viscous (with the consistency of honey) when heated. In many molding processes they are forced, often by very high pressures, which cause them to behave like liquids as they fill the mold cavity, yielding parts with superb detail.

Not too long ago the choices available in liquid-state processing were rather limited and much easier to understand. Thermosets were more or less limited to compression molding, and the injection molding of thermoplastics was fairly straightforward. Today both types of resins can be injection molded, and the process itself, especially for thermoplastics, has become rather sophisticated and complex. The choice of material has become almost as complex with the very large array of materials available. The following discussion is an attempt to describe some of the most common options. They are divided into thermoset and thermoplastic processing categories, but that distinction continues to become increasingly blurred—almost yearly.

9.1.1   Thermosets

Liquid State Forming

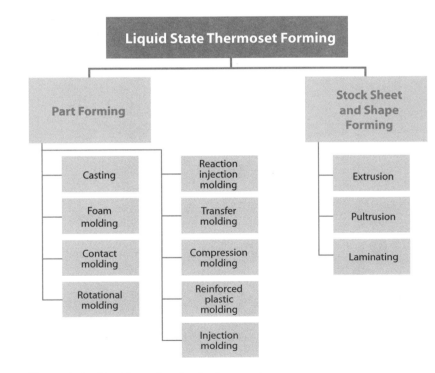

Figure 9–4 *Liquid state forming for thermosets.*

Thermosets and Their Forming Processes	Part Forming								Stock Sheet/Part	
	Casting	Foam Molding	Contact Molding	Rotational Molding•	Reaction Injection Molding	Compression Molding	Transfer Molding	Injection Molding	Pultrusion /Filiment Winding	Laminating
Alkyd	●					●	●	●		●
Allyl	●									●
Epoxy	●	●		●	●					●
Melamine		●				●	●	●		
Urea		●				●	●	●		●
Phenolic	●	●				●	●	●		
Polyester	●		●		●	●			●	
Polyurethane					●					
Silicone	●	●								

Figure 9–5 *Thermosets and their forming processes.*

Figure 9–6 *Potting typical products.*

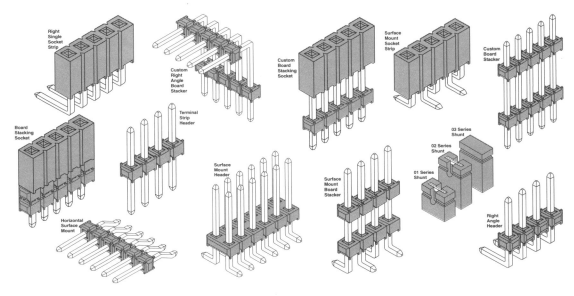

Figure 9–7 *Molded electronic components (Courtesy of Major League Electronics).*

Casting

Casting is a limited production process most often used for part evaluation or preproduction parts. Although mold costs are low, labor and production-time costs are fairly high. Nylon and acrylic are the most common thermoplastics used in casting. Epoxy, phenolic, polyester, and polyurethane are the most-often-cast thermosets. Molds can be rigid or of flexible materials. Casting is usually done with a two-part mixture of a monomer and a catalyst plus additives, such as pigments, fillers, and reinforcements.

Thermoplastics are normally heated before being poured into the mold. Thermoset materials generate their own heat in a reaction with the catalyst during polymerization. Centrifugal casting is typically used to produce small to medium intricate reinforced parts. In the electronics industry potting and encapsulation is used extensively in the production of electrical components, taking advantage of the material's natural insulating property (Figures 9–6, 9–7 and 9–8).

Foam molding or casting is used to produce cushions and other forms in flexible polyurethane resins for the furniture industry. Rigid foam materials are used to produce insulating blocks and foam-core interior and exterior building products for the construction industry. The process uses two or more components, plus surfactants and additives, such as flame retardants, which react to form a cellular structure as they solidify in a mold or part. Foam density depends on the pressure created by the volume of the mixture in the mold.

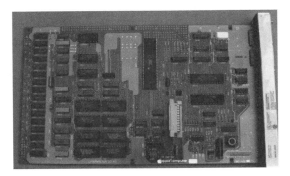

Figure 9–8 *Printed circuit board with molded electronic components.*

Contact Molding

Hand lay-up, or contact, molding (Figure 9–9) is a labor-intensive process typically used in low to moderate production of moderate to fairly large parts. The process uses molds of plastic, wood, or plaster to make boat hulls, tub and shower units, and other large housings. A reinforcement, normally woven of mat fibers of glass, is combined with a thermoset polyester resin mixture in an open mold. A roller is used to compress the reinforcements and distribute the materials in the mold.

A *spray-up process* (Figure 9–10), which uses chopped fibers, can be automated to increase production and provide better uniformity of the reinforced mixture. Although tooling costs are low, only the mold-side of the part is smooth, and the wall thickness is not uniform. A serious problem is that parts are relatively heavy, and the reinforced material is brittle, degrades with time, and can "delaminate" on impact.

BMC Molding

BMC molding mix or "logs" are placed in compression molds. The logs usually contain reinforcements that can be shaped to counter the expected part stresses (somewhat like controlling the grain structure in metal forging).

SMC molding is a resin-fiber mixture that is layered to a required thickness. The ethylene sheets that are used in handling the SMCs are removed prior to forming.

In *vacuum-bag forming* or *pressure-bag forming,* BMCs or SMCs are placed a mold that is then covered with a plastic bag. A vacuum or 50 psi air pressure is used to force the bag against the prepreg and the molds. The molds are usually aluminum but can be of other materials that can withstand the air pressure (Figures 9–11 and 9–12).

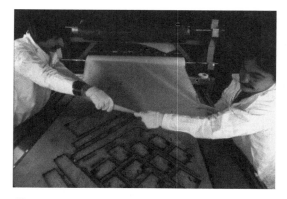

Figure 9–11 *Vacuum bag forming (Courtesy Sikorsky Aircraft Corporation).*

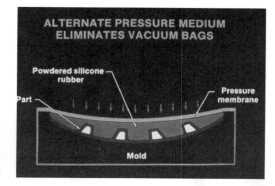

Figure 9–12 *Pressure bag forming (Courtesy Sikorsky Aircraft Corporation).*

Figure 9–9 *Hand lay-up (Courtesy Sikorsky Aircraft Corporation).*

Figure 9–10 *Spray-up process (Courtesy of Hadlock Plastics Corporation).*

Reaction Injection Molding

Reaction-injection molding (RIM) is a process in which a resin-and-catalyst mixture is combined in and chemically reacts in the mold cavity. Glass or graphite reinforcements are normally added to improve part strength. Because the pressures are low, the mold costs are low. As with most thermoset processes, the wall thickness can vary, but only the bottom of the mold-side is smooth (Figure 9–14).

RIM is used to make automotive bumpers, facia and fenders, refrigerator and freezer insulation, structural stiffeners, and other large parts. Because the wall thickness is typically 0.25 inch and the surface is not smooth on all sides of the part, the process has some limitations. It is generally unsuitable for small enclosures.

In *reinforced RIM* (RRIM) usually the reinforcing fibers are woven and shaped to the mold. Because the reinforcements are aligned to meet expected forces, the molded part is usually "structural," meaning it can sustain greater forces than normally expected of an unreinforced part (Figure 9–13).

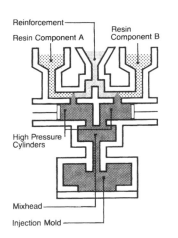

Figure 9–13 *Reinforced reaction injection molding process schematic (Courtesy of Chapman & Hall).*

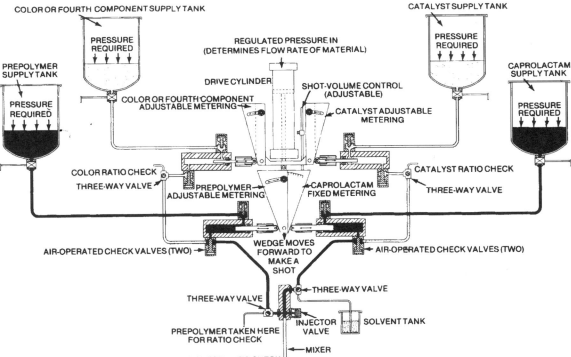

Figure 9–14 *Liquid injection molding (or reaction injection molding) machine that can process different liquid plastics (e. g., nylon etc.) with an accuracy of 0.1%. Mixing action is achieved with the "flying wedge" technique. (Courtesy of Amplan Inc., Middlesex, NJ.)*

Figure 9–15   *Compression molding (Courtesy Hadlock Plastics Corporation).*

Figure 9–16   *Compression-molded Copco melamine dinnerware, by Smart Design Inc. (Courtesy of Smart Design Inc.).*

Compression Molding

Compression molding is used primarily with thermosetting resins and rubbers. Typical parts include container caps and dishes, automotive electrical components, electrical and electronic components and housings, handles and fittings, washing machine agitators, and similar appliance parts (Figure 9–16).

In compression molding, a measured amount or a preform of a partially polymerized resin is placed by hand into a preheated mold. Polymerization or cross-linking takes place in the mold under heat and pressure. Flash normally forms at the parting line and must be trimmed. There are no sprue or runners. Reinforced parts with long fibers can be formed by this process because they are placed directly into the mold, not forced through a gate, as in injection molding.

Compression molds or tools are made of type "P" tool steel, but they cost less than injection molds because they are simpler and lower pressures are used. Because the molds are loaded by hand, inserts are easily added during the loading cycle. Labor costs are higher and cycle times are longer, because the molds are hand-loaded (Figure 9–15).

Transfer Molding

Transfer molding is used to produce electrical and electronic components, and rubber and silicone parts, which can have varying wall thicknesses. The process is an advancement of compression molding. Uncured thermoset material is placed in a heated transfer chamber where it is heated and then injected into a mold. Pressure is provided by a ram, a plunger, or a rotating screw.

Transfer molds are usually more expensive and complex than compression molds. Material is wasted in the runners during mold filling, but some thermosets may now be formulated to be recycled (Figure 9–17).

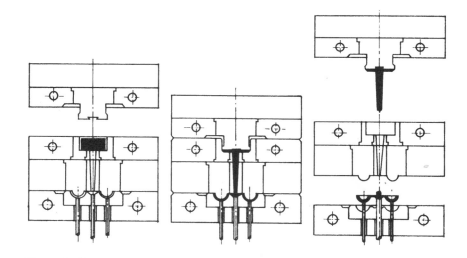

Figure 9–17   *Transfer molding for thermoset plastics (Courtesy of Chapman & Hall).*

Resin transfer molding, a variation of transfer molding, was developed for intermediate to high production. A resin mixed with a catalyst is forced under moderate pressure into a closed mold, usually with mat or woven reinforcing fibers prearranged in the mold (Figure 9–18).

Sheet-Molding Compounds and Pultrusion

Sheet-molding compounds (SMCs) are used to produce large parts especially for the transportation industry. Compression-molding equipment forms large shapes and panels are made of sheet-molding compounds composed of continuous fiber, combined with a layer(s) of resin paste (usually polyester) on an ethylene carrier. SMCs are rolled or placed into containers and stored until ready for molding (Figure 9–19).

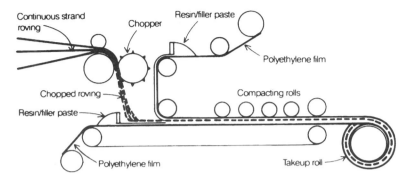

Figure 9–19 *Production of reinforced plastic sheet (Courtesy of Chapman & Hall).*

Pultrusion is in one sense the opposite of extrusion (because the forming shape is pulled rather than pushed through a die). But the process produces shapes that are similar to extruded shapes in that they have a constant profile and indefinite length. Typical products include structural members such as ladders, walkways, and handrails. Other product applications range from golf clubs to drive shafts. In this process, reinforcing material is pulled through a thermosetting viscous bath (usually polyester). The resin adheres to the reinforcement, which is then pulled through a long, heated steel die, curing the reinforced shape or part (Figure 9–20).

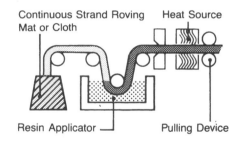

Figure 9–20 *Pultrusion process schematic (Courtesy of Chapman & Hall).*

Filament Winding/ Reinforced Tape

In *filament winding,* a continuous reinforcement and resin are combined and wound onto a mandrel in a cross-reinforced structure of the desired shape (Figure 9–21). This cross-wound reinforced structure with a hardened resin makes parts very strong.

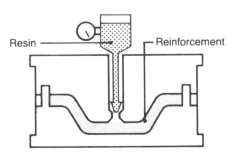

Figure 9–18 *Transfer molding for thermoset plastics (Courtesy of Chapman & Hall).*

Typical products include pressure vessels and large containers (Figures 9–21 and 9–23).

Reinforced tape is fabricated with continuous fibers pulled through a resin bath and then joined with a paper backing. Applications include corrugated architectural panels and structural components for aircraft (Figures 9–22, 9–24 and 9–25).

Figure 9–22 *Reinforced tape production (Courtesy of Sikorsky Aircraft Corporation).*

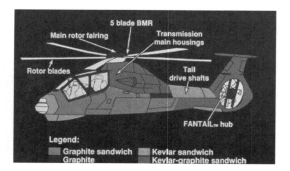

Figure 9–24 *RAH-66 (Courtesy of Sikorsky Aircraft Corporation).*

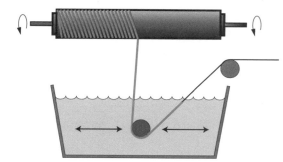

Figure 9–21 *Filament-winding schematic.*

Figure 9–23 *Filament-wound crashworthy fuel tank (Courtesy of Sikorsky Aircraft Corporation).*

Figure 9–25 *RAH-66 first flight (Courtesy of Sikorsky Aircraft Corporation).*

Laminated Plastics

Laminated plastics are essentially composite materials. The most common type is used for kitchen counters with trade names such as Formica and Micarta. These materials consist of printed (and often textured) paper, with a clear melamine top coat, laminated to a substructure of urea-impregnated rein-forcement. This "sandwich" is set using heat and pressure between an upper polished or textured steel sheet and a bottom sheet (Figure 9–26). Formica recently developed Color-core, a laminate that does not have the edge problem common to these materials (Figure 9–26). Other materials used for laminates are silicone, epoxy, polyester, and silicone.

Reinforcements

Paper, cotton cloth, glass fiber (woven fabric or mat), and nylon are commonly used as reinforcements. Asbestos (in the form of paper, mat, or woven fabric) was a common reinforcement and may still be used in some special installations, but asbestos is no longer used for common applications. Other non-metallic reinforcements are elastomers, vulcanized fiber, and cork. Metal reinforcements are mostly aluminum, copper, or steel, which are bonded to one or both surfaces or in a multilayer.

Figure 9–26 *Colorcore table by Lee Payne. (Courtesy of LEE PAYNE).*

9.1.2 Thermoplastics

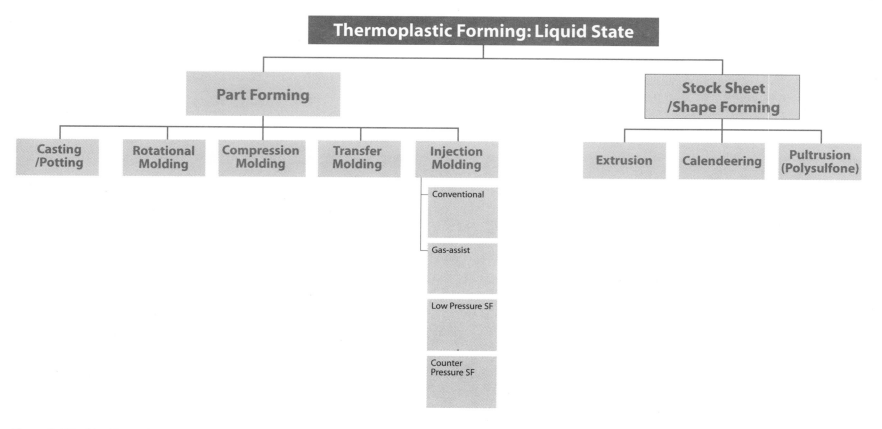

Figure 9–27 *Liquid state forming processes for thermoplastics.*

Thermoplastics and their Forming Processes	LIQUID STATE					PLASTIC STATE		
	LS Compression Molding	LS Injection Molding	LS Extrusion	PS Blow Molding	LS Rotational Molding	PS Thermoforming/Pressure Molding	PS Foam Molding	LS Calendering
ABS		●	●	●	●	●		
Acetal		●	●	●	●	●	●	●
Acrylic		●	●	●		●		●
Cellulose Acetate	●	●	●			●		●
Nylon		●	●	●	●			●
Polyimide		●						
Polycarbonate		●	●	●		●		●
Polyethylene		●	●	●	●	●	●	●
Polypropylene	●	●	●	●	●	●		●
Polystyrene		●	●	●	●	●	●	●
Polysulfone		●	●	●		●		
Polyurethane		●	●	●	●		●	●
PVC	●	●	●	●	●	●	●	●
Polyvinyl Acetate	●	●	●	●	●	●	●	●
Tetrafluroethylene (Fluoroplastics—TFE)	●	●						●

Figure 9–28   *Thermoplastic molding guide.*

Rotational Molding

Parts made by *rotational molding* tend to be large, but can be of any size in limited quantities. Although equipment and tooling costs are low, cycle times are longer than in other molding processes. The process is also labor intensive. Typical large products include boat hulls, recreational-vehicle and transportation parts, storage toys, toy vehicles, medium to very large industrial and chemical storage tanks and housings, trash cans, and other similar containers. Small products span the entire gamut but are feasible only if quantities are low. Because of easy access to the mold, inserts are molded into the parts. Most thermoplastics and some thermosets can be formed by rotational molding.

Premeasured material is loaded inside a two-part metal mold, then heated in a large oven in the second stage of the process, while it is rotated about the two axes (Figure 9–29). This action tumbles the powder, coating the inside walls of the mold. The part cools while rotating in a third, or dwell, stage and then is removed in the unload/load station. Small, complex hollow shapes with wall thicknesses of 0.016 inch to parts as large as $6 \times 6 \times 12$ feet are possible. With no pressure during forming, sharpness in detail is limited.

The process is well suited for short-run products of any size but especially very large parts. With computer-aided machining, cutting into hollow shapes to provide access to the interior of the shape is economical. With creative design the process can be used to provide cleverly designed products (Figure 9–30).

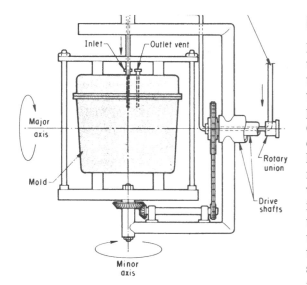

Figure 9–29   *Rotational molding (Courtesy of Chapman & Hall).*

Figure 9–30   *Rotational-molded gas monitor (Courtesy of Bally Design Inc.).*

Injection Molding

Perhaps no other process has changed product design more than injection molding. Although based in hot-chamber die-casting technology for metals, the development of polymer materials, as well as other recent developments for this process, have allowed designers near-total design freedom. Once limited to thermoplastic materials, injection molding is now available for thermosets as well. There have been many new and exciting developments in injection molding, but the process is still relatively new and continues to evolve. Early in its development injection molding had several major limitations, such as limited knowledge of the process and a rather limited selection of materials, some of which had serious drawbacks. The process was often misused, giving rise to the justifiable perception that the materials would not last or would not be durable enough to meet expected demands. Tooling costs were very high, and lead times were long.

Most of these problems have since disappeared, especially with the spectrum of materials now available and the constant development and highly sophisticated use of the basic process. CAD and rapid-prototyping have drastically shortened the lead times for tooling, and EDM has virtually eliminated machining errors. Computer-simulation programs are able to predict all aspects of the molding process, and it is possible to avoid or correct all anticipated problems before the tooling begins.

Today injection-molded products cover the entire spectrum of product design—from consumer products; business, industrial, computer, and communication equipment;

medical and research products; to toys, health and beauty products, and sports equipment (Figure 9–31).

Injection molding is a high-rate production process with molds made of type "P" tool steel. In the injection-molding process, pellets are fed through a hopper into a heated barrel, where they are mixed with additives and melted. The melted resin is then injected into the mold cavity. Older machines use a plunger (much like die-casting machines) to create the required pressure to inject the resin into the mold. These machines are still used to produce marbled products (Figure 9–33). Co-injection is a variation for molding parts with different colors and/or other features. Automobile rear-light covers, instrument panels, and control knobs with different-color lettering are commonly made using these machines (Figure 9–34).

Current machines use reciprocating single or twin screws to create the force required to inject the liquefied materials into a mold cavity at pressures of 1 ton psi. After a thermoplastic part cools or thermosets are cured, the mold is opened and the part is ejected. Elastomers are also injection-molded in these machines (Figure 9–32).

Structural Foam Molding

Low-Pressure Structural Foam Injection Molding

Because of the wall thickness limits and the demands for a force of 1 ton psi for injection molding, part size is limited in standard injection molding. Structural foam injection molding was developed to get economical large molded parts that require only one-

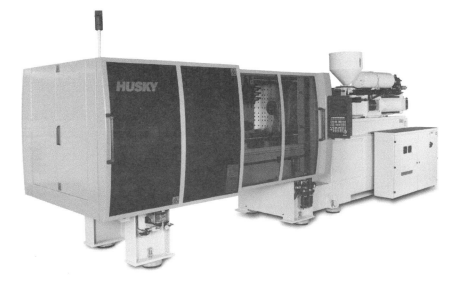

Figure 9–31   *Injection-molding machine (Courtesy of Husky).*

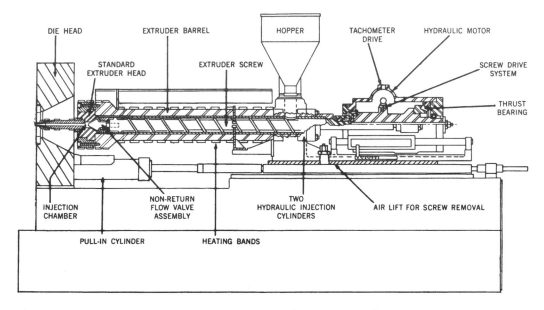

Figure 9–32   *Single-stage plunger machine (Courtesy of Chapman & Hall).*

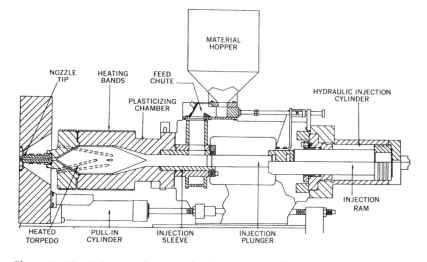

Figure 9–33   *Schematic drawing of an injection end of a single-stage plunger machine (Courtesy of Chapman & Hall).*

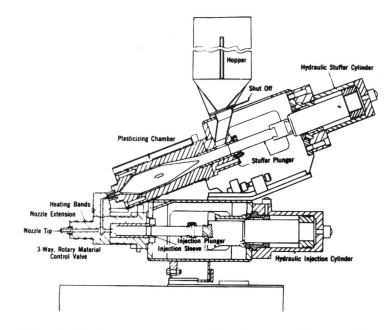

Figure 9–34   *Two-stage injection molding (Courtesy of Chapman & Hall).*

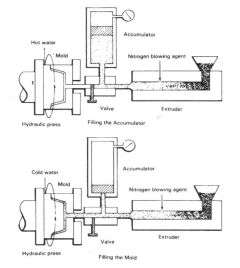

Figure 9–35   *Low-pressure structural foam injection molding (Courtesy of Chapman & Hall).*

quarter ton psi. The parts have wall thicknesses of 0.157 to 0.50 inch, which gives them the high strength and rigidity required for larger structural parts. The process uses inert gas or a chemical blowing agent to make plastic parts that have a solid skin and a cellular inner structure. Typical products are business-machine housings and electronic cabinets. One negative aspect of this process is that the molded parts have a rough surface swirl pattern, called elephant skin. This is caused in part by the lower pressure and, to some extent, by gas escaping to the outer surface along the cavity wall (Figure 9–35).

Counter-Pressure Structural Foam Injection Molding

A variation, called counter-pressure structural foam injection molding, provides a better surface, because it uses near-normal injection molding pressures to force resin into the mold. The pressure is then reversed to allow the foaming action to occur. Parts molded by this process typically have good surfaces and require less post-mold finishing. Thinner wall sections of up to 0.220 inch allow the process to be used for smaller cabinets and housings (Figures 9–36a and b).

(a)

(b)

Figure 9–36   *(a) Structural foam injection-molded product. (b) housing and parts (Courtesy Lesko Design).*

Gas-Assist Injection

Gas-assist injection molding, the latest development in creating greater strengths in large parts, maintains the typical high-quality surface finish of standard injection molding. This process uses an inert gas that, rather than mixing with the resin, forces hollow tunnels in designed-in reinforcement channels that provide the required stiffness for large molded parts. The surface is as good as standard injection-molded surfaces because it uses the standard injection-molding

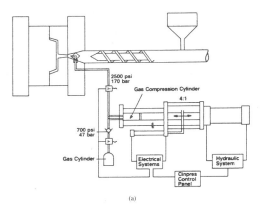

(a)

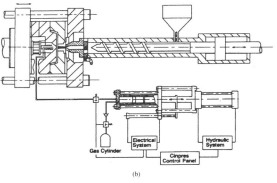

(b)

Figure 9–37   *Gas-assist injection molding (Courtesy Chapman & Hall).*

pressures of 1 ton psi. Although the surface is excellent, there may be some surface-gloss variation. Crates, tables, doors, frames, mounting brackets, base plates, and covers are typical parts that are ideal for gas-assist injection molding (Figure 9–37).

Injection Molding Tools

Injection molding "tools" have a cavity that is the negative of the part to be molded. The molten plastic enters through a sprue centered in the mold, and runners then feed the cavity through an ingate. Cores create hollow shapes and holes, and side-action cams allow undercuts. Other features of an injection molding tool include water-cooling channels, knock-out pins, and a stripper plate and/or ejectors to separate the part from the mold.

The three basic types of molds are:

1. Cold-runner two-plate molds: the simplest mold design.
2. Cold-runner three-plate molds: The runner system is separated from the part when the mold opens. The sprue and runners are generally ejected with the part.
3. Hot-runner molds (also called runner less molds): The molten plastic is kept hot in a heated runner plate. These molds are more complex and therefore more expensive, but cycle times are shorter because only the injection-molded part must be cooled and ejected. No gates, runners, or sprues are attached to the molded part (Figure 9–38a, b, and c).

(a)

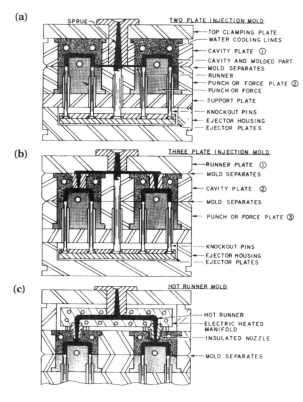

(b)

(c)

Figure 9–38   *(a) Cold-runner two-plate (b) Cold-runner for thermoplastics. (c) Hot-runner for thermoplastics (Courtesy of Chapman & Hall).*

Injection Molding Tooling

Tooling usually accounts for most of the expense of injection molding. In designing a part to be molded, the designer should provide adequate draft, avoid sharp corners, and maintain a uniform wall thickness. The most troublesome aspects of molding are undercuts. A side action can be used to remove a part that has undercuts from the mold, but it is expensive and time consuming to use. Side actions slow down the cycle time and will eventually require maintenance or replacement when they wear out. The least expensive of these options is the cam block (Figures 9–41 and 9–42). The most expensive is the cam action (Figures 9–43 and 9–44).

Other parts of a tool include the stripper plate (Figures 9–39 and 9–40) or knockout pins, which rapidly eject the molded part to clear the tool for the next cycle.

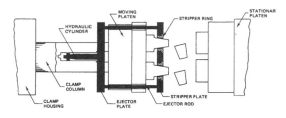

Figure 9–39   *Stripper plate ejecting part (Courtesy of Chapman & Hall).*

Figure 9–40   *Injection-molding machine with tool in open position (Courtesy of Husky).*

Injection Molding

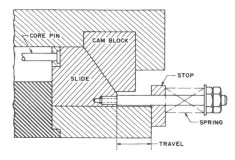

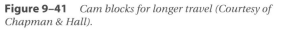

Figure 9–41 *Cam blocks for longer travel (Courtesy of Chapman & Hall).*

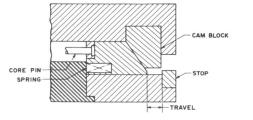

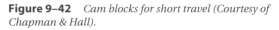

Figure 9–42 *Cam blocks for short travel (Courtesy of Chapman & Hall).*

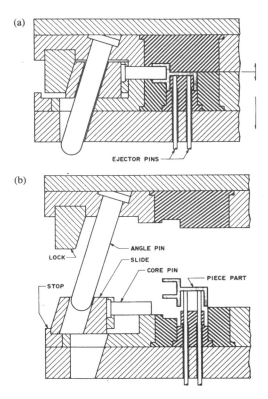

Figure 9–44 *(a) Mold closed. (b) Mold open (Courtesy of Chapman & Hall).*

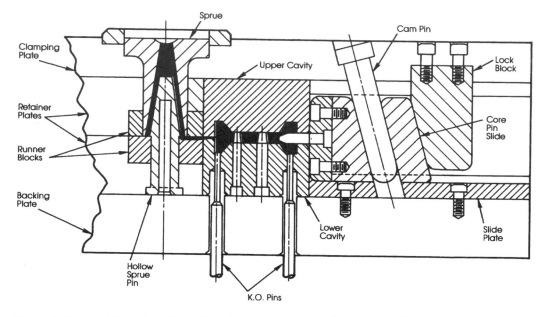

Figure 9–43 *Mold parts including side action core (Courtesy of Chapman & Hall).*

Extrusion

In *extrusion,* polymer pellets are fed into the barrel, where they are melted by electric coil heaters and the internal friction in the barrel created by the drive screw. As the drive screw rotates it blends the pellets with additives and forces the mix forward through the die, forming a continuous shape. As the extruded shape exits the tool, it is cooled by air or passes through a water-filled channel, and (as with metals) it can be coiled or straightened and cut to length. Tooling is normally inexpensive (Figures 9–45 and 9–46).

Nearly any thermoplastic polymer, as well as most elastomers, can be extruded. Typical extruded shapes include solid rods and channels, tubes, pipe, and other stock shapes, as well as window and door frames and other architectural components. Sheet and film can also be extruded. Typical elastomeric parts are window and door seals and bumper edging.

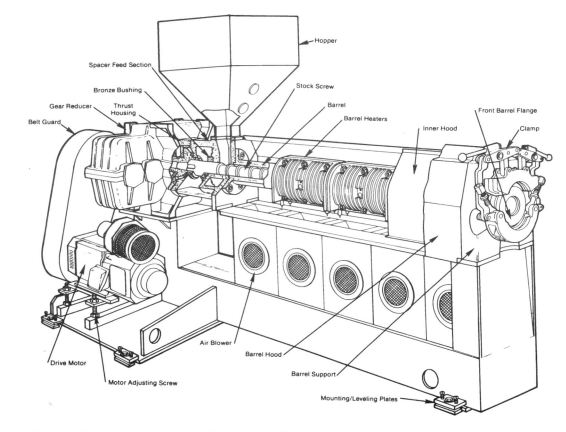

Figure 9–46 *Extruder (Courtesy of Chapman & Hall).*

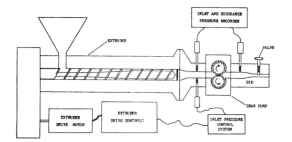

Figure 9–45 *Extrusion line with melt pump (Courtesy of Chapman & Hall).*

Extrusion Coating and Blown Bags

Electrical wire and cable are special extrusion cases wherein wire is fed into the die and combined with extruded plastic (Figure 9–47).

Plastic bags are made from a tube extruded vertically and expanded by blowing air through the center of the extrusion die (Figures 9–48 and 9–49).

Figure 9–48 *Blown film (Courtesy of Chapman & Hall).*

Calendering

In *calendering*, a warm plastic mass is fed through a series of heated rolls and then stripped off in a continuous sheet. Sheet plastic for thermoforming is produced by calendering. Shower curtains and similar sheet-plastic products are manufactured by this process; one of the rollers can be engraved to texture or emboss the sheet (Figure 9–50).

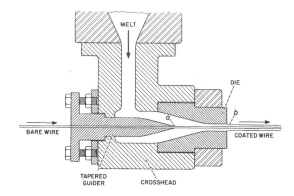

Figure 9–47 *Section of a wire coating die (Courtesy of Chapman & Hall).*

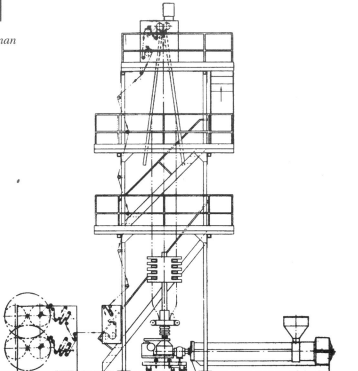

Figure 9–49 *Blown film process (Courtesy of Chapman & Hall).*

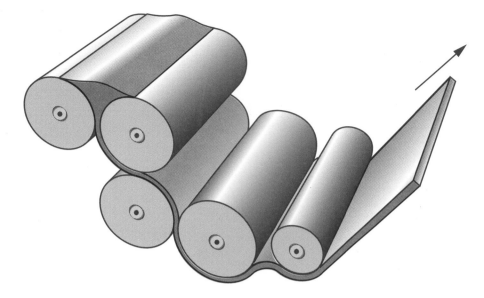

Figure 9– 50 *Calendering.*

9.2 PLASTIC STATE FORMING

Expanded Bead Molding

Expanded PS foam is used to produce molded throwaway foodservice products such as cups and food containers, and expendable recreational life-saving and water-sports products such as small boats, surfboards, and life vests. Insulating blocks and shaped packaging materials, for the purpose of impact-cushioning fragile and valuable products such as electronic, computer, or audio components, are another large market for expanded PS foam (Figure 9–54). It is also used for thermal insulation in rotationally molded and blow-molded coolers and other containers and carriers, and for extruded architectural window and door frames. In addition, it provides high-stiffness-to-weight cores for composite components such as extrusion blow-molded automobile bumpers, and for skis and surfboards.

Expanded PS foams are produced in a two-stage process. First the particles are expanded by heat from 20 to 40 times the size

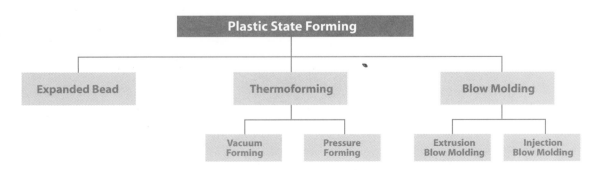

Figure 9–51 *Plastic state forming processes chart.*

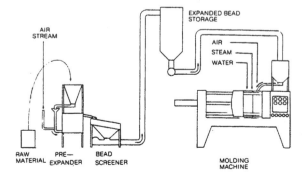

Figure 9–52 *Expandable polystyrene foam molding process (Courtesy of Chapman & Hall).*

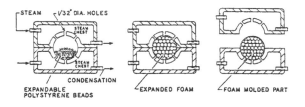

Figure 9–53 *Expandable polystyrene foam mold detail (Courtesy of Chapman & Hall).*

of the original resin particles (color can be added). Then they are poured into aluminum molds and steam heated at pressures below 50 psi. This further softens the particles and expands them, fusing them together. The end product is a closed-cell, void-free shape that is 80 to 95 percent air by volume. Because the shapes are simple and the molding pressures low, tooling costs are low (Figures 9–52 and 9–53).

Thermoforming: Vacuum and Pressure Forming

Thermoforming uses heat and pressure to form thermoplastic sheet. In this process, a vacuum is used to suck a sheet heated to the sag point onto or into a mold. Because the pressures are low, tooling is usually made of wood or aluminum and is relatively inexpensive (Figure 9–57).

Large parts such as advertising signs, appliance and refrigerator liners, bathtubs and shower stalls, and airplane interior panels are usually fabricated by vacuum forming. Limited and low-production parts are also produced using this low-cost process. Because of the potential for the surface on the mold side to be scratched, the tool should be designed with the finished side away from the mold. Colored and textured sheet can reduce finishing costs, but the part

Figure 9–55 *Pressure-formed electronic probe (Courtesy of Bally Design Inc.).*

Figure 9–54 *Expandable polystyrene foam.*

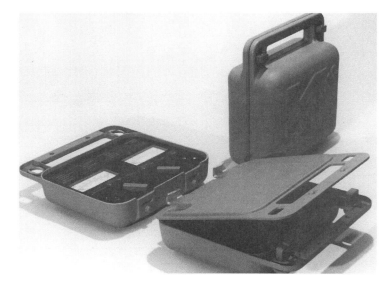

Figure 9–56 *Vacuum-formed case (Courtesy of Bally Design Inc.).*

(a)

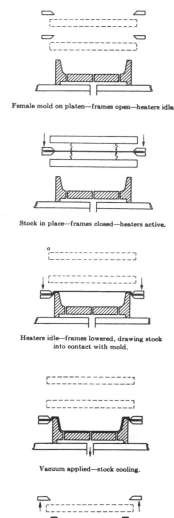

Female mold on platen—frames open—heaters idle.

(b)

Stock in place—frames closed—heaters active.

(c)

Heaters idle—frames lowered, drawing stock
into contact with mold.

(d)

Vacuum applied—stock cooling.

(e)

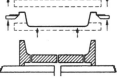

Cycle completed—equipment idle.

Figure 9–57 *Thermoforming process (Courtesy Chapman & Hall).*

must be cut from the sheet and care must be taken with the milled edges. Automated milling machines have reduced this cost considerably and have greatly improved accuracy and quality (Figure 9–56).

A variation of this process is called *pressure forming,* wherein air pressure is used to force the sheet onto a male or into a female pattern or mold, with or without a vacuum assist. Fairly good-quality parts can be obtained, but good tolerance, shrinkage, warping, nonuniform wall thickness, and surface detail can be a problem. The mold costs for pressure forming are higher than for vacuum forming, because of high pressure, wood cannot be used. All of the other features of pressure forming are similar to vacuum forming except that sharper features and detail are much better than in vacuum forming. If designed properly, pressure forming can often compete successfully with other more expensive processes such as injection molding, especially for low-volume production (Figure 9–55).

Injection Blow Molding

Injection blow molding is used to produce beverage and milk bottles and other consumer cosmetics and pharmaceutical products and industrial containers. One of the biggest users is the carbonated beverage industry. When first developed the beverage containers were a failure; the carbonation dissipated through the plastic material and there was a basic structural weakness. These problems were solved by the development of a multilayer structure of various materials that provided a series of barriers to contend with the range of unique demands on the containers. The inner layer provides a permeation barrier to stop or greatly slow the

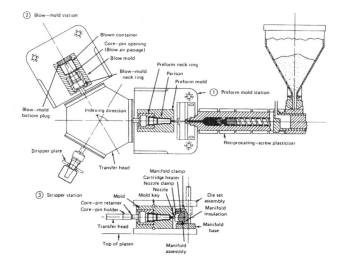

Figure 9–58 *Injection blow-mold 3 station schematic (Courtesy of Chapman & Hall).*

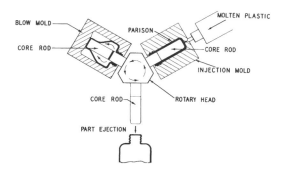

Figure 9–59 *Injection blow-mold system (Courtesy of Chapman & Hall).*

carbonation loss and to provide taste and aroma protection. The outside layer provides scuff resistance, printing capability, and the ability to hold hot fluids. Structural design changes improved the ability of the bottle to sustain impact and other typical abuse in handling.

Injection blow molding is a two-step forming process in a three-station machine. First a parison, a short test-tube-like piece, is injection molded by a conventional injection-molding process, normally with threads or other required features. The parison is then rotated to a station with a blow-molding tool. Hot air is injected into the parison, expanding it into the mold cavity. The last stop is a stripper station, which removes the finished part (Figures 9–58 and 9–59).

Extrusion-Blow Molding

Typical products suitable for the *extrusion–blow molding* process are small- to large-sized double-wall cases for tools and other portable machines, small and large

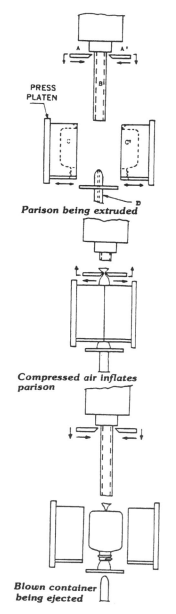

Parison being extruded

Compressed air inflates parison

Blown container being ejected

Figure 9–60 *Extrusion blow molding (Courtesy of Chapman & Hall).*

containers for chemical and detergent liquids and powders (Figure 9–61), and very large hollow shapes such as bumpers for cars and floorboards for truck beds.

In extrusion blow molding, a parison is extruded vertically and then clamped into a tool containing a cavity larger than the diameter of the parison. As the mold halves clamp around the parison, they close off both ends and pinch the parison in selected areas to form ribs and other features. The parison is then blown outward (like a balloon) with 50–100 psi filling the mold cavity. The part cools, the mold halves open, and the part is ejected (Figure 9–60). Multi-layer parts are formed with extruded multi-layer parisons.

Figure 9–61 *Blow-molded modular chemical storage system (Courtesy of Bally Design Inc.).*

Other applications include corrugated pipe and tubing—made by continuous blow molding using a parison extruded horizontally into moving molds.

The extrusion blow-molding process offers many unique opportunities to design part features such as support ribs (called pinch-off), giving the part exceptional strength (Figure 9–66); integral hinges and handles formed at the part line (Figures 9–65 and 9–67) provide reduced assembly costs and provide greater strength. In automotive part design the hollow shapes offered by this process provide air and wireways in dashboard design and exceptional strength-to-weight ratios in front and rear bumper design. Bumpers are often filled with foam for added strength. A unique feature of blow-molded bumpers is that they pop back to their original shape after impact, usually showing little or no damage (Figure 9–64).

The process is relatively fast when compared with competing processes such as rotational molding. Other features made possible by this process are molded-in inserts (Figure 9–62) and the ability to form all of a product's parts and then cut them free, usually by robot-controlled machining centers (Figure 9–63).

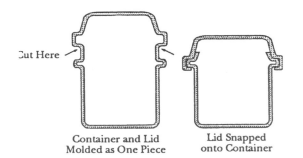

Figure 9–63 *Extrusion blow molding detail—container and lid formed in one piece (Courtesy of Pappago).*

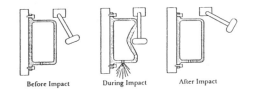

Figure 9–64 *Extrusion blow molding detail—filled bumper (Courtesy of Pappago).*

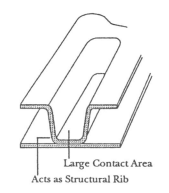

Figure 9–66 *Extrusion blow molding detail—tacked rib (Courtesy of Pappago).*

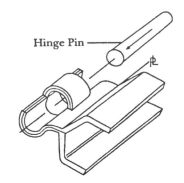

Figure 9–67 *Extrusion blow molding detail—hinge (Courtesy of Pappago).*

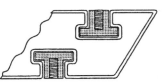

Figure 9–62 *Extrusion blow molding detail—molded-in fastener (Courtesy of Pappago).*

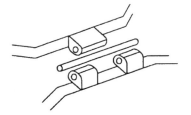

Figure 9–65 *Extrusion blow molding detail—hinge (Courtesy of Pappago).*

9.3 SOLID STATE FORMING

Near Solid State Forming

Cold forming and *solid-phase forming* processes use equipment designed to form metals. Thermoplastics such as polypropylene, polycarbonate, ABS, and rigid PVC are sufficiently ductile at room temperature to accomplish rolling, deep drawing, extrusion, closed-die forging, and coining processes.

Some advantages of cold forming over other shaping methods are:

- Strength, toughness, and uniform elongation
- Use of high-molecular-weight materials, providing parts with superior properties
- Forming speeds unaffected by part thickness because there is no heating or cooling
- Shorter cycle times than in molding processes
- Low forming forces and springback

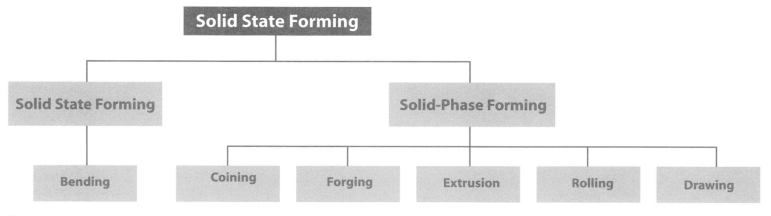

Figure 9–68   *Solid state forming chart.*

10 MACHINING PARTS*

*This section is taken from *Plastic Specification Handbook* by GE Plastics and was used with their kind permission.

There are a number of reasons why machining may be the best solution for shaping parts. Machining parts in resins is economical when the quantity required is so low that molding tooling is too expensive. In addition, parts may require slight variations from time to time, making molding a poor choice. Parts may require machining anyway—for zero-draft or other tolerance requirements that molding cannot accomplish economically. Some resins are difficult to form by standard manufacturing processes. In the past it was necessary to just accept the high cost and slow turnaround of standard machining, but new computer-controlled ma-

chining centers can now compete with some of the standard forming processes, making it a viable forming option.

Types

Machining Techniques

Parts made of most resins can be machined easily with standard high-speed-steel metal working tools. Carbide-tipped tools are recommended for long production runs and, in particular, for glass-reinforced resins. It is important to check with the resin supplier for specific machining recommendations.

The technical information sheet will list general information. The following are conditions recommended for typical machining operations:

Sawing

Standard band, circular, and hand saws can be used with most resins. The best surface is obtained on a band saw with blades containing 10 to 18 teeth per inch.

Drilling

Standard high-speed twist drills with a rake angle of 5° and an out angle of 118° perform

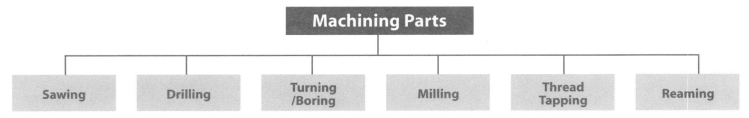

Figure 10–1   *Machining parts (Courtesy of GE Plastics).*

well with most resins. It is important to use sharp drills to maintain the quality of machined parts.

Turning and Boring

Single-edge high-speed steel tools with 15° rake angles are recommended for normal turning operations. If carbide-tipped tools are used in long production runs, the rake angle should be slightly less. Turning speeds of 1500–2500 inches per minute are recommended, with cut depth of 10 to 100 mils. Feed rate may be adjusted to achieve the desired finish.

Milling

End mills and circular mills can be used with most resins. Standard milling cutters with four flutes and a 15° rake angle should produce good results. High feed rate is generally recommended to prevent galling and gumming (Figure 10–2).

Thread Tapping

Concentric-type high-speed steel taps are suggested for tapping. Two fluted taps are suggested for holes up to 0.125 inch in diameter, whereas four fluted tools are recommended for larger holes. Rake angles should be 10° to 15°.

Reaming

Reaming can be accomplished with conventional high-speed tools. Helical fluted reamers give best results, but straight fluted tools are satisfactory. Speeds about two-thirds those used for drilling are suggested.

Figure 10–2 *Machining plastic (Courtesy of GE Plastics).*

JOINING PLASTICS*

*This section is based on information from *Plastic Specification Handbook* by GE Plastics and was used with their kind permission.

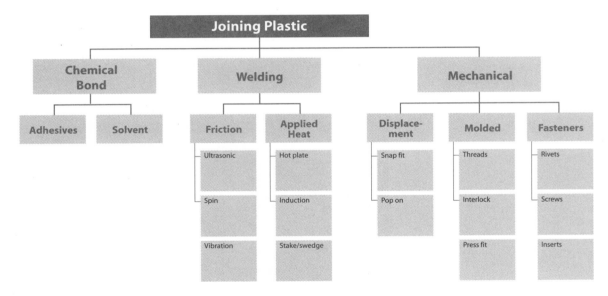

Figure 11–1 *Joining plastics (Courtesy of GE Plastics).*

Adhesive Bonding

Plastic parts and shapes may be bonded to one another as well as to dissimilar materials using a wide range of commercially available adhesives. Because adhesive bonding involves the application of a chemically different substance between two parts, the end-use environment of the assembled unit is of major importance in adhesive selection. Operating temperatures, environments, bond appearance, unit shape, physical properties, production facilities, equipment costs, and production volumes must all be considered. Epoxy or acrylic adhesives are generally recommended owing to their versatile product lines and cure rates.

Factors to consider in selecting adhesives:

- The cure temperature of the adhesive must not exceed the heat-deflection temperature.
- Adhesives not tested for compatibility should be avoided or tested.
- Adhesive testing for compatibility

should consider operational conditions of temperature and stress.

- Bond-strength tests (T-peel, impact, tensile shear) should be conducted on appropriate specimens.

With the exception of holding pressure and cure cycle, the bonding procedures used for solvents can also be used with adhesives. Be sure that part surfaces are free of dirt, grease, dust, oil, or mold-release agents. For maximum strength the surface of the part should be sanded or chromic acid etched before bonding. To ensure against misalignment during the cure cycle, apply only "finger-tight" pressure. Follow manufacturer-recommended cure times and temperatures.

In *solvent bonding* (also called welding), a chemical agent dissolves the outer skin of the resin sufficiently to allow it to be joined with other compatible parts. After the solvent has evaporated, a true bond is created, with no intermediate material. Proper assembly with solvents varies with each application. The area to be bonded, the type of joint design (Figure 11–2), and the assembly speed are factors that may be influenced by the evaporation rate of the solvent used.

Maximum bond strength assembly procedures:

- Remove all surface contaminants.
- Lightly abrade the bond surface, or treat it with acid.
- Wipe a second time with isopropyl alcohol.
- Apply the solvent to both surfaces and quickly assemble the parts.

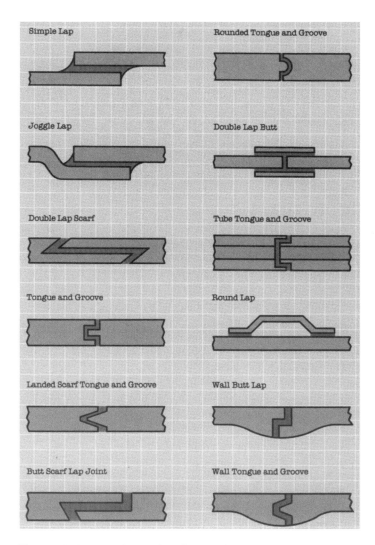

Figure 11–2 *Joint designs for solvent and adhesive bonding (Courtesy GE Plastics).*

- Clamp the parts together as soon as they are assembled.
- Maintain uniform clamping pressure for 30 to 50 seconds.

Important: Always provide adequate ventilation and follow safety procedures when using solvents for bonding. Federal, EPA, and local regulations must be observed. Avoid direct solvent contact.

Welding

Ultrasonic Welding

In *ultrasonic welding* a tool or horn vibrating at an ultrasonic frequency is brought into contact with one-half of the part being assembled (*see* Figure 11–7). Pressure is applied and frictional heat is generated as the high-frequency vibratory energy melts a molded ridge of plastic (energy director) on one of the mating surfaces. Molten material from both surfaces flows together and solidifies when the heat generated by the ultrasonic vibrations stops.

Ultrasonic welding produces uniform results because energy—transferred to the joint and released as heat—is consistent, occurs rapidly, and is confined to the immediate joint area. The finished assembly of two or more parts is strong, clean, and can be accomplished considerably faster than with other methods. Proper design of the mating surfaces and the incorporation of an energy director or shear joint is necessary (*see* Figure 11–3). Tensile shear strengths of up to 3000 psi may be attained in the bond area through the use of this assembly technique. Each application dictates specific conditions

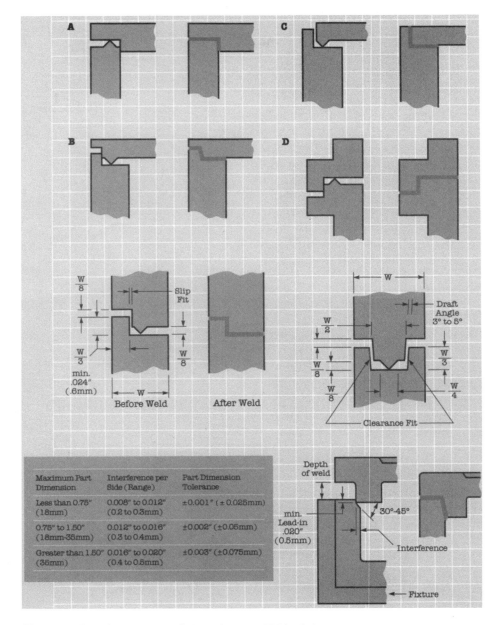

Maximum Part Dimension	Interference per Side (Range)	Part Dimension Tolerance
Less than 0.75" (18mm)	0.008" to 0.012" (0.2 to 0.3mm)	±0.001" (±0.025mm)
0.75" to 1.50" (18mm-35mm)	0.012" to 0.016" (0.3 to 0.4mm)	±0.002" (±0.05mm)
Greater than 1.50" (35mm)	0.016" to 0.020" (0.4 to 0.5mm)	±0.003" (±0.075mm)

Figure 11–3 *Ultrasonic joint designs (Courtesy GE Plastics).*

and designs that must be followed. The use of a common solvent can aid in achieving better welding results in certain resins. Bond strength depends on the materials used and welding conditions. Glass-reinforced grades are more difficult to ultrasonically weld due to the lower amount of substrate material located at the joint surface, and the difficulty in molding a sharp energy director. However, hermetic seals are usually unattainable with glass-filled materials.

Ultrasonic Staking

Most staking applications involve the assembly of plastic to metal or other dissimilar materials. A hole in the part to be joined is located to receive a molded mating stud in the plastic part. The vibrating horn has a contoured tip that, when brought into contact with the stud, melts and reforms it to a locking head. Ultrasonic staking offers many advantages. Because frequency, pressure, and time are consistent during each staking cycle, heat is generated faster and more con-

sistently than when applied with a hot iron. Tight assemblies are assured because the reformed stud is allowed to cool under pressure, eliminating material "memory." With ultrasonic staking there is no degradation of the plastic material, because it is made fluid enough to flow just before it reaches melting temperature.

Set-up

Unlike ultrasonic welding, staking requires that out-of-phase vibrations be generated between the horn and plastic surfaces. Light initial contact pressure is therefore a requirement for out-of-phase vibratory activity within the limited contact area, as shown in Figure 11–4. It is the progressive melting of plastic under continuous but light pressure that forms the head. Optimum staking conditions depend on part design and the particular resin used.

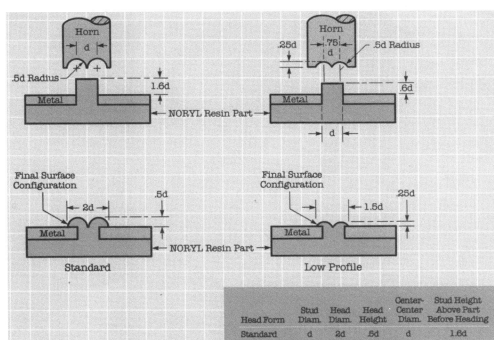

Head Form	Stud Diam.	Head Diam.	Head Height	Center-Center Diam.	Stud Height Above Part Before Heading
Standard	d	2d	.5d	d	1.6d
Low Profile	d	1.5d	.25d	.75d	0.6d

Figure 11–4 *Ultrasonic staking (Courtesy GE Plastics).*

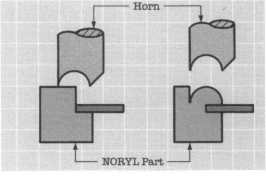

Figure 11–5 *Ultrasonic swaging (Courtesy GE Plastics).*

Staking and Welding

Ultrasonic Swaging

Ultrasonic swaging is a process of melting and reforming a ridge of resin to mechanically encapsulate another component of an assembly (*see* Figure 11–5).

Ultrasonic Spot Welding

In this process, the pilot of the tip, vibrating ultrasonically, passes through the top sheet. The molten plastic displaced is shaped by a radial cavity in the tip and forms a neat, raised ring on the surface. Simultaneously,

energy is released at the interface of the two sheets, producing frictional heat. As the tip penetrates the bottom sheet, displaced molten plastic flows between the sheets into the preheated area and forms a permanent molecular bond. Spot welding replaces adhesives, rivets, staples, and mechanical fasteners. The process is being used in assembling automobiles, all-terrain vehicles, snowmobiles, trailer bodies, furniture, auto-

mobile defroster ducts, and many other large thermoplastic parts (*see* Figure 11–6).

Spin Welding

Spin welding is a process by which two round parts may be joined without the use of adhesives, solvents, or external heating. The spin-welding process requires a specific spin time and a certain nonspin pressure-hold time. The variables depend on the grade of resin used and the joint design. Typical conditions are a peripheral speed of 40 to 50 feet per second, and a pressure of 300 to 400 psi.

Heat Staking

Vibration Welding

In *vibration welding* the lower section of the part is fixtured while the upper section is vibrated at a frequency of 120 Hz and at an amplitude of 0.040″–0.200″ in a horizontal direction. This method is capable of producing

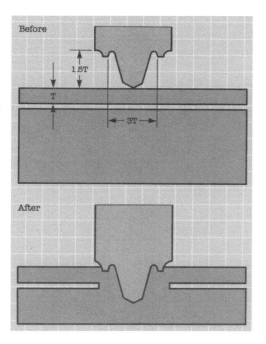

Figure 11–7 *Ultrasonic machine (Courtesy GE Plastics).*

Ultrasonic Welding

Amorphous resins with a broad melt temperature are better than crystalline resins.

Induction Welding

Encased metal or metal particles are passed through a high-frequency magnetic field. This high-cost process is best suited for polypropylene, polyethylene, styrene, ABS, polyester, and nylon.

strong, pressure-tight joints and opens the way for new and innovative design possibilities, especially in the area of large, irregularly shaped parts.

Fusion (Hot Plate) Welding

Parts may be bonded together through the use of *fusion,* or *hot plate, welding.* This technique involves taking two mating parts, placing the area to be bonded of each part onto a hot plate, removing the hot plate surface, then forcing the two parts together until the bond has formed.

Electromagnetic Induction Bonding

Parts may be joined by a technique known as *electromagnetic induction.* Heat is generated directly at the interface by a magnetic field

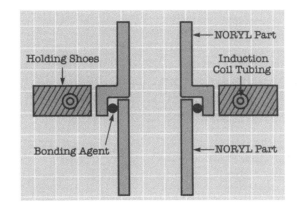

Figure 11–9 *Electromagnetic induction bonding (Courtesy GE Plastics).*

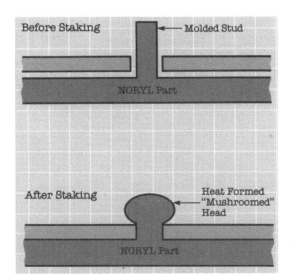

Figure 11–8 *Heat staking (Courtesy GE Plastics).*

that reaches through the materials being joined. With a properly designed coil, the magnetic field energizes sub-micron-size metallic particles uniformly dispersed in the bonding agent, producing heat effective for joining (*see* Figure 11–8).

    Heat staking, another assembly technique, is similar to ultrasonic staking except that the forming head is heated and temperature is controlled. The equipment can be shop-made or purchased and is relatively inexpensive (*see* Figure 11–9).

Displacement

Snap-Fit Assembly

A method of assembly that works well with many resins is the molded snap-fit (Figure 11–10a). Since no additional components are needed, the mating parts can be assembled

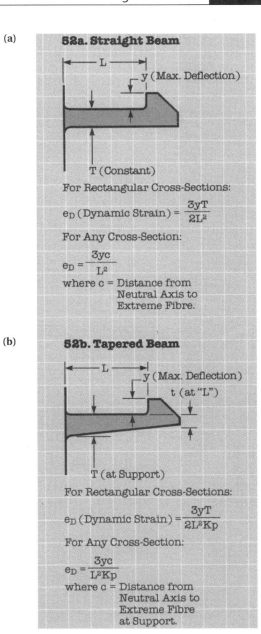

(a)

52a. Straight Beam

For Rectangular Cross-Sections:

$$e_D \text{ (Dynamic Strain)} = \frac{3yT}{2L^2}$$

For Any Cross-Section:

$$e_D = \frac{3yc}{L^2}$$

where c = Distance from Neutral Axis to Extreme Fibre.

(b)

52b. Tapered Beam

For Rectangular Cross-Sections:

$$e_D \text{ (Dynamic Strain)} = \frac{3yT}{2L^2 K_p}$$

For Any Cross-Section:

$$e_D = \frac{3yc}{L^2 K_p}$$

where c = Distance from Neutral Axis to Extreme Fibre at Support.

Figure 11–10 *(a)–(b) Snap-fit (Courtesy GE Plastics.)*

rapidly and economically on the assembly line, or at the final-use location.

The following guidelines should be observed in designing the flexing finger:

1. Do not exceed the recommended dynamic strain limit.
2. Make sure the flexing finger is under little or no stress after it is snapped into place.
3. Plan the snap-fit location so there are no sharp corners, gates, or knit lines on the flexing finger, which could lead to shortened life.
4. A snap-fit assembly is generally used less than 10 times, so if a large number of cycles is expected, fatigue life could be a consideration and a lower strain limit may be required. Consult the resin Technical Marketing Group for more information.

Since a tapered beam will provide a more efficient, equally stressed flexing finger, Figure 11–10b also includes the necessary guidelines for calculating the strain level on such a beam.

Hinges and Snaps/Locks

Products with lids or covers are normally designed with molded hinges and snaps. These lids and housing can be easily designed to incorporate hinge and locking mechanisms, as shown in Figure 11–11. Limited resins are available for living hinges.

Threaded Assembly

Threaded Metal Fasteners

Metal screws and bolts are commonly used to assemble parts or for attaching various components. Common Bolted Assemblies

1. Through Nut and Bolt

    In this case, the metal assembly puts the part into compression under the bolt and nut. The following guidelines must be observed:

    a. The parts must go into compression without causing high bending stresses or distortion at the molded part. The loose-fit "gap," shown in Figure 11–13a, should only be large enough to make the assembly a snug-fit.

    b. Uncontrolled assembly torques with this type of assembly can cause excessive compression forces in the molded parts. If the resultant compressive stress is beyond the recommended working stresses, either the torque must be controlled to a lower value, or the areas under

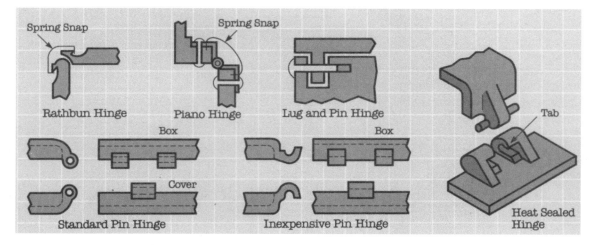

Figure 11–11 *Hinge designs (Courtesy GE Plastics).*

Figure 11–12 *Pneumatic screwdriver (Courtesy GE Plastics).*

(a)

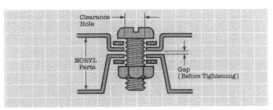

(b)

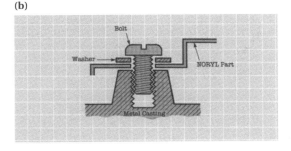

(c)

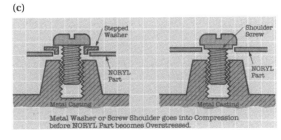

Metal Washer or Screw Shoulder goes into Compression
before NORYL Part becomes Overstressed.

Figure 11–13 *(a)–(c) Threaded assemblies (Courtesy GE Plastics).*

compression must be increased with a larger screw head or with metal washers.

c. Since the areas are usually under moderate stress, lubricants, oils, thread-locking compounds, and other substances should be avoided.

2. Attaching to Metal Part

This is similar to the through bolt and nut design in that excessive compression stress can create problems. If large washers or lower torque are impractical, a shoulder screw or stepped washer is a practical solution (*see* Figures 11–13b and c).

Self-Tapping Screws

There are two general classes of self-tapping screws, each with certain advantages and disadvantages. When using thermoplastic resins in injection-molded parts, the use of thread-cutting self-tapping screws is recommended. This type of screw cuts its own threads during installation, and has a slot cut out of the bottom to provide a channel in which the chips may accumulate. Thread-cutting screws offer the advantage of low residual stresses in the area around the boss.

General design criteria for using self-tapping screws with resins are:

1. The receiving hole diameter should be equal to the pitch diameter of the screw.

2. Boss OD should be adequate to resist possible hoop stresses developed during insertion. Usually, a boss OD equal to twice the screw diameter is sufficient.

3. Thread engagement should be at least twice the screw major diameter. A small increase in thread engagement will result in a significant increase in pull-out strength, but an increase in screw diameter will result in only a minimal increase in pull-out strength.

4. Boss height should not exceed two times the boss OD. Hole depth should be slightly longer than the screw length, to allow for chip accumulation.

5. Repeated assembly operations are not recommended.

6. Use minimum torque to keep screw assembly stress within the design limits of the material (Figure 11–12).

Other Mechanical Fasteners

Ultrasonic Inserts

Ultrasonic insertion is a fast and economical method of installing metal inserts into molded parts. This technique offers a high degree of mechanical reliability with excellent pull-out and torque retention combined with cost savings resulting from rapid production cycles. If the assembly is properly designed, ultrasonic insertion results in lower residual stress compared to molded-in or pressed-in techniques, since a uniform melt occurs and a minimum amount of thermal shrinkage is involved (Figure 11–14).

Rivets

Care should be taken when riveting resin parts to avoid the high stresses inherent in most riveting techniques. Using a shouldered rivet (Figure 11–15) limits the amount of stress imposed on the part. Aluminum riv-

ets also limit the force that can be applied, since the aluminum will deform under high stress.

In general the rivet head should be 2.5 to 3 times the shank diameter, and the flared end of the rivet should have a washer to avoid high, localized stresses. Clearance around the shaft should allow easy insertion but shouldn't be so great as to allow slippage of the joined parts (Figure 11–15).

Boss Caps

A *boss cap* is a cup-shaped metal ring that is pressed onto the boss by hand, with an air cylinder, or with a light-duty press (Figure 11–17). It is designed to reinforce the boss against the expansion force exerted by self-tapping screws, and works well with resin parts in light-duty applications.

Figure 11–14 *Nuts and stud inserts for plastic materials (Courtesy GE Plastics).*

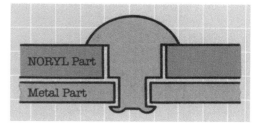

Figure 11–16 *Shouldered rivet (Courtesy GE Plastics).*

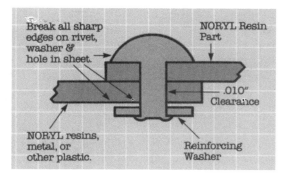

Figure 11–15 *Standard rivet (Courtesy GE Plastics).*

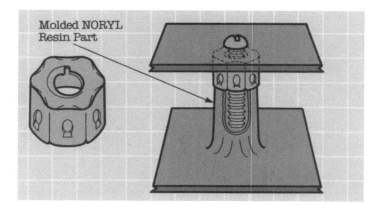

Figure 11–17 *Boss cap (Courtesy GE Plastics).*

FINISHING PLASTICS*

*The information in the section is largely taken from *Plastic Specification Handbook* by GE Plastics and was used with their kind permission.

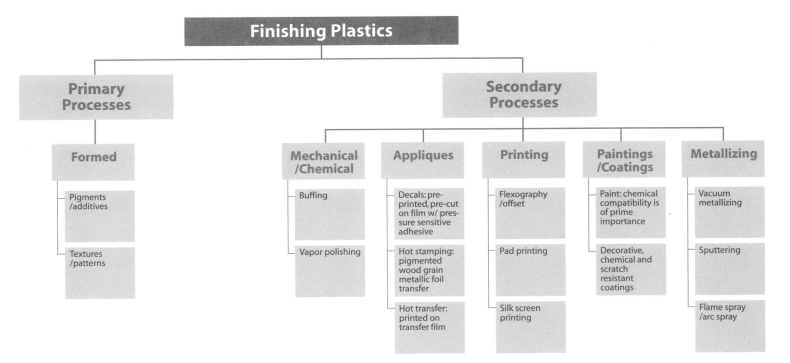

Figure 12–1 *Finishing plastics (Courtesy of GE Plastics).*

Primary Processes

Pigments, Additives, and Textures/Patterns

Most resins, whether transparent or opaque, can be pigmented to provide a spectrum of molded-in color. Surface textures, from ultra-gloss to matte, as well as near infinite patterns, can be molded in by altering the molds. Textures are also used to cover minor molding glitches, to resist an abusive environment, to provide a gripping surface, and to color- or texture-match adjacent parts composed of different materials.

Other Additives

Additives can enhance a part's resistance to weathering and chemical attack, and also help minimize the color degradation common to most resins when exposed to UV or fluorescent light. Flame retardants and/or smoke suppressants can greatly improve the UL acceptance for critical applications. Metal additives can provide electrical conductivity, required for shielding against radio frequency interference (RFI) or electromagnetic interference (EMI).

Patterns

Mold-Tech is a well-established company that specializes in altering plastic and metal tooling to provide patterns and textures that are molded-in the final part. Most parts have depth and therefore a draft (textures will increase the draft requirement). The rule of thumb is 1° to 1.5° draft for every 0.001 inch of depth of texture that must be added to the original draft (Figure 12–2). As is usual for internal draft, internal textures may require an additional draft. Many standard patterns are available—more than 10,000—which may be altered photographically to provide a unique variation. Virtually any pattern can be provided, but the cost for unique patterns may be high, and it may take time-consuming trial-and-error modifications to produce a successful new pattern. A good source for textures is the Letratone patterns by Letraset USA (Figure 12–3).

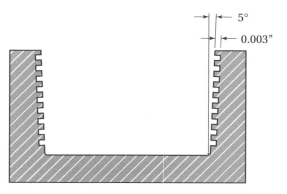

Figure 12–2 *Rule of thumb is 1° to 1.5° draft for every 0.001 inch of depth of texture that must be added to the original draft.*

Figure 12–3 *Patterns (Courtesy of Letraset).*

Secondary Finishing

Finishing

Aesthetic and functional finishing options include: painting, electroplating, sputtering, vacuum metallization, vinyl draping, flocking, flame/arc spray, hot stamping, decals, and numerous printing techniques. Coatings are also used to shield sensitive electronic components from electromagnetic radiation and to protect against ultraviolet radiation.

Even though finishing is one of the final production stages, concern for it should begin in the design stage. The quality, durability, and environmental compatibility of a finished part depends extensively on early design considerations. If the part requires a particular finish or printing needs, then it is important that the industrial designer discuss these needs early in the design process to ensure that the part geometry and resin used will be sufficient for the desired finish.

The design criteria needed for a high-quality, long-lasting finish include:

- Draft angles—to eliminate the use of mold-release agents that can adversely affect finishing adhesion
- Rib and boss design—to eliminate visible sinks on finished parts
- Wall thickness and part geometry—to withstand hot stamping pressures

Fabricated parts can often be finished by buffing and vapor polishing.

Printing

Decals

A *decal,* a pigmented decoration printed on a piece of precut transparent plastic, has a pressure-sensitive adhesive backing protected with a release sheet. When the release sheet is removed, the decal is easily applied to the plastic surface. Decals are available in limitless colors, designs, and styles, but care must be taken in their selection to ensure that the plastic film and adhesives used are compatible with end-use requirements, particularly in high-impact applications. For a listing of recommended materials and suppliers available, consult the resin supplier Technical Services Group.

Hot Stamping and Hot Transfers

For selective decorative effects, *hot stamping* offers exceptional economy. During the hot-stamping process, pigmented, wood-grained, or metallic designs are sandwiched between special coatings on a release tape and then transferred to the part surface using a heated stamping die. In designing parts to be hot stamped, special care must be taken to obtain part walls thick enough to withstand stamping pressure. Large areas to be imprinted should be as flat as possible, and all parts should be designed to avoid the use of mold-release agents. Also, molds should be polished in those areas where hot stamping is to be applied.

When a design is to be hot stamped over a painted part, proper drying of the paint system is essential. No special masking is needed over the painted area, as hot stamping applies a very selective, permanent image.

In the *hot transfer process,* a preprinted decal-like transfer is applied to the part's surface using heat and pressure. Although hot transfer is more expensive than silkscreening or hot stamping, improved color registration can be obtained.

Printing

Numerous printing techniques are currently in use for molded resin parts, including:

- *Flexography:* an economical method limited by shape to simple parts
- *Autoroll padflex:* usually limited by cost considerations to difficult shapes that can't be silkscreened
- *Pad printing:* recommended for parts requiring precise registration of print design
- *Silkscreening:* inexpensive and yields a high-quality print with good physical properties. The silkscreening process exerts only slight pressure on the part during decoration. However, as a wet system, silkscreened designs must be air- or force-dried after each color is applied. Since registration on intricate designs is difficult, this process is usually limited to two colors. The printing technique selected will usually determine the type of ink to be used. Assistance in choosing the correct process and chemically compatible inks is normally available from the resin supplier.

Painting and Coating

Choosing a Paint

A variety of alkyd, urethane, polyester, acrylic, and epoxy-based paints have been used with great success on many molded and fabricated parts. Paint selection for each application requires consideration of the functional, environmental, and other end-use requirements, as well as the desired aesthetic effect. Consult the resin Technical Sheet for recommended paints with past histories of proven performance, and use a paint and painting technique recommended by the resin supplier to achieve a wide range of decorative and functional effects. In addition to providing a special surface appearance, many paints enhance the part's resistance to weathering and chemical attack. Paint coatings can also help minimize the color degradation common to most resins when exposed to UV or fluorescent light.

Metal-pigmented paints provide the electrical conductivity required for shielding against radio frequency interference (RFI) or electromagnetic interference (EMI). A coat/spatter coat is one of the easy-to-apply texturing techniques for concealing minor molding imperfections as well as fingerprints, scratches, and other normal signs of daily use.

Preparing the Surface

Mold-release compounds, molding-tool rust preventatives, lubricants, and oils—even ordinary dust or dirt—can affect paint adhesion and surface appearance. In order to remove these surface contaminants, wipe the part with a solution of water and detergent, or with a (recommended) nonaggressive solvent such as isopropynol, methanol, or hexane. In more critical applications, an automated alkaline power wash system should be used.

Paint Application

Air, airless, electrostatic, and plural component spraying (Figure 12–4); curtain and flow coating; pad transfer; and silk screening all have been used with great success. The application method you choose, of course, will depend on the paint you've selected.

In electrostatic spraying, parts are first coated with a conductive prep coat, or primer. Then the part is grounded and an electrically charged paint coating is applied. The electrical attraction of the paint to the part eliminates much of the wasteful 70 percent overspray associated with many conventional spraying techniques.

Figure 12–4   *Spray painting (Courtesy GE Plastics).*

Curing an Finishes

Curing

Circulating warm-air ovens, infrared ovens, and conventional air drying techniques are all common methods of curing painted resin parts. Ultraviolet light exposure is a fast, energy-efficient method, but the parts may have to be coated with a specially designed polymeric resin. Curing times and conditions for all of these techniques will vary according to part design and the paint or coating employed. The heat deflection temperatures (HDTs) of resins should be considered before bake drying. Parts that are relatively free of stress and have no thin sections can be baked at temperatures in excess of the rated HDT for short periods of time.

Texturizing and Other Finishing Techniques

A number of finishing techniques are used to achieve a padded or suede look. Other special textures available range from various wood-grained surfaces to brightly colored decals.

Vinyl Draping

By adhering foam-backed vinyl or vinyl composites to a resin part, a soft, padded feeling can be obtained in most applications. The process—called *vinyl draping*—is surprisingly simple. First, a compatible adhesive is applied on the plastic surface, and the padded vinyl is heated to the specified temperature. Then the heated vinyl is draped over the part, and vacuum suction is applied. When a recommended adhesive is used in

conjunction with a properly designed part, the vacuum-formed vinyl will produce a durable, well-fitted skin over the entire part surface.

Flocking and *suede-coating flocking* are two unique methods for putting that special soft touch on resin parts. In these processes flocking fibers are first adhered to the part surface, followed by the application of an electrical charge to stand the fibers up in a regular fashion. The final composite resembles a soft, fuzzy rug in appearance—an unusual decorative advantage in countless automotive and household applications.

Environmental Legislation

Recent environmental legislation has impacted the coatings industry in two basic areas:

1. Federal Environmental Protection Agency (EPA) and various state requirements limit the amount of volatile organic solvent emission permissible at the work site.
2. FCC regulations control the acceptable levels of electromagnetic and radio-frequency radiation emitted by a wide variety of electrical and electronic products.

Volatile emissions can be controlled by employing high-solid or water-reducible paints in conjunction with high-efficiency paint application techniques, such as electrostatic spray.

Electromagnetic and radio-frequency emissions can be reduced through the application of a conductive barrier coating on the interior walls of emissive products. Silver reduction, metal-pigmented paints, vacuum metallization, flame or arc spraying, cathode sputtering, and electroplating of parts will all serve this purpose to varying degrees.

Assistance in meeting the specific state and federal environmental regulations that may apply are normally available from the resin supplier Technical Service Group.

Metallization

Metallization is available via electroplating, sputtering, vacuum metallization, and flame spraying/arc spraying.

Electroplating

Specifically formulated resins are normally available for plated applications where high performance is required. As an example, Nonyl PN235 is a highly stable substrate material with superior dimensional stability under heat and load, providing reliable platability with low reject rates during manufacture. In the electroplating process, a molded part is first etched by strong acids, then an electroless process is used in conjunction with activators and accelerators to deposit a copper or nickel finish on the part's surface. Electrical deposition of various layers of copper, nickel, and chrome follows, resulting in a bright, durable metallic finish. In selective plating, the electroplating process remains basically the same, but a layer of stopoff paint is first used to cover areas that are not to be plated. It's important to remember that optimum plated-part appearance, performance, and economy demand a well-coordinated effort among the designer, the molder, and the plater.

Sputtering

Sputter coating provides a bright, durable metallic finish with abrasion resistance comparable to that of exterior automotive topcoats, yet it offers price, weight, and environmental protection advantages over electroplating. In sputter coating, the surface atoms of the metal chosen to finish the part—including alloys such as chrome or stainless steel—are bombarded with ionized molecules. The atoms then break away from the target metal and deposit on the plastic surface in a thin, uniform layer. Sputter coating usually requires the use of a basecoat and topcoat that sandwich the metallized layer. The basecoat helps to level the plastic part's surface, thereby increasing the brightness and improving adhesion of the metal deposit. Basecoats also help to reduce the amount of outgassing (release of gases from the plastic substrate in the vacuum), which occurs by effectively sealing the part surface. The topcoat, which can be transparent or tinted to give a variety of attractive effects, helps to protect the metal deposit from abrasion and physical abuse, while providing improved corrosion resistance.

Vacuum Metallization

Vacuum metallization produces a high-polish, metallic-mirror effect that closely matches the look of chrome or solid plating. It involves a process similar to sputtering, but only pure metals—such as aluminum—can be deposited. The resulting reduced corrosion resistance usually limits the use of vacuum metallized parts to interior or non-corrosive applications. Nonetheless, vacuum metallization is a versatile, economical alternative to sputtering or electroplating, and is normally compatible with a number of resins. During the vacuum metallization process, the part is first sprayed with an organic basecoat that promotes adhesion. The finishing metal is then heated to the point of vaporization in a vacuum chamber, and the condensing metal deposits on the part surface. (Alloys cannot be used because their component metals would separate during the evaporation process.) After metallization is completed, the part is removed from the vacuum chamber and sprayed with a second organic coating to protect the thin metal film. A gas plasma discharge is set up between a cathode of the coating material and an anode of the plastic substrate.

Flame Spray/Arc Spray

Metal powder is melted by a superheated inert gas, fusing the metal onto the plastic surface.

Flame Spray/Arc Spray

Metallization

Metallic finishes are available for resins without the weight, cost, processing problems, or regulatory limitation of a standard metal part. Two other methods of metallization, flame and arc spraying, produce a thick sandpaper-like finish quite unlike the smooth, reflective surfaces obtained with other metal-finishing techniques. Their use is commonly limited to nonaesthetic, inner-part applications, such as shielding for electromagnetic and radio-frequency radiation. To improve metal adhesion, the surface of a resin part to be flame or arc sprayed should first be sandblasted or texturized. In *flame spraying,* a metal powder is metered into a special spray gun, melted by contact with a superheated inert gas, and sprayed directly onto the part (Figure 12–5).

In *arc spraying,* two metal wires are fed through an electric arc produced by a hand-held pistol. The arc melts the ends of the target wires, causing a layer of metal to be sprayed on the part surface (Figure 12–6).

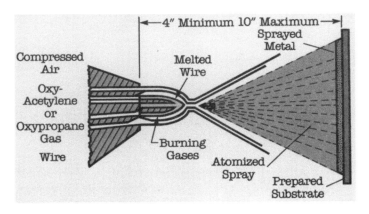

Figure 12–5   *Flame spray (Courtesy GE Plastics).*

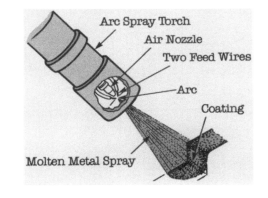

Figure 12–6   *Arc spray (Courtesy of GE Plastics).*

RUBBERS AND ELASTOMERS

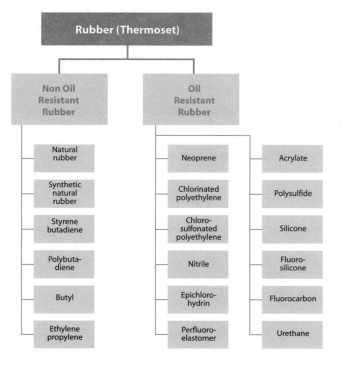

Figure 13–1 *Rubber thermosets.*

Rubbers and elastomers are materials that return to their original shape after being stretched to several times their length (*see* Elasticity page 10). The difference between a rubber and an elastomer is based on how long it takes a deformed sample to return to its approximate original size after a deforming force is removed, and the extent of its recovery.

Rubber is defined as "a material that is capable of recovering from large deformations quickly and forcibly, and which in its modified state, retracts within one minute, to less than 1.5 times its original length after being stretched at room temperature to twice its length and held for one minute before release."

An *elastomer* is defined as "a macromolecular material which, at room temperature, is capable of recovering substantially in shape and size after removal of a deforming force." No time is given for full recovery.

Thermoset Rubber

Natural and synthetic rubber is used for shock absorption, noise and vibration control, sealing, electrical and thermal insulation, and waterproofing. Styrene butadiene rubber (SBR) is the dominate material used, accounting for nearly one-half of all rubber used in the United States. More than half is used for passenger-car tires. Natural rubber is used for truck, bus, aircraft, and off-highway tires.

Manufacturing selection requires consideration of:

- Mechanical or physical service requirements
- Operating environment and life cycle
- Part manufacturability and cost

Rubber parts are formed by transfer molding, compression molding, or injection molding.

13.1 RUBBERS

Non Oil-Resistant Rubber Materials

Natural Rubber (NR, AA)

Properties:

- The best of the general-purpose rubbers
- A large deformability capacity with strength while deformed
- Service temperature range is –65 to 250°F
- Poor oil, oxidation, and ozone resistance

Uses:

- Tires
- Shock mounts and energy absorbers
- Seals
- Isolators
- Couplings
- Bearings and springs

Synthetic Natural Rubber (SNR)

Synthetic polyisoprene (IR, AA)

Properties:

- Closest to natural rubber
- High unreinforced strength with good abrasion resistance

Uses:

- Same as natural rubber

Styrene Butadiene (SBR, AA, BA)

Properties:

- Must be reinforced for acceptable tensile strength, tear resistance, and general durability
- Does not have the processing and fabricating qualities of natural rubber

Uses:

- Tires

Polybutadiene (BR, AA)

Properties:

- More resilient than natural rubber
- Made the solid golf ball possible
- Superior to natural rubber in low-temperature flexibility
- Lacks the toughness, durability, and cut-growth resistance of natural rubber

Uses:

- Blending with other polymers
- Industrial tires and vibration mounts

Butyl (IIR, CHR, AA, BA)

Polyisobutylene with isoprene with or without chlorine

Properties:

- Outstanding impermeability to gases
- Excellent oxidation and ozone resistance

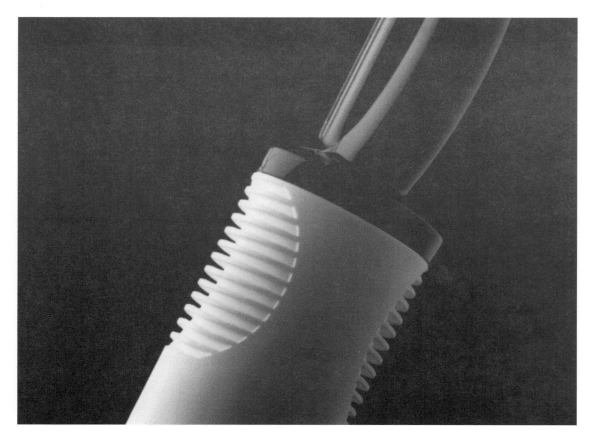

Figure 13–2   *OXO Good Grips by Smart Design (Courtesy Smart Design Inc.).*

- Flex, tear, and abrasion resistance approach those of natural rubber
- Lack toughness and durability of general-purpose rubbers

Uses:

- Belting
- Steam hoses

- Curing bladders
- O-rings
- Shock/vibration products
- Structural caulks and sealants
- Water-barrier applications
- Roof coatings
- Gas-metering diaphragms

Ethylene propylene (EPR, EPDM, AA, BA, CA)
EPR—copolymer of ethylene and propylene
EPDM—copolymer of ethylene and propylene
plus diene monomer

Properties:

- Good property retention when exposure to heat, oxidation, and ozone
- Bonding is difficult
- Broad resistance to chemicals (except oils and hydrocarbon fluids)
- Good electrical properties

Uses:

- Automotive hoses
- Body mounts and pads
- O-rings
- Conveyor belting
- Wire and cable insulation
- Window channeling and other products requiring resistance to weathering, such as roofing, and as liners for water-conservation and pollution-control systems

Oil-Resistant Rubber Materials

Oil-resistant rubbers are suitable for service at temperatures to 250°C with maximum resistance to oils and greases—considered specialty materials. Some are expensive.

Neoprene (CR, BC, BE)

Properties:

- Family of rubbers with properties approaching those of natural rubber with better resistance to oils, ozone, oxidation, and flame
- Age better and do not soften with exposure to heat

Uses:

- Hoses
- Belting
- Wire and cable
- Footwear
- Coated fabrics
- Tires
- Mountings
- Bearing pads
- Pump impellers
- Adhesives
- Window seals
- Curtain-wall panels
- Flashing and roofing

Neoprene latex uses:

- Adhesives
- Dip-coated goods
- Cellular cushioning jackets

Chlorinated Polyethylene (CM, DE)

Tyrin: Dow

Properties:

- Excellent ozone and weather resistance
- Heat resistance to 300°F
- Dynamic flexing resistance with good abrasion resistance

Uses:

- Automotive hose applications
- Premium hydraulic hose
- Chemical hose
- Tubing
- Belting
- Sheet packing
- Foams
- Wire and cable

Chlorosulfonated Polyethylene (CSM, DE)

Hypalon: Du Pont

Properties:

- Total resistance to ozone
- Excellent resistance to abrasion, weather, heat, flame, oxidizing chemicals, and crack growth
- Low moisture absorption
- Good dielectric properties
- Wide range of colors (does not require carbon black for reinforcement)
- Very good oil resistance
- Low-temperature flexibility is fair at −40°F
- Special-purpose rubber—not recommended for dynamic applications
- Outstanding environmental resistance

Uses:

- Coated fabrics
- Maintenance coatings
- Tank liners
- Protective boots for spark plugs and electrical connectors
- Cable jacketing
- Sheeting for pond liners and roofing

Nitrile (NBR, BF, BG, BK, CH)

Properties:

- Copolymers of butadiene and acrylonitrile
- Used primarily for applications requiring resistance to petroleum oils and gasoline
- Excellent resistance to mineral and vegetable oils
- Poor resistance to acetone, methyl ethyl ketone, and other ketones
- Good resistance to acids and bases except those having strong oxidizing effects
- Good resistance to heat aging—often a key advantage over natural rubber
- Poor tear resistance
- Electrical insulation
- Often used instead of natural rubber, has increased resistance to petroleum oils, gasoline, and aromatic hydrocarbons

Uses:

- Carburetor and fuel-pump diaphragms
- Aircraft hoses and gaskets

Epichlorohydrin (CO, ECO, CH)

Properties:

- Moderate tensile strength
- Elongation properties
- Low heat buildup

Uses:

- Bladders
- Diaphragms
- Vibration-control equipment
- Mounts
- Vibration dampeners
- Seals
- Gaskets
- Fuel hoses
- Rollers
- Belting

Ethylene/Acrylic

Vamac: Du Pont

Properties:

- Moderate price, heat and fluid resistance surpassed only by the more expensive, specialty polymers such as fluorocarbons and fluorosilicones
- Constant damping characteristic over broad ranges of temperature, frequency, and amplitude

Uses:

- Applications requiring a durable, set-resistant rubber with good low-temperature properties and resistance to the combined deteriorating influences of heat, oil, and weather
- Automotive components such as mounts, gaskets, seals, boots, ignition-wire jackets

Perfluoroelastomer (FFKM)

Kalrez: Du Pont

- High-performance, high-priced rubber
- Perfluoroelastomer parts are used primarily in demanding fluid-sealing applications in the chemical-processing, oil-production, aerospace, and aircraft industries

Acrylate (ACM, ANM, DF, DH)

Properties:

- Highly resistant to oxygen and ozone
- Superior heat resistance
- Poor water resistance—not recommended for use with steam or water-soluble materials (methanol or ethylene glycol)

Uses:

- Bearing seals in transmissions
- O-rings and gaskets

Polysulfide (PTR, AK, BK)

Properties:

- Outstanding resistance to oils, greases, and solvents
- Unpleasant odor
- Resilience is poor
- Heat resistance is only fair
- Abrasion resistance is half that of natural rubber, and tensile strength ranges from 1200 to 1400 psi. However, these values are retained after extended immersion in oil.

Uses:

- Gasoline hose
- Printing rolls
- Caulking
- Adhesives
- Binders

Silicone (VMPQ, PVMQ, MQ, PMQ, FC, FE, GE)

Properties:

- Versatile family of semiorganic synthetics that look and feel like organic rubber, yet have a completely different type of structure.
- High end of the cost range for rubbers
- Withstand temperatures as high as 600°F without deterioration
- Chemically inert

Uses:

- Surgical and food-processing equipment
- One- and two-part silicone sealants
- Structural adhesives
- Weatherseals in commercial buildings

Fluorosilicone (FVMQ, FK)

Properties:

- Improved resistance to many hydrocarbon fluids
- Moderate dielectric properties
- Low compression set
- Excellent resistance to ozone and weathering
- Expensive, special purpose

Uses:

- Seals
- Tank linings
- Diaphragms
- O-rings
- Protective boots in electrical equipment

Fluorocarbon (FKM, HK)

Viton: Du Pont Fluorel: 3M

Properties:

- High-performance, high-cost rubber
- Outstanding resistance to heat, chemicals, oils, and solvent
- Moderate tensile strength with reinforcements

- Low elongation properties
- Resist oxidation and ozone
- Do not support combustion
- Hardness range of 65 to 95 Shore A

Uses:

- Seals
- Gaskets
- Diaphragms
- Pump impellers
- Tubing
- Vacuum and radiation equipment

Urethane (AU, EU; BG)

Properties:

- Outstanding abrasion resistance
- Excellent tensile strength and load-bearing capacity

- Elongation potential with high hardness
- Low-temperature resistance
- High tear strength
- High or low coefficient of friction
- Good radiation resistance
- Good elasticity and resilience

Uses:

- Seals
- Bumpers
- Metal-forming dies
- Valve seats
- Liners
- Coupling elements
- Rollers
- Wheels
- Conveyor belts (especially with abrasive conditions)

13.2   ELASTOMERS

Thermoplastic elastomers can be molded or extruded on standard plastics-processing equipment. The cycle times are considerably shorter than required for compression or transfer molding of conventional thermoset rubber materials. Other advantages are lower energy costs required for processing and the scrap can be recycled. They are also available in standard or uniform grades.

Types

Polyurethanes

Properties:

- First major elastomers that could be processed by thermoplastic methods
- Do not have quite the heat resistance and compression-set resistance of the thermoset types
- Available in a wide range of hardness grades
- Outstanding abrasion resistance
- Good low-temperature flexibility
- Excellent oil resistance to 180°F
- Load-bearing capability ranks with the best of the elastomers
- Tubing is used for fuel lines
- Fluid devices and parts requiring oxygen and ozone resistance

Uses:

- Bumpers
- Gears
- Rollers
- Sprockets
- Cable jackets
- Chute linings
- Textile-machinery parts
- Casters and solid tires
- Gaskets
- Diaphragms
- Shaft couplings
- Vibration-damping components
- Conveyor belts
- Sheeting
- Bladders
- Keyboard covers and films for packaging.

Copolyesters

Hytrel: Du Pont
Riteflex: Hoechst-Celanese
Ecdel: Eastman Chemical

Properties:

- Generally tougher over a broader temperature range than the urethanes
- Hardness from 35 to 72 Shore D

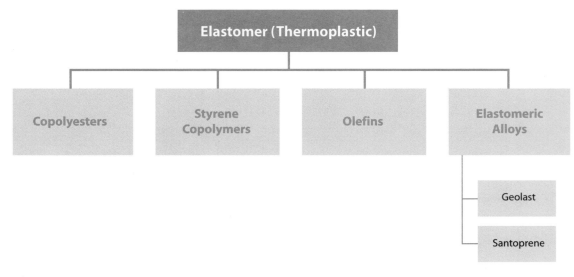

Figure 13–3   *Elastomer thermoplastics.*

- High-priced elastoplastics
- Excellent dynamic properties
- High modulus
- Good elongation and tear strength
- Good resistance to flex fatigue at both low and high temperatures
- Weathering resistance is low—can be improved by UV stabilizers and carbon black

Uses:

- Hydraulic hose
- Fire hose
- Power-transmission belts
- Flexible couplings
- Diaphragms
- Gears
- Protective boots
- Seals
- Oil-field parts
- Sports-shoe soles
- Wire and cable insulation
- Fiber-optic jacketing
- Electrical connectors
- Fasteners
- Knobs
- Bushings

Lomod: GE

Properties:

- General-purpose
- Flame-retardant
- High-heat grades

Uses:

- Connectors
- Wire
- Cable
- Hose
- Tubing
- Specific grades for airdams, fascias, filler panels
- Excellent impact resistance down to −40°F

Styrene Copolymers

Lowest priced thermoplastic elastomer: Shell-Kraton

Properties:

- Molding/extrusion grades with hardness from 28 to 95 Shore A
- Lower tensile strength
- Higher elongation (than SBR or natural rubber with similar weather resistance)

Uses:

- Disposable medical products
- Food packaging
- Tubing
- Sheets
- Belting
- Mallet heads
- Shoe soles
- Used as sealants
- Hot-melt adhesives
- Coatings
- Wire and cable insulation

Olefins: TPO (mid-range cost)

Properties:

- Available in several grades
- Room-temperature hardness from 60 Shore A to 60 Shore D
- Remain flexible down to −60°F, hot brittle at −90°F
- Autoclavable, used at service temperatures to 275°F in air

Elastomeric Alloys

TPV (thermoplastic vulcanizates) Santoprene and Geolast
MPR (melt-processible rubbers) Alcryn: Du Pont

Properties:

- Middle performance range
- Available in black and colorable grades
- Hardnesses from 55A to 80A

Uses:

- Automotive protective boots
- Hose covering
- Electrical insulation
- Seals
- Gaskets
- Medical tubing
- Syringe plungers
- Architectural glazing seals and roofing sheet

NATURAL ENGINEERING MATERIALS

Surprisingly, one of the more exciting developments in materials is in the tried-and-true older engineering materials: glass, ceramics, and carbon.

New high-performance demands have spawned the development of new classes of materials made from combinations of materials. These new combinations provide greater strength, corrosion resistance, dimensional stability, heat resistance, and other properties unavailable in a single material. To achieve these new standards of performance, materials engineers have combined ceramics with metals, carbon with plastics, and other new combinations of materials.

These old-but-reborn materials in new combinations are now appearing in a variety of applications, ranging from supercomputers to high-performance cutting tools; and from high-temperature engines to high-end sports equipment.

Recently a new form of carbon was discovered. It is called Fullerine, in honor of

R. Buckminster Fuller, for his life's work in developing geodesic structures—the basic structure of this newly discovered material. The discovery of Fullerine, or "Bucky Balls," will bring on a new generation of materials.

14.1 ENGINEERING CERAMICS

Types

Engineering Ceramics

Engineering ceramic structural parts provide high strength, light weight, and corrosion resistance for applications at extremely high temperatures and in highly corrosive environments. Ceramic engine components permit efficient burning of fuel at higher temperatures and eliminate the need for a cooling system. Other uses include cutting

tools, valves, bearings, and chemical-processing equipment. In the electronics industry ceramic materials are used for chips, superconductors, magnets, capacitors, and transducers. The cost is low because there are abundant raw materials for making ceramics. Brittleness is a problem in using these materials, but new combinations with reinforcing fibers or whiskers have increased the ductility and toughness of ceramic materials.

Metal Oxide Ceramics

Aluminas serve at 3000°F but with limited thermal shock/impact resistance and poor performance in corrosive atmospheres.

Beryllia resists thermal shock, and has a low coefficient of thermal expansion and high thermal conductivity.

Zirconia is inert to most metals with the highest strength to 4000°F.

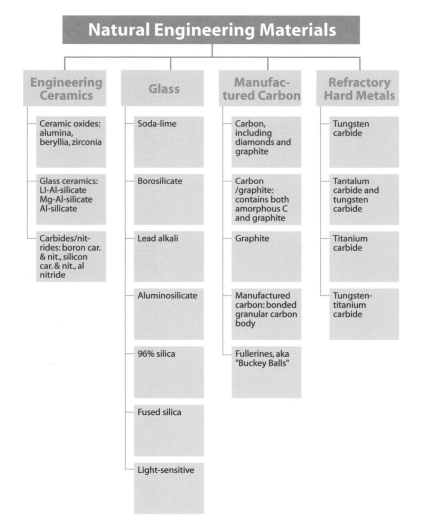

Figure 14–1 *Natural Engineering Materials chart.*

Glass Ceramics

Glass ceramics are used for consumer and commercial cooking vessels, tableware, cooktops and radomes for microwave ovens and for industrial and technical applications. They are formed from molten glass and then crystallized by heat treatment. The common glass ceramics—lithium-aluminum-silicate, magnesium-aluminum-silicate, and aluminum-silicate—are composed of oxides that form complex, multiphase microstructures, have near-zero coefficients of thermal expansion, and resist high-temperature corrosion. Macor by Corning can be machined with conventional tools and has the strength of alumina and many high-temperature and electrical properties of the other glass ceramics. A photosensitive glass ceramic can be chemically machined, and is used for disk-memory read/write heads, wire guides for dot-matrix printers, cell sheets for gas-discharge displays, and substrates for thick-film and thin-film metallization. A moldable/machinable ceramic called a "ceramoplastic" can be pressed into a preform and heated and transfer or compression molded into shapes or sheets and rods that can be machined with conventional carbide tools.

Carbides and Nitrides

Boron carbide and nitride, silicon carbide and nitride, and aluminum nitride qualify as engineering ceramics. Boron carbide, which has very high hardness and low density, is used for bulletproof armor plate. It has excellent abrasion resistance and is used for pressure-blasting nozzles and other high-wear, low-temperature applications. The others have a higher cost and are used for the more critical applications.

Forming and Shaping

Forming and Shaping Ceramics

1. Crush or grind raw materials into very fine particles.
2. Mix with additives to achieve desirable characteristics.
3. Shape, dry, and fire.

The three basic forming processes for ceramics are casting (LSF), plastic (state) forming, and pressing (SSF) (Figures 14–2 a, b, and c).

Liquid State Forming

In *slip casting* a suspension of ceramic particles in water is poured into a porous mold. The dry plaster mold absorbs most of the water from the outer layers of the suspension, leaving a layer of ceramic slip on the inner surface of the mold. The mold is inverted and the remaining suspension is poured out (Figure 14–3 a through e). The top of the cast part is trimmed, the mold is opened, and the part is removed and fired. Small and simple to large and complex parts, from bathroom products to *art objects* and *dinnerware,* can be made by this process. Dimensional control is limited and the production rate is low. It is labor intensive, but the other costs are low.

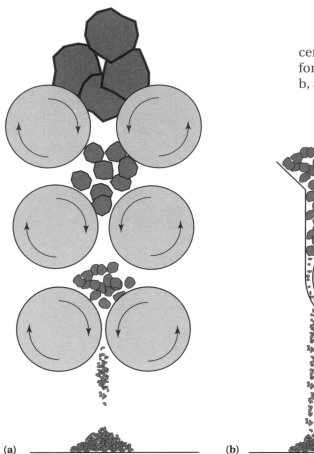

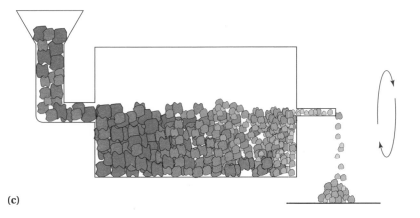

(a)   (b)   (c)

Figure 14–2   *(a)–(c). Methods of crushing ceramic raw materials.*

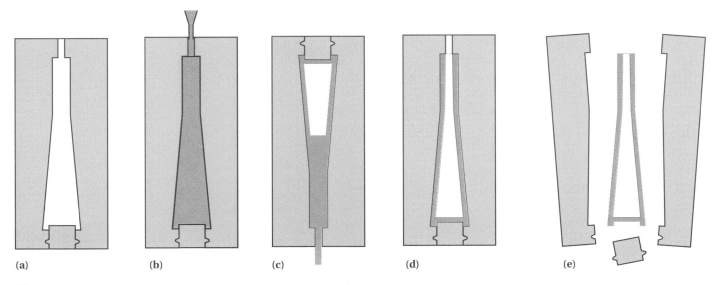

(a)   **(b)**   **(c)**   **(d)**   **(e)**

Figure 14–3   *(a)–(e). Sequence of operations in slip casting a ceramic part.*

Plastic State Forming

Plastic (state) forming (also called soft or hydroplastic forming) of ceramics includes: extrusion, injection molding, and jiggering. These forming processes tend to orient layers of clays along the direction of material flow.

Pressing

Dry pressing is used to produce simple ceramic shapes such as whiteware, refractories, and abrasive products. The process is similar to powder-metal compaction with high production rates and close control of tolerances.

    Wet pressing is used to make small, intricate molded ceramic shapes under high pressure in a hydraulic or mechanical press.

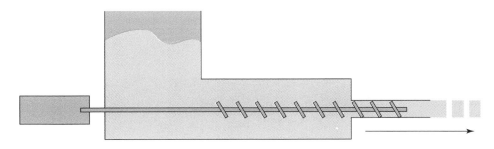

Figure 14–4   *Extruding clay blanks.*

This process has high production rates, but dimensional control is difficult due to shrinkage during drying. Tooling costs can be high because of the high pressure.

In hot pressing or *pressure sintering,* pressure and temperature are applied simultaneously, which reduces porosity, making the part denser and stronger.

Jiggering is used to make ceramicware. Clay slugs are extruded, formed over a plaster mold, and then jiggered with templates or rollers on a rotating mold. The part is then dried and fired, and usually glazed. The process, which can be automated, is limited to symmetrical parts with limited dimensional accuracy because of shrinkage during drying and firing (Figures 14–5 a through e).

Injection molding is used to form precision ceramic parts for high-technology applications. Alumina, zirconia, silicon nitride, or silicon carbide clay is mixed with a thermoplastic binder and forced through a die by screw-type equipment (Figure 14–4). The binder is removed by pyrolysis and then the part is sintered. As in metal extrusion, there is a constant cross section of the extruded part with some limitations to wall thickness. Die costs are low and production rates are high. There may be some postextrusion shaping operations.

Drying and Firing

After the ceramic part has been shaped, it is dried and fired, which gives the part strength. During drying and firing there is a tendency for a part to warp or crack because of variations in moisture content caused by differences in wall thickness and the complexity of its shape. Shrinkage of up to 20 percent of the original wet size is common.

In firing or sintering the part is subjected to an elevated temperature in a controlled environment, which gives it strength and hardness. Firing creates a strong bond between the complex oxide particles in the ceramic and reduces porosity. The process is similar to sintering in powder metallurgy.

Finishing Operations

After firing, additional operations such as grinding, lapping, and ultrasonic, chemical, and electrical-discharge machining may be used to give a part its final shape and tolerances, and to remove surface flaws and improve the finish, which can increase its strength. A ceramic product is usually glazed and fired, giving it a final glassy coat that improves appearance and strength and makes it impermeable.

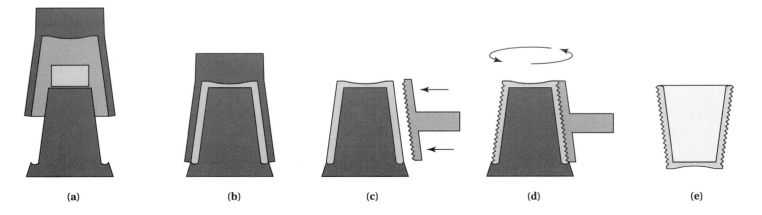

(a)   (b)   (c)   (d)   (e)

Figure 14–5   *(a)–(e). Jiggering sequence.*

14.2   GLASS

Glass is an amorphous (noncrystalline-atomic-structure) transparent solid that is hard and brittle with excellent resistance to weathering and most chemicals except hydrofluoric acid. Glass is composed of silica, lime, and sodium carbonate and is organized into three basic types: soft glass, hard glass, and very hard glass. There are also three grades of light-sensitive glass and specialty architectural glasses.

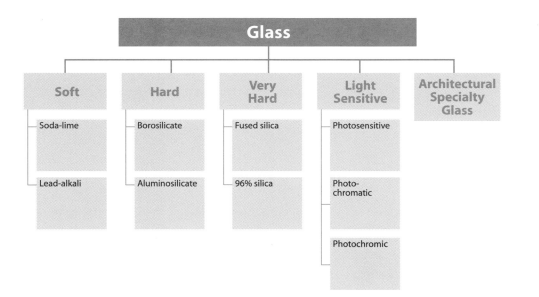

Figure 14–6   *Types of glass.*

Soft Glass

Soft glass softens or fuses at relatively low temperatures.

Soda-lime glass accounts for 90 percent of all glass produced, is inexpensive, and is used to make commodity products such as bottles, drinking glasses, windows, and light bulbs. It is not very resistant to high temperatures, abrupt temperature change, or chemicals.

Lead-alkali glass, developed in 1676, contains lead monoxide, which was used for "lead crystal" and "cut glass" stemware. It is no longer being sold in certain states, and lead crystal tableware will soon be banned throughout the United States. It is called crystal because of its high index of refraction (not its atomic structure), and it is used for optical prisms and lenses. It is a better electrical insulator than soda-lime or borosilicate glasses, and is used to shield atomic radiation. Lead glass has little resistance to high temperatures and to thermal shock.

Hard Glass

Hard glass softens or fuses at relatively high temperatures.

Borosilicate glass, developed in 1912 under the trade name Pyrex, is the first to be resistant to thermal shock and high temperatures. It is used for consumer and commercial coffee makers, oven and laboratory glassware, headlamp lenses, and other high-temperature uses. It has excellent resistance to acids and chemical attack, has a low coefficient of thermal expansion, and is used to make telescope mirrors and other precision parts as well as reinforcing fibers for plastic.

Aluminosilicate glass, developed in 1936, costs more than borosilicate and is more difficult to fabricate. It is used in high-performance applications such as high-temperature thermometers, space-vehicle windows, and as resistors in electronic circuits.

Very Hard Glass

Very hard glass softens or fuses at very high temperatures.

Ninety-six percent silica glass, a borosilicate glass, is a highly heat-resistant glass developed in 1939 by a proprietary (Corning Glass Works) process. It can be formed more readily and into more shapes than fused silica. Its properties are close to those of fused silica, and it is sometimes used as a substitute in optical components and spacecraft windows. It can withstand the heat of reentry into the Earth's atmosphere, and is used as a heat-resisting coating applications on space-shuttle exteriors. Other uses include laboratory ware and lighting components such as arc tubes in halogen lamps.

Fused silica, developed in 1952, is the most expensive of all glasses. It consists simply of silica (silicon dioxide). It has the maximum resistance to thermal shock of all glasses, with operating temperatures of 900°C for extended periods.

Many new glass products are composites, with different properties for each material. High-strength products are made of a low-expansion glass with a high-expansion glass core. Optical communications fibers are drawn from glass with a controlled variation in composition. Space-vehicle windows have multiple panes of glass, each with a unique property from heat resistance to high mechanical strength.

Light-sensitive glasses are available in three grades:

1. *Photochromic glass* is used to make sunglasses that darken when exposed to sunlight or ultraviolet radiation and fade when the stimulus is removed. They also fade when heated. The rate of change can also vary.

2. *Photosensitive glass* changes from clear to opal when it is exposed to ultraviolet energy and is heated.

3. *Photochromatic glasses,* developed by Corning in 1978, are used for information storage, decorative objects, and other transparent containers and products. They have true color permanence.

Glass used in architectural applications can be treated to filter or reflect sunlight or ultraviolet radiation.

Liquid State Forming

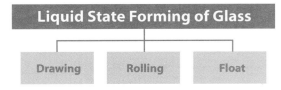

Figure 14–7   *Liquid state forming of glass.*

Glass products include:

- Flat sheet or plate 0.03 to 0.4 inch
- Rods and tubing
- Bottles, vases, headlights, and television tubes
- Glass fibers

Glass sheet, tubing, and fibers are formed or shaped in a liquid state or viscous syrup heated in a furnace or tank.

Forming and Shaping Glass

Glass sheet is made by a rolling process somewhat similar to the calendering of plastics. Flat sheet or plate is formed in a machine in which the molten glass is drawn through a series of rollers, solidifies, and is then cut to size. This process produces sheet and plate that has a rough surface. Both surfaces have to be ground and polished, or they can be textured by the rollers (Figure 14–8).

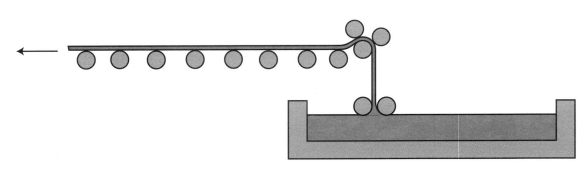

Figure 14–8   *Continuous process for drawing sheet glass from a molten bath.*

Figure 14–9 *Float method of forming sheet glass.*

In the *float method,* molten glass is fed into a controlled-atmosphere bath of molten tin. The glass floats on the bath of tin as it is passed on rollers into a lehr, where it is fire-polished as it solidifies. Float glass needs no further polishing (Figure 14–9).

Float Method

Glass tubing is drawn out of the crucible by rollers as it is formed around a rotating mandrel. Air pressure blown through the mandrel keeps the tube open. Solid rods are made the same way except that air pressure is not used (Figure 14–10).

Glass fibers for fiber-optical cable are made by a drawing process similar to the drawn wire process except that the process uses multiple orifices in heated plates. The fibers are drawn at speeds of 1700 feet per second.

Thermal and acoustic insulating glass wool is made by a rotating head in a centrifugal spraying process similar to making cotton candy.

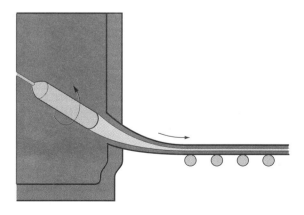

Figure 14–10 *Manufacturing process for glass tubing.*

Plastic State Forming of Glass

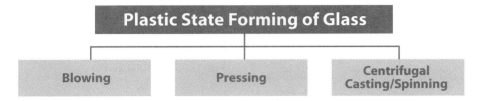

Plastic State Forming of Glass

| Blowing | Pressing | Centrifugal Casting/Spinning |

Figure 14–11 *Plastic state forming of glass chart.*

PLASTIC STATE FORMING

The *blowing process* is used to make thin-walled containers such as bottles and flasks, and high volume products such as light bulbs. In this process air pressure expands a hollow blob of heated glass into a mold coated with a release agent. While the surface finish may be acceptable for most products, the wall thickness cannot be controlled. Automated glass blowing machines are capable of producing over 1000 bulbs per minute (Figures 14–12 a through g).

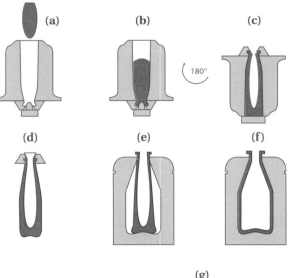

Figure 14–12 *(a)–(g). Stages in manufacturing a typical glass bottle.*

(a) **(b)**

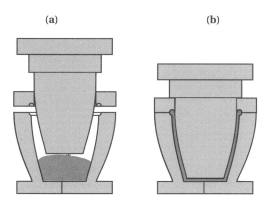
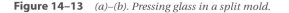

(a) **(b)** **(c)**

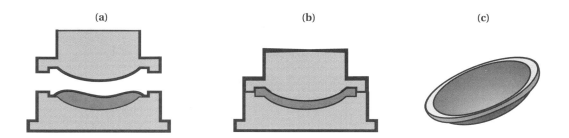
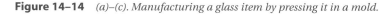

Figure 14–14 *(a)–(c). Manufacturing a glass item by pressing it in a mold.*

Figure 14–13 *(a)–(b). Pressing glass in a split mold.*

Pressing is used to form fairly simple open shapes with good dimensional accuracy. A plunger forces a gob of molten glass into a one-piece or split mold. The process cannot be used on thin-walled parts or closed shapes (Figures 14–13a and b, and 14–14a, b, and c).

Centrifugal casting or spinning is used to make symmetrical products such as TV picture tubes and large industrial and aerospace high-performance parts such as mis-sile nose cones. The process is similar to centrifugal casting for metals, where the centrifugal force pushes the molten glass against the mold wall (Figure 14–15).

Sagging is a process to shape lightly embossed glass parts such as dishes, lighting diffusers, and sunglass lenses in a shallow mold. Heated glass sheet sags by its own weight and takes the shape of the mold as it cools. Shallow shapes with little detail are formed by this inexpensive process.

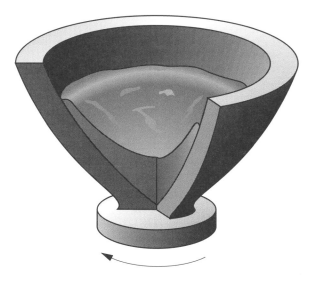

Figure 14–15 *Centrifugal casting of glass.*

Treating Glass

Glass products are strengthened by:

- *Thermal tempering* (or *physical/chill tempering*), a short process that quickly chills the surfaces, causing tensile stresses to develop on the surfaces. The process improves the strength of glass sheet, and the energy stored from the residual stresses causes tempered glass to shatter into many small pieces when broken.
- *Chemical tempering,* a longer-term process that uses a bath of molten chemicals. Atoms are exchanged, resulting in residual compressive stresses that develop on the surface.
- *Laminated,* glass commonly used for automotive windows is made with tough plastic sandwiched between two pieces of glass. The plastic holds the pieces if the glass is broken.

Other Processes

- Glass can be annealed (in a manner similar to stress-relieving or annealing of metals). The glass is heated and then cooled gradually, usually at room temperature.
- Glass sheet, which has a surface tension, is usually "cut" by scoring the surface and then snapping it, causing the sheet to break along the score or "notch". This is called *notch sensitivity.*
- Glass can be cut, drilled, and ground with special tools and polished with appropriate abrasives. Sharp edges and corners can be smoothed by sanding, grinding, or fire polishing.

14.3   CARBON

Manufactured carbon is composed of coke and graphite powder bonded with carbon. Its properties make it indispensable for applications such as electric motors. Carbon is:

- A good conductor of electricity and heat
- Self-lubricating (slides on metals without galling or welding)
- Corrosion resistant
- Unaffected by solvents, caustics, and most acids

Carbon is available in plates, rods, tubes, and rings and in hundreds of grades. It is formed by compression molding or extrusion and fired at high temperatures. Parts are machined using carbide- or diamond-tipped tools.

Properties

Manufactured carbon is brittle, but is not notch sensitive (to surface scratches or nicks). Its fatigue resistance exceeds that of most metals.

Applications

Beside its use as brushes to transfer electrical current to the rotating commutator in electric motors, manufactured carbon is used as sliding elements in mechanical devices, as a rubbing face in mechanical seals and piston rings, and as cylinder liners for air pumps and liquid dispensers. It is used for pistons and valves in chemical and gasoline pumps.

One of the newest uses is as a reinforcement in advanced composites. Carbon-reinforced plastics are dramatically changing the design of high-performance sports equipment as well as high-performance vehicles from racing cars to commercial and military aircraft. Carbon-reinforced plastics are replacing metals for weight reduction, vibration dampening, and for stealth purposes. As the technology advances, the use of these new materials has increased from 13 percent to as much as 54 percent in one generation of helicopter design (Figures 14–16 and 14–17).

Figure 14–16   *Cross section of an advanced composite reinforced plastic helicoptor rotor blade (with honeycomb fill).*

Figure 14–17   *CH-53E with Graphite-Epoxy Sponsons. A 220-pound weight saving and a 40% cost saving.*

14.4 REFRACTORY HARD METALS

Refractory hard metals (RHMs) are ceramic-like materials made from metal-carbide particles bonded together by a metal matrix. They have extreme hardness and wear resistance and are more ductile and have better thermal shock and impact resistance than ceramics, but have a lower compressive strength at high temperatures and lower operating temperatures than most ceramics.

The four RHM systems used for structural applications are:

1. *Tungsten carbide*—the most common structural RHM. It is used for applications requiring wear resistance. Saw blade tips are often made from this RHM. High-cobalt grades serve where impact resistance is required.

2. *Tantalum carbide* and *tungsten carbide*—suited for a combination of corrosion and wear resistance. Applications include nozzles, orifice plates, and valve components.

3. *Titanium carbide*—characterized by high tensile and compressive strengths, hardness, and oxidation resistance. It is used in welding and thermal metalworking tools, valves, and seals.

4. *Tungsten-titanium carbide*—used for metal-forming tooling. Typical uses are draw dies, tube-sizing mandrels, burnishing rolls, and flaring tools.

Parts are made by conventional powder-metallurgy compacting and sintering methods.

COMPOSITES

Charles Eames was one of the first designers to recognize the advantages of using new materials called *composites.* Plywood is a composite, but it wasn't until Eames and Eero Saarinen used this material in their 1944 competition furniture that its design potential was understood (Figures 15–2 and 15–3). The limitations of plywood led Eames to look for other materials. He discovered that fiberglass gave him the strength, lightness, and design freedom that he was looking for in a material for a chair. The low cost of this material was another factor that excited designers because it meant that their design could reach a very large market.

Today this same excitement continues in the search for new material combinations that will do the impossible or what was thought to be the impossible. Even today it seems inconceivable that it is possible to design an all-plastic aircraft. But nearly all-plastic aircraft exist today, and tomorrow all-plastic aircraft, reinforced with carbon and other new materials, powered by ceramic engines, may be commonplace.

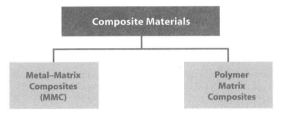

Figure 15–1   *Composite materials chart.*

Figure 15–2   *Molded plywood chair, by Charles Eames (Courtesy herman miller co.). Photograph: Bill Sharpe.*

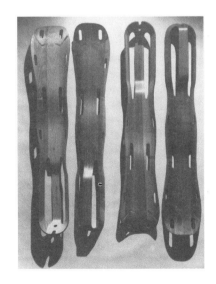

Figure 15–3   *Ray Eames designed molded plywood splints for the war effort—an example of the uses that the Eameses saw in this new material concept. The photograph was taken in 1945 by Charles Eames. (Courtesy herman miller co.).*

15.1   METAL COMPOSITES

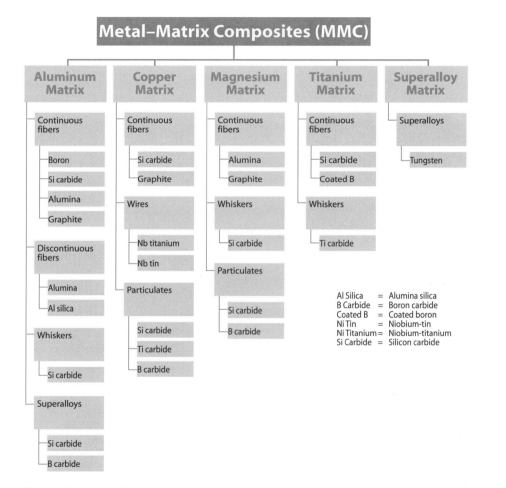

Metal–Matrix Composites (MMC)

Aluminum Matrix
- Continuous fibers
  - Boron
  - Si carbide
  - Alumina
  - Graphite
- Discontinuous fibers
  - Alumina
  - Al silica
- Whiskers
  - Si carbide
- Superalloys
  - Si carbide
  - B carbide

Copper Matrix
- Continuous fibers
  - Si carbide
  - Graphite
- Wires
  - Nb titanium
  - Nb tin
- Particulates
  - Si carbide
  - Ti carbide
  - B carbide

Magnesium Matrix
- Continuous fibers
  - Alumina
  - Graphite
- Whiskers
  - Si carbide
- Particulates
  - Si carbide
  - B carbide

Titanium Matrix
- Continuous fibers
  - Si carbide
  - Coated B
- Whiskers
  - Ti carbide

Superalloy Matrix
- Superalloys
  - Tungsten

Al Silica	= Alumina silica
B Carbide	= Boron carbide
Coated B	= Coated boron
Ni Tin	= Niobium-tin
Ni Titanium	= Niobium-titanium
Si Carbide	= Silicon carbide

Figure 15–4   *Metal-matrix composites chart.*

Advantages of MMCs Compared to Monolithic Metals

Better:

- Fatigue resistance
- Elevated temperature properties
- Wear resistance

Higher:

- Strength
- Strength-to-density ratios
- Stiffness-to-density ratios

Lower:

- Creep rate
- Coefficients of thermal expansion

Advantages of MMCs over PMCs

Higher:

- Temperature capability
- Traverse stiffness and strength
- Electrical and thermal conductivities

Better:

- Fire resistance
- Radiation resistance, with no moisture absorption or outgassing; conventional production equipment can be used with whisker and particulate-reinforced MMCs

Disadvantages of MMCs compared to monolithic metals:

- Higher costs of some material systems
- Relatively immature technology
- Complex fabrication methods for fiber-reinforced systems (except for casting)

15.2 PLASTIC COMPOSITES

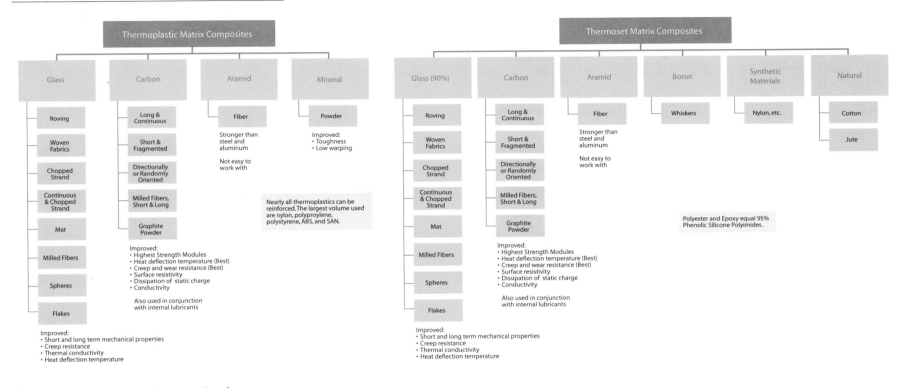

Figure 15–5 *Polymer matrix composites chart.*

15.2.1 Advanced Composites

Advanced composite materials grew out of the very high demands placed on materials for the aero-space-defense industries. Some of the demands are very low weight-to-strength-ratios, ballistic tolerance, electro-magnetic hardness, low observability, nuclear-biological-chemical hardness, and crashworthiness. Sikorsky Aircraft Corporation's advanced composite materials program uses new toughened epoxy resins, bis-maleimide resins, improved stiffness and strain graphite fibers, and fiberglass and Kevlar fibers. These advanced composite materials have allowed dramatic weight reductions of approximately 20% per generation. A spin-off is the dramatic performance increase in recreational and sports equipment, such as tennis rackets and skis. These materials are also being used to manufacture private and commercial aircraft with similar weight reduction and performance advantages.

Figure 15–6 *Composite plastics airplane built by Sikorsky for Aerofetti.*

16

RAPID PROTOTYPING

Just as plastics dramatically changed product design and manufacturing following World War II, the minicomputer perfected for the cold war has revolutionized manufacturing today. No development has been more dramatic than *rapid prototyping* and *rapid tooling*. Using advanced computer and polymer technology, a prototype part can now be produced in a matter of hours after it has been drawn using a computer-aided drawing (CAD) program, and a tool can be obtained in as fast as five days.

The main benefits of rapid prototyping (RP) and rapid tooling (RT) are a dramatic cut in part/product development time, and a shorter time to market. In today's highly competitive, international market, getting a new product on the market early is a great advantage.

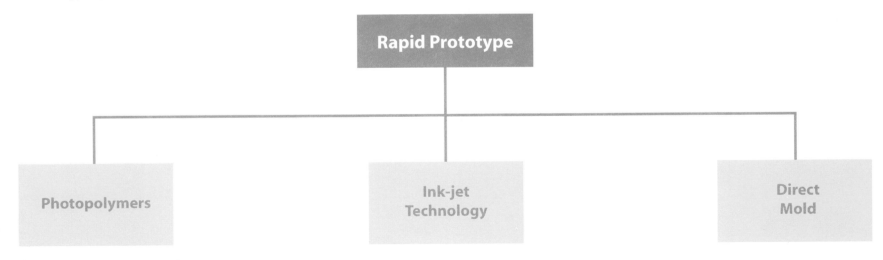

Figure 16–1 *Rapid prototype chart.*

Laser/Photopolymers

Stereolithography (STL), or *3D systems,* was the first RP system, developed by Charles Hall in 1986. The 3D systems process uses part geometry computer drawing files to produce solid parts up to 12 inches square using a photosensitive resin. No drawings are necessary, no model shop is used, no hard materials—just a liquid resin that is hardened in layers by stereo laser beams.

Fused deposition modeling (FDM), developed by Stratasys Inc., also uses a liquid resin to build models.

Solid ground curing (SGC) by Cubital America uses machinery that exposes design layers of a photopolymer. The resin is removed from the unexposed regions and replaced by wax, which supports the model as it evolves.

Laminated object manufacturing (LOM), developed by Helisys, uses adhesive-coated paper. The paper is indexed, laser-cut, and bonded in layers to build the model.

Ink-Jet

3D printing and deposition milling (3DP), developed by Sanders Prototype, uses piezo-electric ink-jet heads to deposit thermoplastic model material and support wax.

Ballistic particle manufacturing (BPM) uses microparticles of molten resin from a piezo-electric nozzle. The system uses a five-axis robotic head to position the nozzle, which deposits particles that harden and create a model.

Direct Mold

Direct shell production casting (DSP) uses the negative of an STL file to produce molds directly (without the usual step of building a positive to make the mold).

Selective laser sintering (SLS) from DTM Corp/DTM GmbH, developed the DTM RapidTool process, which uses laser-sintered powdered metal to create metal molds with a total time from design to molded part of 5–10 days.

The SLS Process

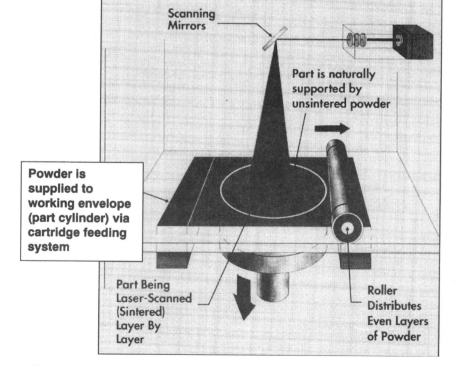

Scanning Mirrors

Part is naturally supported by unsintered powder

Powder is supplied to working envelope (part cylinder) via cartridge feeding system

Part Being Laser-Scanned (Sintered) Layer By Layer

Roller Distributes Even Layers of Powder

Figure 16–2   *Selective laser sintering process drawing (Courtesy of Casting Design and Applications).*

Figure 16–3   *The RapidTool process (Courtesy of DTM Corp.).*

INDEX

213